SEMI QUEER

SEMI QUEER

INSIDE THE WORLD OF GAY, TRANS, AND BLACK TRUCK DRIVERS

ANNE BALAY

THE UNIVERSITY OF NORTH CAROLINA PRESS

CHAPEL HILL

This book was published with the assistance of the
Anniversary Fund of the University of North Carolina Press.

Designed by April Leidig
Set in Arnhem by Copperline Book Services, Inc.

The University of North Carolina Press has been a member
of the Green Press Initiative since 2003.

Cover illustrations: Rainbow image © iStockphoto.com
/Sonya_illustration; truck image © iStockphoto.com/gorodenkoff

Library of Congress Cataloging-in-Publication Data
Names: Balay, Anne, author.
Title: Semi queer : inside the world of gay, trans, and black truck
    drivers / Anne Balay.
Description: Chapel Hill : University of North Carolina Press, [2018] |
    Includes bibliographical references and index.
Identifiers: LCCN 2018008644 | ISBN 9781469647098 (cloth : alk. paper) |
    ISBN 9781469659039 (pbk. : alk. paper) | ISBN 9781469647104 (ebook)
Subjects: LCSH: Gays—United States. | Women truck drivers—United
    States. | Transgender people—United States. | African Americans—
    United States. | Truck drivers—United States. | Trucking—United
    States—Social conditions.
Classification: LCC HQ76.3.U5 B355 2018 | DDC 306.76/60973—dc23
    LC record available at https://lccn.loc.gov/2018008644

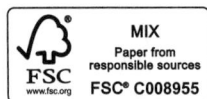

For Marilu, Michelle, and all the others,
to honor your work

CONTENTS

ILLUSTRATIONS

SEMI QUEER

It's All On The Driver

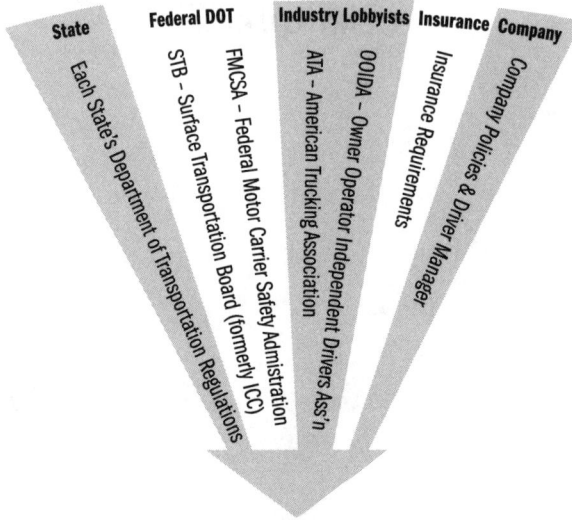

State **Federal DOT** **Industry Lobbyists** **Insurance** **Company**

Each State's Department of Transportation Regulations

STB – Surface Transportation Board (formerly ICC)

FMCSA – Federal Motor Carrier Safety Admistration

ATA – American Trucking Association

OOIDA – Owner Operator Independent Drivers Ass'n

Insurance Requirements

Company Policies & Driver Manager

Daily Trucking Equation

Logging Legal Hours
Meeting Load Delivery Deadlines
Finding Parking
+ Unexpected Obstacles on the Route
= Day-In, Day-Out Stress

It's All on the Driver: Daily Trucking Equation.
(Created by Patricia A. Wright.)

Get the Load

LOAD OFFER VIA ONBOARD COMPUTER (FROM DRIVER MANAGER OR BROKER)
☑ Accept or Reject unless it's "Forced Dispatch."

FIND A ROUTE

5 6 5

PICK UP THE LOAD
- Wait until the customer opens or the loading dock is available.
- Live Load (inefficient) or Drop & Hook (efficient).

WALK-AROUND INSPECTION BY THE DRIVER
The driver is responsible for the truck's mechanical condition, compliance with all rules and regulations, and any tickets or fines.

Obstacles

ROAD CONSTRUCTION

TANDEM ADJUSTMENTS & BRIDGE LAWS
Laws restricting weight on bridges, and placement of tandem wheels on a semi-trailer vary from state to state, so truckers need to plan routes accordingly and often adjust tandems.

INSPECTIONS
Conducted by DOT officers on the roadside, at a weigh station, or at truck stops.

WEIGH STATIONS
Pre-pass allows many truckers to skip weigh stations. Others need to pull in and get weighed.

Weigh Station

BREAKDOWNS & ACCIDENTS

WEATHER

FUEL STOPS & BREAKS
Must be logged as "on duty, not driving."

Get It There & Keep It Legal!

EACH 24 HOURS

EVERY 8 DAYS
The driver must "run off recap" after accumulating the maximum of 70 drive-hours allowed by law in an 8-day period.

30 min break per 8 hours of drive time.

14 Working Hours – 11 Hours Max for Driving

10 Consecutive Hours of Downtime

P

PARK & SLEEP
Need to find a legal parking spot built for truck weight with bathroom and (hopefully) shower facilities.

Unload & Get Paid

SETTLEMENT (GETTING PAID)
Settlement, via direct deposit into a bank account. Calculated either by reported mileage or by "straight ruler" (direct line from point-to-point, irregardless of truck routes).

DROP OFF LOAD
- Wait until customer opens or loading dock is available.
- When empty, wait for a new preplan.

Get the Load: How Long-Haul Trucking Works.
(Created by Patricia A. Wright.)

INTRODUCTION

CAROLYN IS A TALL, GORGEOUS, charismatic transwoman who has driven a big rig in Texas and the rest of the South for the past eight years. The day I spoke to her, she had pulled into a truck stop for the night in South Carolina. It was 2016, maybe a month after North Carolina had passed House Bill 2, widely known as the "bathroom bill" because it required people to use the bathroom that agreed with the gender on their birth certificate. Carolyn told me how she planned to respond the following day after crossing into that state: *"If I get anywhere near the capital of North Carolina and I need to use the restroom, I'm going to use the steps of the courthouse. Or the capitol building. That's just because I know I can't get anywhere near the governor's mansion, or I'd go take a whiz on their azaleas."*

So much is said here, and so much is not. I want you to imagine this scene: an eighteen-wheeler, underlit, with chrome stacks and an airbrushed eagle on the door, drives right up to the steps of the governor's mansion. Out steps a tall, immaculately made-up transwoman wearing a sundress and high heels. She possesses poise, elegance, effortless grace. She turns and, carefully keeping three points of contact with the truck at all times, steps down from that enormous vehicle. She takes a few steps away from her cab, whips out her dick, and pees on the azaleas.

Justice.

It doesn't matter whether Carolyn is pre- or post-op. What matters is that we think about Carolyn's words along with what she is *not* saying: that she is scared, angry, and vulnerable. She tells me, *"I wound up going back into trucking because, being different, that's the only place I could really make money. I drove a school bus for a while, but unfortunately I couldn't get the better runs, and I know it was a direct result of being different, because at that time, my two immediate supervisors cornered me, wanting to know what I had down below. So I called the ACLU and talked to lawyers, and they straight-out told me there was nothing I could do about it, uh-huh, so I said screw it and I went back into truck driving. I put my hair up under a hat, wore a pair of baggy clothes, and went and got a job, and they never looked at my driver's license until they hired me. Once they saw my driver's license, they told me if they ever saw me getting out of the truck looking that way [like a woman], I was fired. Back then I basically had to do that, because there was absolutely no laws that would even remotely protect me. That hasn't changed much. About four years ago I was doing a gig hauling sand down to the oil fields, and I was delivering in Alabama and I had to use the restroom, and I asked them where it was and they pointed it out. And I went and used the ladies' restroom, and all of a sudden I was never allowed back there, and they say that it was because of that."* Her plan to "whiz on their azaleas" is a fantasy of retaliation and release that responds to these experiences.

Carolyn and I had this conversation in 2016, when life had gotten better and work had gotten safer for many queer and trans people. Nevertheless, when Carolyn faced workplace discrimination, the ACLU and lawyers offered her no help. Here, not without irony, she relates that "they straight-out told" her that their rights-based advocacy doesn't extend to people like her. Mowing over my dismay, she adds "uh-huh" and describes her escape via trucking work, in a story that uses humor to gain control of the narrative, and thus of her life. She finds herself alone and without legal protections, yet neither anger nor despair are available to her, because she needs to keep her job, and her sanity. Carolyn, the many other truckers I came to know, and countless other Americans share this situation. They feel trapped, voiceless, and isolated because they—we—are. To respond with humor, with toughness, to be like Carolyn, is our best hope to change that.

This book tells the story of truckers and trucking in the twenty-first century, with a focus on the gay, trans, and minority truckers who are now gaining a foothold in the industry. To write it, I spent years talking formally and informally to truckers in an effort to understand their lives. Quotations from these conversations appear in italics, I assigned an alias to each trucker, and I describe each of these narrators in appendix 1. I include photographs of narrators who gave permission. I identify them in the captions by their real names and detached them from their stories for their protection. I learned that trucking is a shitty job: dirty, underpaid, and demeaning. And I learned that trucking work is important, adventurous, exciting, and available. As Marilu, one of the truckers I talked to, says, *"If you can put your butt in the seat, you can get a job driving truck."* In this job market, for the people I talked to, that is often enough.

Though trucks are everywhere and enormous, though 3.5 million people currently work in trucking, and though every single person depends on the work truckers do, trucks and their drivers remain oddly invisible. Within the trucking industry, queer, female, and minority drivers experience yet another level of erasure. It's difficult to document how many of these truckers there are, or how different their experience is from that of more traditional truck drivers, but this book attempts to do just that. Two accidental conversations I had on airplanes illustrate this problem.

Once, I chanced to sit near a recruiter for the trucking megacarrier TMC. When I outlined my sense of the changing trucking workforce, he told me I was wrong, saying that only about 7 percent of truckers are women, that there are very few nonwhite truckers (I won't repeat his reasons), and that gay and trans people don't get or stay hired as truckers. There was no doubt in his (white, straight, male) mind about any of this.

On a separate flight, I happened to sit next to a contractor who paves truck stops, a process he explained to me in detail. I was interested, since I had never thought about what goes into making asphalt able to withstand that weight and heat, or what that costs. When I told him about my narrators for this book, he exploded into stories about a culture in transition. He said that the people who work and hang out at truck stops, and how they interact with the truckers who cycle through them, have all shifted dramatically in the past ten years. His language around all of this was colorful, and I wasn't recording him so I won't try to duplicate it, but the gist was that emerging conflicts on the national stage around issues like antitrans violence or Islamophobia were already well under way in trucking. And that though the industry continues to present itself as white, male, and socially conservative, that's more a nostalgic fantasy than a representation of current reality.

Certainly, most people who drive trucks are white men who understand themselves as straight. But in the twenty-first century, the incursions into that homogeneity are many, and snowballing. I aim not only to understand and explain trucking as a whole, but also to focus on some of the new entrants to the trucking workforce. By exploring both industry-wide shifts and particular truckers' experiences, both historical changes in how gendered bodies see and understand themselves and individual instances of contemporary sexual life, I weave an account of the meaningful differences that gender and sexuality make in a particular vocational field. While I would argue that learning about the experiences of truck drivers—even about only queer, trans, or black truck drivers—is a valid and valuable end in itself, I also contend that we can't understand sexuality, work, attitudes about the regulatory power of government, or race and racism without thoughtfully attending to these people's stories.

Marilu Fanning driving to Louisville, 2016.
(Used with permission of the subject.)

The myth of the lone-wolf, rebel trucker still has a powerful hold on the public imagination. It's an extension of the frontier myth: truckers are their own bosses, liberated from domestic obligations and cozying up to danger in exchange for financial rewards and independence. Currently, this couldn't be further from the truth. Instead, truckers work within a tightening web of regulations imposed by federal and state governments, insurers, and employers. Ironically, the term for this historical shift is *de*regulation. This change has happened gradually, and it will take me many pages to unpack; essentially, however, the government has switched from regulating corporations and freight to regulating drivers. Truckers, like so many contemporary workers, are now at the mercy of corporate and government structures that treat them as disposable. In the interest of corporate profits, and in the name of highway safety, truckers are regulated often to death. When queer, black, trans, and immigrant workers enter the trucking labor force, their limited employment options and social vulnerability increase the existing micromanagement—and consequent mistreatment.

As a result of deregulation, truckers are subject to state, federal, and company rules and to a wide array of technological controls; together, these refute the popular image of a freewheeling life on the road. Bridget, who drives an eighteen-wheeler, told me: *"Everybody's got their own little fantasy about being able to sleep on the road, and seeing America, all the freedom it offers you—and I find it the most restrictive, the most unfree thing I have ever done. They told me at my company . . . that I was captain of my own ship. And I'm controlled by the Qualcomm [an electronic monitoring device], I'm controlled by the DOT [Department of Transportation] clocks, I'm controlled by the size of my vehicle, I'm controlled and told where to go, what to do, how to do it. They don't always tell me whether I'm unloading or dropping, because they want you to call in at some point to ask a question to see if you're still thinking. Or they don't want you calling in to find out what's going on because they don't want you to know. It's a 'need to know' basis—well, I need to know! And everything is dictated to you, how you're going to spend your day, except how you're going to drive, and that's limited by law, so there's no freedom. There's no freedom in this job in any way that I can figure out."*

The people who drive trucks are also shifting, and more women, immigrants, gays and lesbians, trans folks, racial and religious minorities, veterans, and people with disabilities are entering the industry. The increasing regulatory burdens are driving more-experienced truckers out of the industry, making it possible to attract only more marginalized and therefore exploitable workers. At the same time, limited economic opportunities for such marginal workers compel them toward the grindingly difficult realities of life on the road. Minimal data has been collected breaking down the race, ethnicity, sexuality, and gender of the people who drive trucks, but my narrators and my own experience tell me that white men are less dominant than they once were. Desiree says that *"there's enough of us out here now that we can feel more bold, and be more visible."*

Coming In Loud and Proud

Trucking, as a job and as a cultural phenomenon, had its heyday in the 1970s: citizens band (CB) radio slang was trendy, truckers were unionized under the Teamsters, and average salaries were high. Movies like *Convoy* and country ballads like "White Line Fever" give the flavor of this time. But the Motor Carrier Act of 1980, signed by President Carter, changed all that. Of course, change didn't happen overnight, and Presidents Kennedy and Ford had both signed incremental legislation leading up to the big deregulation bill attributed to Carter. Each piece of legislation drew support from anti-big-government conservatives, but also from lefties like Ralph Nader, who hoped to reduce corruption in the Teamsters and limit price collusion in the shipping business. In practice, deregulation made storing and shipping goods vastly cheaper, creating a "just in time" delivery model and leading to increasingly cheap consumer goods. For example, in 2017, Amazon and Walmart competed to see who could deliver goods for less by increasing the sizes of their fleets and reducing their drivers' pay. Deregulation increases the number of corporations like these involved in trucking and eliminates drivers' unions or any effective grassroots resistance. Perhaps most important, it shifts the responsibility for highway safety off of the government and the employer and onto the individual trucker.

This change has happened across the workforce, with risk shifting down onto the smallest, most vulnerable unit: the worker. Because truckers work on highways, driving deadly machines right next to everyone else, the government has an interest in monitoring their working conditions. Increasingly, instead of, say, requiring employers to ensure an eight-hour workday or to guarantee pay rates, the government, the companies, and the industry treat truckers like small children who need to be told exactly what to do, when, and how. Their sleep, schedule, health, speed, fuel, and pay are subject to a network of regulations imposed by the federal government, companies, and the states they drive through. Nontruckers might think that such regulations increase highway safety by ensuring that truckers are rested and monitored, but in fact I observed countless instances where overlapping or excessive regulations, combined with a lack of structural support (including simple things like sufficient parking), forced truckers to drive tired. Since their work is difficult and dangerous, they resent this treatment and chafe at it. This situation helps explain why antigovernment rhetoric and antiregulation politicians like Donald Trump appeal to some truckers and other blue-collar workers. Finally, deregulation reduces the price of everything, which makes change unlikely.

In 2016, 5.1 percent of truckers were women (Hsu). About 8 percent of truckers were African American or Latino, but how many of those are also women was not reported. No data is kept on gay or trans truckers. But my narrators assert that the trucking workforce is changing much faster than this data implies. According to Frankie, *"A lot has changed, a lot of the old-timers are getting out of the industry, so women are more acceptable, and there's the transgenders, and the gays and the lesbians. I'm kind of waiting to see how that's all going to fall out, 'cause right now there's a whole lotta backlash."* In parts of California, it's rare to see a white trucker. Like any last-choice job, trucking is getting browner, more female, and more queer. Some white workers blame increasing regulations and decreasing pay on these new workers. They feel threatened by what they perceive as the increasing political power and visibility of these groups and resent their access to some of the last remaining decent jobs. Of course, this does not make the new truckers' lives any easier.

With each additional restriction, whether legal, regulatory, or techno-logical, trucking becomes more dangerous, both for truck drivers and for everyone who shares the roads with them. On my drive to work, I pass a bill-board that claims that one-third of road accidents involve a semitruck and provides a lawyer's name and phone number. This reinforces fear of trucks and implies that we should not only blame truckers but also sue them. Such messaging ignores the reality that almost all road accidents involve cars and that automobile drivers are the ones who cause most accidents.

There's plenty written about truckers. Entire government agencies study them, in the United States and elsewhere, and ample data is collected by private and public researchers. There's a lot we can know about the real ex-periences of truckers and the effects of their professional lives on their per-sonal ones. And truckers do write prolifically about their own experiences, from formal ethnographies to blogs and posts in Facebook groups. When a federal agency debates a rule change — something that seems to happen weekly — the media often covers it. But the volume of words produced doesn't lead to a feeling of being heard. Whatever media coverage might exist, and regardless of the urgency and articulateness of truckers' statements about what is wrong and how to fix it, we tend to overlook their voices in much the same way we overlook trucks themselves, even though they are enormous.

Road Warriors

Like any good superhero, the Incredible Hulk has both a power and a prob-lem. Once transformed into the Hulk, Bruce Banner is a majestic, mascu-line, invincible green victor: you definitely want him on your side. But he can't control when his transformation happens or what he does once he gets transformed. He's a hero and a savior but at the mercy of an arbitrary system.

Truckers are a lot like that. I've never met people tougher and more fiercely independent. Truck drivers work eleven- to fourteen-hour days, driving enor-mous machines in all weather, over mountain passes, through crowded cities, on ice, at night, alone. They have more courage, and more modesty, than you can begin to imagine, and their own stories provide better proof of this than my testimony. Readers who meet some of these truckers in the coming pages will see their similarity to the Incredible Hulk. They look like regular people we see every day and barely notice, but once we know what the truckers do—what their daily lives entail—they begin to seem superhuman. At the same time, like Bruce Banner, they are allowed very little control over the circumstances of their own heroism.

Being behind the wheel of a semitruck is magic. Typically, there are nine to thirteen gears and the transmission is not synchronized, so truckers monitor the tachometer to time their shifting. The trailer is fifty-three feet long, and turning something of that length that's attached to a tractor via a kingpin requires depth perception and grace. The driver sits high and looks down at the road and at other motorists across a vast array of knobs and gauges. When a trucker turns the key and hears the engine respond, anger and frustration fade. Like most jobs, trucking becomes tedious and mind-numbing, but the stakes—the very real risks—of the work generate a physiologic level of arousal that keeps it interesting. Once they build up confidence, drivers move in rhythm with the vehicle, feeling connected to it and thus sharing its power. For queers and other stigmatized truckers, the power conferred by the enormous machine provides both a defense and a visceral, tangible reward. As Sisyphus says, *"I see a lot of transwomen out here. I think a lot of transwomen choose this career because it's a place where we can work—we're by ourselves, no one's going to harass us while we're in the truck. When I worked in the printing plant, I was being harassed. I couldn't go to work a single day without being harassed. I had my tires sliced, I had nails put under my tires, I had hate messages put up. One day I walked into work and saw a sign up: 'All fags must die.' That was in my face every single day. When I'm in the truck I don't have to deal with that. The fact that people hate me 'cause I'm trans, well then they'll hate me, but say hello to my truck."*

Trucking is usually not a first-choice job. It's where you wind up if you're desperate—out of options. Patrick is a black gay man born and raised in Gary, Indiana, who reminds me that educational and employment opportunities are few and far between for people like him. He puts it like this: *"I never said, 'Mommy I want to be a truck driver'; it was just something I thought of instead of doing something illicit, selling drugs or whatever. It was something I thought of that's in my area, that would be a good fit because there's a lot of industrial working here, and so I did it, and when I did it, I hated it. I got my license, and when I got laid off from my other job, I felt like I was obligated to go back to truck driving, either that or do something crazy. So the second time I went into it, it was paying the bills, and it took care of what needed to be done, so I'm not going to complain. But you have only one day off, you work midnights, and you get off early Saturday morning, sometimes late Saturday morning, and then you go back to work Monday night. So I was working six nights a week, twelve, fourteen, sixteen hours straight, I had no time for my personal life—I made good money, this is true, but my personal life sucked. I didn't have time to pay my bills, all I did was a lot of stuff I missed out on, and so much I couldn't do—I hated my life. I really did."*

Manual labor is stigmatized in the present knowledge economy, with truckers experiencing increasing waves of disrespect. Sandy Long, a force behind the group Women in Trucking, describes this stigma as one of trucking's biggest problems. She confides, *"One of the problems that we have right now is we're riding the tail of the tornado of our image. . . . It's just that we have been so vilified. You know the statistics. You* know *the statistics. We're the safest people in the world. According to the government, we're the most unsafe people; we're all fat, and we all have sleep apnea, and we're all unhealthy, and we all drive tired."*

When I met up with Adele, another trucker, for breakfast in Lake Station, Indiana, I asked her what the main problem was with trucking, in her view. She immediately responded: *"The lack of respect, disrespect, the regulations being changed and set up and mandated by people that can't even move their rolling chair from one end of their office to the other without falling off. Listening to these antitruck groups that lobby against us, when all we're trying to do is provide a service for our country; we're taking care of our country. Productivity, of course, gets disrupted."*

In practice, truckers are met with either undisguised disgust or legislative management. The public maintains two cultural abstractions about truckers: mythological and intellectual. On one hand, they're independent heroes, and on the other hand, we tolerate them only because they're necessary for the functioning of our society. Living this contradiction—being both symbolic and grudgingly tolerated—is what the Incredible Hulk is all about, and what American truckers have to manage every day. What does it feel like to be glorified, crucial, pervasive, and yet simultaneously invisible and beneath contempt?

Trucking is a culture that isn't fixed in place—we see trucks all the time, but only in passing. It's a set of circulations and networks that, though enormous and ambient, remains hidden. Trucking is central to how the United States imagines itself as a set of possibilities about class and geographic mobility. We imagine the frontier, cowboys, road trips, cars. We hope for meritocracy, the American dream, self-reliance. These myths intersect powerfully in the body of the trucker.

Truckers' situation at the start of the twenty-first century is a more intense version of a struggle we all share. The pace of technological change and the increasing, though uneven, acceptance of queer and trans lives, combined with the permeability between private and public spheres along these axes, is so destabilizing that the culture is almost in free fall. I don't focus on truckers to fetishize them (though I'm not ashamed to say that I find them fascinating, fun, and even heroic) but rather to view them as a microcosm of this inconceivable change. The trucking industry's almost magical ability to be both enormous and elusive, and culture's extreme curiosity about truckers, which somehow coexists with obliviousness about them, combine to make trucking a source of insight into labor, gender, and contemporary life.

The rise and dominance of systems of technology and surveillance shape how truckers function. Each additional regulation is intended to reduce highway dangers, to increase profit to the trucking companies, and to reduce consumer costs. Yet regulations also infantilize truckers and make their daily lives much harder. In response, they often rebel, taking risks to retaliate against these increasing regimes of control. Most smoke, and many engage in sexual behavior that's potentially dangerous. Donovan says she and others truckers are sending a message to those who control their lives: *"If you're going to wreck my body, I'm going to wreck it first—I own this, asshole."*

Dragging an Anchor

The following chapters unfold in the shape of an imaginary truck run, alternating between driving ("rolling" or "running") and stopping. Chapters about truck stops, customers (shippers and receivers), and accidents alternate with chapters about driving while black, dealing with severe weather, and coping with excessive regulations. The chapters weave together queer, trans, and minority truckers' stories that illuminate gay life, working-class life, and meaningful, transformative change. Collectively, my narrators' experiences give a sense of what it's like out there, who does it, and how all of that is changing.

Each of these chapters opens with a relevant piece of trucker slang; "hammer down," for example, means to speed up or to just get out there and get 'er done. There's a cloud of nostalgia around this lingo now, since cell phones are replacing CBs, and trucking work now proceeds in a less colorful, more universal language. And yet the slang persists as a means to create community; with faces and places constantly shifting, embodied community doesn't usually happen, so truckers create an insider-type bond through slang and stories. For example, "four-wheeler" is a term truckers use to describe automobiles and their drivers. It's not a compliment. "Driver" is a term truckers use to describe each other. One trucker will hail another with the title "driver" as a means of invoking professionalism: of seeing and naming trucking community. Because I have been a trucker, I can draw on that sense of community. But as an ethnographer, I'm also outside the community, observing it. My training in language and narrative provides a way into the culture, an understanding of how words ground community. Yet they also create distance from that community. The stories—the words of my sixty-six trucking narrators—give me access to the trucking lifestyle and enable me to share it with readers.

"Dragging an anchor" is a trucker term with many meanings. The trucker sits in the cab and drags the trailer up and down the road. You get a feel for this running passes such as the Grapevine, Cabbage, Donner, or Snoqualmie. The trailer holds the weight and literally pulls or pushes the tractor up, down, or sideways. Since you're in the tractor grinding the gears, it feels like you're dragging the freight up the hills personally—it's a very embodied, visceral process. It's fun.

But "dragging an anchor" has other meanings. Sitting there behind the wheel, truckers feel like they're pulling the entire weight of regulations and micromanaging rules through time and space. It feels like this web is pulling you down—dragging you back—and you have to twist, plan, accommodate, you have to haul it physically down the road with you: an added burden.

And sexual and social mores and cultural logics are other anchors truckers drag. Trucking serves as a common fantasy of escape, especially in this century of limited freedoms and of fear. Trying to take care of family and other responsibilities while also impersonating badassery, sexual voracity, and a refusal to be tied down is a complicated, if delicious, burden.

"Good buddy" used to be a casual trucker greeting. When there was a flurry of interest in truckers and CB radios in the 1970s, "Hey, good buddy" was how truckers (and others) greeted each other. According to a trucker slang website, "good buddy" "was the stereotypical term for a friend or acquaintance on a CB radio. It is now the modern term for a homosexual" (Fringe62). That's a powerful elision, and one that this book unpacks and explores.

1

STARTING

WHOOP 'N' RIDE

Why People Choose Trucking,
and How They Prepare

I'LL START WITH MY OWN STORY, which I found to be quite typical, and weave it into related stories I heard from my narrators. I was drawn to trucking out of a mixture of desperation and desire. I have always loved driving. I physically love how it feels: the machine's response to me, the need to monitor my surroundings and react to my environment, the strange combination of tedium and surprise. This mundane fact is the essential core of the cowboy-trucker legend. The expression "whoop 'n' ride" captures the enthusiasm of trucking, movement, escape. Truckers use it as a sign-off, as a way to emphasize the thrill of trucking in the face of its many mundane details. One of trucking's rewards is the isolation: truckers like to be alone with their thoughts. There's some magic in the combination of movement, endurance, and productivity that frees our minds and unleashes an addictive inner satisfaction.

Yet, to get that reward, truckers have to walk away from their lives. Most truck drivers give up both a presence at home and control of their lives and time. People don't make that choice until they're driven there by some degree of desperation. For example, take Ulrike's case: *"[I] worked in a factory and the factory was shipped overseas, and they said we could transfer companies or we could get some schooling. The training options was mostly computers. This was like the late 80s and computers was so new back then, and that wasn't something I wanted to do. But I couldn't sit there in North Carolina and not do anything at all, so I took the truck driving course."* In my case, I had been denied promotion and tenure as a professor (essentially, I had been laid off), been unsuccessful at fighting the decision, and been unable to land any other stable employment. My anger and my panic about finances began to mount. Being jobless was my motivation to become a trucker, but it combined with more emotional preconditions: the shame of career loss and the lure of the open road.

Ciara had a similar experience: *"I got into driving because of the fact that my job as an autoworker was going kaput; I was then at the Chrysler Plant in Dayton, Ohio, when it happened. We had been laid off for about six weeks, and I thought, well, I had to do something. My unemployment was about to run out, I lost my apartment, I was behind on all my bills—but I'm not the only one, believe me. I had gone to a union meeting about hopefully going back to school, and I thought about going into medical accounting, but they said, 'Well, you can't do that because we don't have a need for that. You need to go into a field that's needed.' All I kept seeing was ads for truck drivers and nurses, so I answered an ad for a flatbed company, and I found out that they'd put me through school. The whole experience of learning to drive a truck was probably one of the most rewarding things I've ever done. At the same time it was so hard. For everything I did right, I did five things wrong. It was two steps forward and five steps back. In reverse. It tests your emotional capacity and how strong you actually are as a person, because there were days I wanted to stop because I was just fighting with it and asking, 'How come everybody else can do this and I can't?'"* She stuck with it, got her license on her second try, and started driving.

Vito turned to trucking because he *"was actually running away from quite a few problems."* These included drug and job problems, not directly related to being gay but not unrelated either. Jobs are hard to come by, especially full-time, decent-paying jobs, and trans, minority, and queer people report that trucking jobs hire them when no one else will. This may be because the recruiting typically happens by phone, so they can slide in under the radar. Odette says, *"When I first came out as transgender nobody would hire me. I would fill out job applications and they would probably run background checks and see my birth name and throw my application in the garbage. I just could not get a job. After a few years of chronic unemployment, the state offered me a grant to go to school to get my CDL [commercial driver's license], and I read up on it, and I thought it was the kind of thing that could be kind of accepting for a job."* She's never had a hard time getting or keeping a trucking job, though the schedule remains difficult for her. Many trans and intersex truckers report choosing trucking because being alone is physically and emotionally their safest option. This book's narrators had a hard time getting

A truck stop at dusk. (Photo by the author.)

and keeping nontrucking employment because of bias from coworkers and employers, so once they secure a trucking job, working alone can be a boon. For instance, Ingrid says, *"I tend to get nervous around people no matter how well I know them, so this job — with so little contact dealing with people — it's perfect."* Though she tries to *"smile and be friendly,"* she characterizes both the public and her own family as *"more curt than courteous,"* so she chooses isolation. Gracie, who learned about their own intersex condition as a teen, reports, *"I really felt like I was an alien"* and that they *"really do think it makes you feel disconnected from everyone else."* Trucking provides Gracie a way to both escape and work through these feelings.

Liam, who transitioned in 2006, worked in the financial industry, where he was harassed at work to the extent that his coworkers figured the company was trying to force him to quit. But he persisted until he was laid off in 2008, and then the only work he could get was delivering pizza. With limited work history in his new name, he decided that trucking was his only option. Even once he got his CDL, Liam struggled to get hired, but eventually, he says, *"I talked to a recruiter and I just told them straight up, 'Before we waste any more time, I'm transgender, this is what you're going to find on the background check. So it's no problem, just tell me now, and we'll move on.' And he's like, 'You do realize you're not the first, right?' So that's how I ended up in trucking."*

It was basically like starting all over again. I'm going through my second pu-
berty and getting the same type of jobs that a teenager going through puberty
would have."

Trucking serves these marginalized workers well by giving them a job
that, in its isolation, allows them to craft and defend queer and trans em-
bodiments. Almost all the truckers I spoke to described themselves as introverted and characterized life on the road as facilitated by interactions
that are impermanent and therefore tolerable. Liam went on to say, *"It's just*
not cool when you're in your forties and need to support a family. I'm luckier
than my male-to-female counterparts because nobody looks at me and says,
'Oh, look at that trannie.' So they just see some other person out here trucking.
I tend to . . . stay mainly stealth for safety reasons. I really feel like trucking is
a very conservative, redneck—for lack of a better word—industry. When I sit
in the truck stop having dinner, I listen to these other truckers talking about
how wonderful Trump is, and how it's about time we got someone with balls in
[the White House]. Oh man, there is no way I'm going to be an out-and-proud
trans person out here. What a way to ruin my appetite. I just feel safe because
nobody knows." The loneliness of this life, isolated from what scant community truckers can manage, is both a problem and one of the job's appeals.

Training

Having spent many hours driving in all weathers, I had seen countless trucks
and their drivers, and the romance of that life appealed to me. I can drive all
night, I don't need to pee very often, and I love the mental state long drives
put me in; they're pretty much the only time I feel relaxed. I love that feeling,
and almost every trucker I've talked to does too. That's what we mean when
we say trucking is addictive—it's not just a job but a lifestyle. Further, all
that time behind the wheel means truckers spend copious hours thinking,
and that's why we resent being considered brainless or treated like we're just
steering-wheel holders. As a group, truckers spend lots of time in their own
heads and have plenty to say if someone asks.

When I ran out of other options, I decided to look into trucking, and since
I had been an English major, and then an English professor, the trucking
company called CR England appealed to me. It had a nearby training facility and was very eager to sign me up and train me, demanding no financial
contribution. The company's offer seemed too good to be true, though, so I
did some research.

It turns out that England is one of many companies that lure trainees in, offering "free" education in exchange for driving contracts that pay back the training expenses in a form of indentured servitude. School, lodging, meals, and testing are all "free," but you pay for them liberally out of your first paychecks. I've spoken with countless truckers trained and then trapped by this system. One such trucker, LaToya, had served a short prison stint in Georgia for stealing from her employer (a friend "returned" items to the big-box store where LaToya worked, and they split the profits), and she was having a really hard time getting hired with that felony on her record. However, *this lady at the unemployment office saw me and asked if I'd tried trucking,"* LaToya says. *"I think she thought I was a dude when she said it, but it lit a lightbulb up in my head."* That office indicated that many trucking firms were hiring, even people with felony convictions. LaToya said she wanted to show her family (who had been supportive during her incarceration and her coming out) that their belief in her was justified and that she could be as independent financially as she was in spirit. She says, *"I called England, and they were willing to give me a chance. Even after everything that's happened, I still remember how good that felt. Maybe this was my answer. I got on the bus like they told me and came to Indiana."*

LaToya traveled to Gary, Indiana, where she signed lots of paperwork and got assigned a roommate, who she said looked more scared that she was gay than that she was black. The company van drove trainees from the hotel to the training site and back, and if they wanted to go anywhere else, they walked. Except for breakfast, the food was inedible (cold boxed lunches), and trainees typically dragged around plastic grocery bags full of snacks they bought at convenience stores, which were the only walkable options. LaToya remarks that the best part was that her roommate quit almost immediately, leaving her a room to herself, since she was then the only remaining woman. There were classes and written tests, physical exams, lots of waiting, and minimal time behind the wheel, with even less guidance. LaToya recalls her experience during training: *"I can do it. I can drive, that's not the problem. I actually picked it up pretty fast. But there was only one teacher to ask questions, and he usually ignored me or didn't know. And we all had to take turns, so there was more waiting than anything. When I showed up to test, that time in the truck was the most time I had driving, by a lot."* She failed twice before passing, but that's par for the course, and she valued the drive time anyway. But she was motivated: *"I had run out of cash, and I just wanted to get out there and start collecting a paycheck."*

For her first six weeks, she drove with a trainer, making a flat hourly wage. But she saw almost none of that money, since she was reimbursing the company for her room and board, testing, and training. This is when she started to get angry. She ran constantly, since having two drivers in a truck allows the company to log almost continuous miles and thus maximize profits, but almost none of that went into her pocket. This pattern held true when she was assigned to her own truck and drove solo. We met up early in this period, when her pride and glory in the truck itself, and in her ability to handle it, made her almost shine. Seeing her walk across a dusty parking lot radiating confidence made her frustration at her working conditions even sadder. This worker is loyal, fierce, and utterly dedicated to a job that shows her no respect. *"Knowing I can't quit, they send me out west to, like, Montana or Wyoming,"* she says. *"Great money getting there, sure, but these are locations with no freight, so then I sit for days waiting for my DM [driver manager, who assigns freight to company drivers] to call, constantly checking to see if I missed a message, eating that crappy truck stop food, and watching the money I made driving west flow down the drain. And there's still months till I'm out of debt to these people. I feel like a slave. I just want to tell other drivers to go to community college instead — borrow the money if you have to. As soon as I can, I'm switching — other carriers want me, and they'll treat me right."*

Trucking recruiters' misrepresentations and lies are legendary, so I have no reason to hope that what she has been promised will actually materialize, but I didn't opt to share that information with LaToya, whose morale was low enough already. Because I had heard many horror stories like hers, I decided to visit an independent truck driver school in Gary, where I lived, to pursue my own training. When I stopped by to inquire, they suggested I climb into the cab of one of their training vehicles, and sitting there, feeling the challenge and the thrill of it, I could feel the bitterness and humiliation of getting fired drain away. I enrolled on the spot. The school was owned and operated by an affable former trucker named Lou. His son Johnny, a teacher at the school, became my nemesis. Jimmy and Bob, my other teachers, were great: patient, full of stories, encouraging, warm but challenging, and above all, clear. I remember every other student in that class. They were all better than me by a mile, and all gracious about that, and helpful.

I drove fine. Changing gears was hard because you have to clutch twice — once to get in the gear and once to get out — following a rhythm that varies slightly in each truck. But I could do that. I had been a car mechanic for years, and I had a feel for transmissions. True, "the button" tripped me up sometimes. The shifter has a button, and to reverse and go through the low gears you need to have the button up, then you flip it down to go through the second set. The escaping air makes a *pfft* noise that is one of the sensory joys of driving truck. If you forget this step, you can't get in gear, which is dangerous, so the teacher yells, reminds, and begs.

Turning was more challenging. To this day, when I drive around a curve, I hear Bob's voice reminding me to "hang it high and watch the tandems." In a car, the back basically goes where the front goes, but in a truck, you need to radically overcompensate with the front of the truck to get the back to end up where you need it. Hard to get the hang of, but again, not impossible.

Then there's backing. There's no rearview mirror, because you can't see through fifty-three feet of solid mass. And the rear wheels don't swivel, they only rotate. So essentially you are at the front of a very large train, pushing the rear by turning only the front. People who play video games have an advantage here because they're used to moving something that affects the direction of something else. Or maybe I just used the fact that I don't play video games as an excuse for why I struggled with backing way more than the other students did. One by one, each of them internalized this process, and could back our three practice trucks into the various designated spots in the yard. However, when it was my turn, I'd get discombobulated, pull forward to regroup, and then repeat. Not infrequently, I would find myself in the very front of the yard, in the disused area that served as a barrier between the driving school and the road. This frustrated the instructors almost as much as it frustrated me, but they worked with me and helped me brainstorm solutions. Johnny, however, was belligerent. "What the fuck do you think you're doing?" he would yell, jumping up on the step and glaring into the cab at me, as though I had gone out on an unauthorized joyride. Every student was older than Johnny, and we had all found ourselves in school because our other plans had derailed, so his ungenerous response felt dehumanizing. The tactic that worked best for me was to calmly reply, "I think it's clear that I don't know. Would you please explain this to me again?" But sometimes I was too angry—or too near tears—to pull this off, and then his bullying eroded my confidence.

Jimmy, Bob, and Lou all tried to teach me, as did every other student in my class, which added to my shame because, as the only woman, I didn't want to fail. Ultimately, I did catch on. Though I was never a fast backer, I could get into a zone where, if I trusted myself and didn't overthink, I could move the steering wheel so that the rear of the truck went where I wanted it to. I passed the road test, went to the DMV, and was issued a CDL. This license qualified me to sign on with a megacarrier, where I then got another week of training and passed another test. Next, I trained "over the road" (which is what it's called when truckers leave their terminal with a load knowing they will be gone at least several days, picking up various kinds of freight) with another trucker and took one final road test.

Because I paid for my initial trucking school up front, and the subsequent trainings were paid for by the company, I escaped the pattern of debt and indenture many truckers share. The popular press, scholarship, and the Internet, however, are crowded with such stories. In 2015, *Bitch* ran an article that was then picked up by *Utne* and others called "Rigged System," about the vulnerability of female truck drivers. It relates stories of trainer harassment, class-action suits, and trainee anxiety and lack of options. One informant "had gone through trucking school and now owed them $6,000. 'I wasn't in the position to just cough up thousands of dollars; if I was, I wouldn't be here in the first place,' Tracy said" (Asgarian, 43). This practice of debt servitude, combined with the vast intimidating machine and with truckers' isolation from social protection and from each other, often makes the training process a trial by fire.

My training experience was hard, but it was nothing compared to the stories I heard. Many of my female narrators had trainee horror stories, including Fanny, whose male trainer told her, *"You have to prove yourself with the paperwork the first day, the second day you have to prove yourself behind the wheel, and the third day you have to prove yourself in the bunk."* When she reported it, the company laughed it off, saying the trainer probably meant something innocuous and pointing out that he had never said the word "sex." Fanny responded, *"You can go ahead and play stupid, but I'm not getting back in his truck."* They got her a different trainer but did nothing about the first guy, who presumably got assigned someone with less ability to fight back. My trainer was a lesbian and not a source of anxiety. Further, I knew if I didn't make it, I had other options. And in fact, I only wound up trucking for a few months, including company training with a firm in Wisconsin. I mostly ran giant rolls of paper from Mississippi to Minnesota and huge volumes of Trident gum or other "food" from Minnesota to distribution centers on the Gulf Coast.

The end of my trucking career came when a family member had a medical emergency. I informed my driver manager, drove my truck to the terminal, turned my keys in, and left. Several days later, I called to report back to work and was told I had no job to return to. Trucking companies prefer drivers who prioritize shipping schedules over their own needs, and they are perfectly happy to let noncompliant drivers go. In fact, each megacarrier has a yearly turnover rate of over 100 percent. I hadn't known that at the time, nor was I aware of the employment history files from Drive-A-Check, which pays companies to submit data on all their truck drivers and serves as a clearing-house for trucker information. It's an unmonitored clearinghouse, in which the company's explanation of an employee's work history goes unchallenged and often unknown to the driver. Since my Drive-A-Check report indicated that I had abandoned my load, I could not get rehired by that company or any other, at least not soon. I could request (and then purchase) a copy of my report and attempt to get it corrected, but the odds of that succeeding are not in the driver's favor. I was told that my chances of getting hired by a different carrier would increase after six months. By then, if I had no other employment options, I would be thoroughly desperate and grateful for any chance to try again: an ideal trainee.

You don't have to be paranoid to imagine why companies treat drivers this way. They value loyalty and want to select drivers who are more than a little desperate, docile, and compliant. It's not different from the preferences of any other employer, really, but trucking companies accomplish these goals unusually well. Unions are practically nonexistent. The Teamsters Union was in its death throes when deregulation happened in the late 70s, and by the time Reagan fired the air traffic controllers in 1981, trucking unions were in full retreat. Only about 8 percent of truck drivers are unionized now, and federal oversight focuses on road safety via micromanagement rather than on protecting workers. I'll have more to say about these circumstances in the coming chapters, but here I want to specifically point out how vulnerable truckers are to unfair termination because of the Drive-A-Check employment history file, to which employers, but not workers, have access.

Solitary Confinement

There are profound social costs to the isolation of trucking. People are drawn to its perceived renegade lifestyle for personal reasons or because of stigma or outright bigotry in other work or social settings. But once there, the lonely trucker lifestyle pushes them further away from community. Vito describes this poignantly: *"It's hard to get invested. For people with relation-ships, you can tell that there's always a strain on the relationship, any type of relationship, because as a truck driver, you can't call your friends up and talk to them about your experiences and what you're going through. They look at trucks going through the city, but they don't pay attention. And the discussion that they want to have is on a personal level, so it's hard to have those types of conversations that make you not want to be on the road, which is your career, so yeah, it's hard to stay in relationships. So there's times where I go home and I don't see anyone. My first day home, everyone in my life knows that's my rest day—don't call, don't—I need to mentally detach from being on the road. And then there's times where the second and third day, I don't want to go out, I don't want to go do anything. And you almost crave to get back in the truck, and once you get in the truck you just want to go back home, but for a split second there you're like, 'I don't want to deal with people—I just want to get in my truck and go as far away as possible.' So especially for very social people it's—you're always teetering on one or the other—you want to be home, but you don't. Where, because you can't be there in the type of way that another person needs you to be there, it's better if you keep it very simple or very distant. Typically that's what keeps you being out on the road."*

Some queer and trans truckers report having struggled for years to do and be what is expected of them. These narrators often experience the solitude of trucking as an opportunity to finally be themselves instead of pleasing others. Josephine, when I spoke to her in Rolla, Missouri, reflects: *"Getting all this time alone is just about enjoying my life. And me. And I listen to audiobooks, and I can listen to any book I really want to."* She laughs. After a lifetime of trying to gain approval, trucking is about her. It gives her the opportunity to be out, to meet people on her own terms, and to exchange a life focused on service for one focused on her. Still, harassment is constant for Josephine, and it causes health problems. She tells me, *"I do know my blood pressure spikes when I get screamed at by men, for crying out loud."* Odette feels safe and welcome on the road, yet reports, *"I'd say the two biggest stressors for me are being away from my family and just being alone. The solitude really bothers me a lot."* Though many truckers tell me that as long as they keep their butts in the seats, trucking jobs don't discriminate, others suspect they have been covertly denied good freight and thus forced to seek better work. Echo, who presents as a butch lesbian, was dismissed after she was in an accident. Her company told her that she had *"met the threshold of damage,"* though she knew straight men who had cost the company more yet continued to work there. *"Clear discrimination,"* she adds.

Freedom and the open road are attractive options for my narrators, but their reasons are important. Even those who are running away from problems at home are experiencing those problems because of stigma; they are running away not from their life, but from people's reaction to their life, and specifically to their sexual or gender expression. Lori says trucking is perfect *"because it gets [her] away from having to deal with people a whole lot."*

Dealing with people means interacting, but it also means tolerating their hostility and antitrans bullshit—and a job that lets you escape all that can feel like a very good fit. Hanna went into trucking because she was harassed so much in her previous factory jobs. She thinks, *"Probably so many trans girls truck [because] they're not welcome at home. Or if they're single, they don't have to have a home, so it's easier to save up for surgery. Also, it's harder for people to bother you, and they definitely don't want to be around people. I was so stressed by the crap at Valeo that I was throwing up every night. And I tried working at another factory, [a] Toyota Industrial Equipment Manufacturing plant in Seymour, Indiana, and I remember one girl making a comment when I put my shirt on: I looked like I was built like an anime character. But they put me in a job where everybody outcasted me, and so I just ran away from it."*

People get driven into trucking usually out of desperation, and this is more true the more socially marginalized they are. Even the traditional straight, white trucker tends to be a loner or down on his luck, but when the job offers more freedom and pays better, it can provide a way out of society's margins. Marilu says what it comes down to is that *"T-girls truck because it's open, y'know, we're able to get jobs. And they don't care what you wear, or how you act— they just want you to show up and sit there, get from A to B."* Once hired, the isolation of the job and its financial challenges make it hard to integrate socially. For many, the transience and the power conferred by the truck become sufficient reward, but others quit and are worse off than ever. Donovan became a trucker because she *"got fired for being trans in my last job as a bus driver, and I didn't have money anymore to pay for a place, so I ended up taking the first job that was offered to me."* Though she drove truck for more than three years, Donovan quit after our interview, choosing homelessness over signing a new contract. The hardest part, she says, was having to give away her dog, because she couldn't imagine living on the street with a pit bull.

Hanna and I spend as much time talking about fandoms we share as we do about trucking; she seems happy to find another sci-fi viewer and hobbyist. She concludes our conversation by saying, *"I've had other drivers ask questions about the gender thing. But I'm pretty quiet, I keep to myself. I went into trucking for self-security. You don't have to be around a lot of people. But I love that I can wake up in a different place every day. Every day is different, no load is ever really the same, and I have the best office window you could ask for. I've woken up to some beautiful scenery."* Truckers often cherish the beauty and freedom of the road as rewards for the loneliness and as ample compensation for society's marginalization. While it may seem contradictory that Hanna and others love the job in spite of its difficulty, this ambiguity is something they share with many truckers who embrace the freedom and excitement that was once the defining shape of the job and that still can be found in it. They fight fiercely to retain and expand those aspects. In addition, socially stigmatized folks may identify with the job even more tenaciously because their options are limited, and because in trucking, both their bodies and their outsider status are valued, however problematically.

2

ROLLING

SAILBOAT RACES

*The Web of Regulations That Shape
the Work of Trucking*

RECENTLY, I WAS HAVING DINNER with a lovely collection of faculty members from the liberal arts college where I teach. I was talking about truckers, of course, and trying to explain the difficult situation in which many find themselves. My assertion that they are overregulated and underpaid was met with surprise. People who only see truckers from their cars, and get information about trucker pay only from recruitment billboards and mileage rates posted on trucks, might think truckers are doing well. There's a liberal assumption that when people complain about regulation, they're overreacting; that regulations keep us safe, make life fair, and are the price of civil society.

That's not truckers' experience, and it's not because they're childish or unreasonable. It's because over the past forty years a web of regulations, rules, company policies, corporate noncompetition agreements, and laws have shifted all the restriction and risk away from large corporations and down onto individual truckers, while denying those same truckers access to choice, options, or financial reward. Further, truckers are often seen as nostalgically clinging to old patterns and values, rather than embracing change, technology, and daily yoga. What this assessment misses is that truckers *were* better off forty years ago: The rules under which they operated were more flexible and their pay rates higher. They could shape their schedules, have fun, and experience a certain renegade respect. The job has gotten steadily more regulated, less enjoyable, and less lucrative just as women and immigrants have entered it. Which came first, and how they are related, is an ongoing question. Many truckers believe regulations were put in place to curtail bad behavior by immigrants and to make the job safe for weak and whiney women. Though GPS, power steering, air ride seats, and cell phones have all vastly improved trucking, these advances don't outweigh the lost income, autonomy, and respect or make up for the sense of being hemmed in by endless, incompatible regulations and expectations. Thus, truckers' nostalgia is justified, but its target is misplaced.

This chapter explains some of the regulations governing truckers and gives examples from my narrators' experiences about how the rules work to increase driver exhaustion and danger, thus reducing highway safety for everyone. Relating actual situations, including their causes and consequences, is the best way I know to make that point. But I'll also discuss the regulators' motivations, since we can assume that their intention is not to punish or harm people, but rather to save lives, fuel, and stress. Though I went to trucking school, had significant further training, and have talked extensively to many truckers, the network of governmental and intra-industry rules and policies continues to overwhelm me, so I can imagine that nontrucking readers often get lost in the weeds.

When the interstate highway system solidified in the 1950s, the U.S. government began to regulate truck weights and freight. Since 1938, the federal government (then the Interstate Commerce Commission) has regulated truckers' hours of service with increasing stringency. Initially, truckers were required to sleep eight of every twenty-four working hours, but they could choose when those hours occurred, and they kept track of them in paper logbooks, which were easy to manipulate. With the Motor Carrier Act of 1980 and the concurrent collapse of the Teamsters Union, the regulations governing truckers (now under the Federal Motor Carrier Safety Administration, or FMCSA) began to increase. In brief, truckers can now drive seventy hours in the space of eight days, provided they stop for ten consecutive hours in every twenty-four and take a thirty-minute break during their first eight hours of driving. In any twenty-four-hour period, they can only drive eleven hours and only work fourteen. At any point, they can "reset" this seventy-hour limit by taking a thirty-four-hour break. The more flexible schedule had allowed truckers to stop for an hour or two to nap if they got tired and do the rest of their sleeping later. By planning ahead, they could stagger their driving to avoid tight parking situations and rush hours. Though their time was supervised, they had enough control within that system to make smart, profitable choices. With the newer, more rigid regulations (but with trucking companies, weather, and industry demands remaining constant) truckers report working tired, doing many, many hours of unpaid work, and feeling hopeless and angry. Produce, for example, still has to be loaded onto a pallet as soon as it gets picked, then chilled, and then transferred into a truck, from which it must reach store shelves within a set number of hours so that it will be fresh enough to sell. In addition, technological surveillance mechanisms are available now that allow truckers to be monitored when they're out driving. Two-way cameras are increasingly common, and electronic logging devices (usually called e-logs or ELDs) that record and transmit data about when a truck is in motion are required by law. When compounded regulations and technologies interfere with getting their work done on time, truckers are the ones who pay in lost income, added stress, and exhaustion.

Speed Limiters

Appropriately, my first example of government regulation is the "governor," also known as "speed limiter." Increasingly, truck engines have a feature built in that prevents them from driving over a certain speed. You've probably been in a situation where there is a truck in the right lane, and another truck takes the left lane to pass the first one but seems to take forever to do so. This happens when the passing truck's engine is governed just a few miles higher than the right-lane truck, so overtaking it takes a long time. This is frustrating for the drivers behind them, who probably don't understand why the truck in the passing lane doesn't give it a little more fuel to let traffic move again. But that trucker can't. The driver is probably hoping that the right-lane trucker will back off a bit to let the truck pass. Often a driver will, but not always. "Sailboat races" is the term truckers use to describe this frustrating situation.

In 2016, the American Trucking Association, a loose private coalition of trucking company lobbyists, proposed a new rule that requires all trucks and busses over a certain weight to have speed limiters installed, and the rule became open for public comment before ratification. One of my narrators, Reba, tells me that the American Trucking Association is owned by the megacarriers — huge companies like Swift, Schneider, and U.S. Xpress — that unfairly influence the FMCSA. Megacarriers are the only places where new CDL holders can get hired, because since the companies self-insure, these enormous companies can shoulder the risk of hiring inexperienced truckers. Smaller companies have to buy insurance for their drivers, which makes it prohibitively expensive for them to hire truckers with under a few years' experience. So new drivers get that experience driving for Knight, or Prime,

or Con-way, and then may hope to switch to a smaller firm with better pay
and more respect, where they can be a name, not a number.

Meanwhile, the megacarriers take new drivers and train them. In exchange, they get very cheap labor. But they also get high-risk labor, which
they feel the need to monitor and control. This makes sense; however, these
companies use their influence to pressure federal regulators to control everyone else in roughly parallel ways. Reba summarizes it this way: *"Prime
got the e-logs before they had to. They cut off their own nuts. Then to be com-
petitive, they tried to make everybody else do it, but since they also have speed
limiters, they say the playing field is still not even, and they're pushing through
speed limiters for everybody. Then all drivers would only be able to run 660
miles a day on e-logs."* Now, drivers with open (ungoverned) trucks have an
edge; they can drive faster, so they log more miles. Reba and other narrators
who work for smaller trucking companies defend their right and need to
run those extra miles because the megacarriers, with their huge fleets and
low mileage pay, can easily underbid smaller operations and thus control
all the freight and hog all the profits. The drivers further argue that speed
limiters don't make roads safer, that evidence and practical experience show
roads are safer when everyone drives at around the same speed, and that any
vehicle occasionally needs to accelerate to avoid road hazards or otherwise
respond to rapidly changing circumstances. Speed limiters get all truckers
down to the level of their least free, least respected counterparts, clog up the
roads, increase danger for truckers and other drivers, and heighten everyone's frustration.

Regulations on truckers are implemented to maximize corporate profits
and minimize automobile danger. There's no real pretense that they protect
truckers at all. We can ask why posted speed limits are not enough. They are
considered adequate for cars, and an enforcement system is in place. What
makes it acceptable to regulate trucks more and protect their drivers less?
Trucks don't come equipped with airbags, and that's a regulation that might
save truckers' lives. But it would cost companies money and wouldn't affect automobile drivers directly. Requiring airbags would be a regulation on
companies, not on truckers, and that's not the preferred regulatory strategy.

Being at once micromanaged and treated as disposable creates under-
standable bitterness among truckers. Alix summarizes it like this: *"When
I came into the game, e-logs and governors were already pretty standard with
a lot of these big companies, so I came in really not knowing any difference. I
came in on e-logs and a castrated truck. I understand the frustration a lot of
truckers have, but at the same time, I'm of the mentality that people need to*

Cheryl and her rig.
(Used with permission of the subject.)

embrace more of the change because, with as lawyer-happy as our country is, the regulations aren't just going to go away. So I do embrace the change. I'm not keen on the truck governors; it's the only issue that bothers me. I do believe that some of the companies are setting speeds so low they're actually hazardous. I've never felt the need to have a wide-open truck. Sixty-eight has always been my number, it will get you up and past a lot of the goofballs. Sixty-eight is a great, fuel-efficient number; you can safely pass a lot of people and then go back to cruising without much fuss. But if you're governed at sixty-one or sixty-two miles an hour, oh my God, it makes me want to bash my head against a wall. It's a safety issue—you'll have a bunch of four-wheelers that will bunch up, and when they're playing bumper cars, you can't get away from them. You're stuck at that same speed, and here they are going down the interstate with you, and there's nothing you can do about it unless you back the fuck off. This truck that

I'm in currently was initially governed at sixty-one, and I went about two or three weeks running at sixty-one instead of sixty-four, which isn't much better, but it's enough that I actually lost two different loads because that two or three miles, over the course of an eleven-hour day, it added up. Like I said, it was enough that I lost several different loads." Alix's experience demonstrates that governors aren't about the safety of truckers or other drivers as much as they are an indirect structure that manages freight and the truckers who run it.

The Trucker's Time Clock

The Hours of Service regulations are the central mechanism by which trucker life is managed. Like speed limiters, this set of rules is often changed, so truckers need to stay up to date. Before a change becomes enforceable by the DOT, it gets introduced to the FMCSA, and there's an open comment period during which the public can respond to the proposed ruling. Public hearings are scheduled, usually in locations that truckers can't access, and even when shuttles are provided from nearby truck stops, most truckers can't control their schedules precisely enough to make getting there possible. But comments are also collected online, via a public platform called regulations.gov. The government is careful to project the image that it wants input from the people who will be affected by its decisions. But based on the rulings the government makes and enforces, it's clear that it doesn't listen to what it hears. Earlier, I quoted Reba's claim that this happens because megacarriers buy off the regulatory agencies. Whether that's true or not is immaterial, because the results of the rule changes are the same either way: the risks (financial, physical, and emotional) of trucking have been directed down onto the driver, while the profit from trucking is directed up to large corporations.

Two different systems overlap in discussions of keeping track of hours of service, so I'll start by explaining what they are and how they relate. Hours of Service is the network of rules that regulate when truckers drive, rest, and sleep. Though any summary of this complex system oversimplifies it, truckers can drive eleven hours per day and work fourteen. Then, they are required to spend eight consecutive hours in bed and take two additional non-driving hours. Further, they can drive no more than seventy hours in eight consecutive days, unless they do a reset (stop driving for thirty-four hours). To meet their deadlines and make money, they juggle these restrictions impressively smoothly. Recent changes to this system have involved the thirty-four-hour reset, by which truckers clear themselves to begin another stretch of driving days, and the thirty-minute break now required before eight hours of driving elapse.

These scheduling restrictions can be kept track of in any number of ways. Theoretically. But a different regulation now requires all trucks to have an ELD, or e-log, to keep track of their hours of service. Once it's installed, when the truck's wheels are moving, driving hours get recorded. A computer installed in the truck and linked both to the engine and to the Internet monitors the truck's movements to ensure compliance with the Hours of Service. This became a requirement in all trucks in 2017, and many truckers said that they were going to quit then, while others worked to prevent or delay its installation. There were rallies in DC and urgent reminders to call senators and pressure the president, whose expressed opposition to new regulations led some truckers to believe that he might be sympathetic. Nevertheless, the new regulation was added, albeit with (temporary) exceptions for steer haulers, for trucks built before 2000, and for short-run-only drivers. In the daily life of most truckers I met, Hours of Service and ELDs are interconnected conversations—and linked problems.

Hours of Service and electronic logging might seem like good things. Before e-logs, truckers had to keep written accounts of their worked hours, and these were confusing, time-consuming, and easy to cheat on. Truckers routinely kept three logbooks concurrently so they could produce one for inspectors that would make them appear compliant at any point. A culture of widely accepted, almost required, rule breaking is probably not a good thing. In addition, this "system" was very hard to learn. Keeping three records that dance around rules yet are up to date requires an agile mind, a very clear understanding of how complex legal structures intersect, and the ability to manipulate numbers. Acquiring this skill set takes years and a very good teacher. Like in any apprenticeship program, this resulted in drivers acculturating new drivers with whom they were comfortable (people like them) and thus keeping trucking white and male. Further, it kept new drivers out of the most lucrative runs. By contrast, ELDs are easy to learn and consistent. Certainly, there are strategies for how best to interact with e-logs that increase available drive time and thus earning potential, and different drivers are given different degrees of flexibility with the e-log system, but a new driver can get up to speed quickly. To summarize, the argument in favor of using ELDs to enforce the Hours of Service are that road safety will increase if there isn't a widely acknowledged culture of corruption in the industry, and an easier and fairer system increases equity in the workforce. These are valid reasons and might seem to outweigh the arguments against e-logs, unless you have spent some time doing, or learning about, actual trucking. My narrators' stories tell a different story.

Maci explains the wage and regulation structures, which she attributes to *"corporate America and our government. And corporate America is paying our government so we'll have low wages and they'll get the profits. . . . It's set up to get the driver punished for what the industry is doing."* Natalia gives a concrete example: *"With the electronic logs, you get to Walmart, say, and they take six hours to unload you, your clock ran out three hours ago, what do you do? Walmart doesn't even want you on their property—they're done, so you take the violation [decide to drive when you're out of legal hours to do so, risking a ticket or dismissal], and where do you go? They're going to say, 'Go to a safe haven'—well, where the hell is that? That's the frustration of it—it doesn't take into account what is real. Like, I read somewhere 60 percent of all loading and unloading takes longer than three hours. That can really mess up your day if you've got to drive six or eight hours to get somewhere."*

Tammy has been trucking for more than eleven years, and she has seen regulations change significantly during that time. Like many of my narrators, she doesn't want to complain, because staying positive is important to her. There are things she likes about driving truck, so she doesn't want a critique of the system to detract from that. Still, she says, *"You get tired, you know? Even in the middle of the day, and evening comes around, and it just wears you out, driving through all that traffic. The fatigue it just . . . I don't want to call it just a job because it is my career, driving truck, and I've done it for ten years, going on eleven, and I like doing it. Things were so much different a long time ago: you didn't have all these rules and laws. I'm not trying to get too political, but it's the federal government. You remember the safety manual, that thick and that's only a part of it, updated monthly. It's like, OK. That was yesterday's law. The regulations are not about safety. It's all about control, and their version is to make the roadways safer by controlling us. Trucking is the most—THE most—federally regulated industry out there. They have more rules and regulations, guarding, watching us. Your big container ships coming from China—I would be so inspecting those. They have no idea what's on there. They just don't take security seriously enough in the ports—I've been in a lot of the ports. But give us a break! There's only so much you can push down on somebody."*

Zoe makes a similar argument, delivered in less gentle terms: *"This modern technology, I mean, they got the public thinking that these electronic logs are safer, but really it's not about safety, it's all about revenue. All this candy-ass Qualcomm stuff—electronic logs doesn't make truckers safer. I mean, you got grown people out here that are used to sleeping at night, but sometimes the way things happen, you're driving at night and you're supposed to be sleeping in the daytime. But your body is so used to sleeping at night that you don't get to sleep till an hour before time to ride, and yeah, you're sleepy as hell come eleven o'clock at night, but you're still driving because the freight got to be there about one or two in the morning."* Before the industry started stacking regulations up, truckers could sleep their required eight hours whenever they wanted. They still had to log eight hours of sleep, but when they did so was up to them, so if the freight schedule got challenging and they found themselves driving tired, they could pull over, sleep for an hour or two, and then return to driving and still make the deadline. Now, the eight hours must be continuous, so truckers keep driving until they can deliver their freight, no matter how tired they get.

Vito offers a different perspective. He defends the e-logs, which he says make it harder for companies to push their drivers to drive tired in order for them to meet deadlines. He says, *"I've ran paper logs, I've ran electronic logs. I love electronic logs, and the reason I say that is the truckers used to cheat the logbooks, but the companies used to cheat them too. Now, the company can't push you any more than what's on that clock, and you can't push yourself to any more that what's on that clock, which keeps everyone that's out on the road a lot safer."* If truckers running e-logs are out of hours, their companies run risks if they pressure them to drive anyway. Thus, if the timing works for the trucker, e-logs can increase safety and rest. But there are other types of timing regulations that Vito classifies as intrusive, such as a now-suspended rule that the thirty-four-hour reset contain two overnight periods. This stipulation shortened his available drive hours significantly, but the FMCSA has let it revert to the system he liked, so Vito no longer objects to the e-logs.

The e-logs are easier to learn than paper logbooks, and harder to cheat. But they can be revised or deviated from, and companies offer drivers some discretion about this. One trucker said the company allows three violations per month before the trucker gets in trouble. Others report feeling panicked and vulnerable if they go over the allowed drive time in even a single instance, including for reasons such as road construction delays or lack of parking at truck stops. Spaces where it's legal to park a truck are limited, and truckers report circling truck stops and rest areas for hours looking for a legal spot, especially in the popular evening hours. Typically, there just aren't enough spaces and truckers must either park illegally (risking a ticket for which they are personally responsible), drive illegally (past legal drive time limits) searching, or stop driving before their legal hours run out in the attempt to find a spot early, before the pressure mounts. Truckers thus juggle parking and other time pressures within a very rigid time frame, which they must manipulate very effectively in order to make a profit. In this context, there's some flexibility in how e-log technologies are deployed. Tricks and tips for how to sneak things by them or how to physically disengage them and not get caught circulate in trucker spaces.

During my ride-along with Reba, the Qualcomm (a common brand of ELD) was almost a third personality in the truck. Reba often pointed to it contemptuously, detailing the stupid and illegal steps it forced her to take. For example, as soon as we reached a customer, she'd update our status on the e-log to "on duty, not driving" and specify that we were at a customer. We would sit there and wait five minutes. Then we'd change our status again to "off duty, in sleeper berth" and get out of the truck and go confer with the customer. We would figure out where to go and whom to talk to, try to determine where to put the truck and when. Then, driving slowly so as not to trigger the e-log into driving mode, we'd back up to the assigned dock, handle paperwork, and generally do a trucker's job. All while logged as asleep in bed.

This practice is common among experienced truckers because the requirement that they spend ten hours off duty not driving, eight of which have to be logged as continuous hours in the sleeper berth, makes it very hard for them to do their jobs. Strategies like these logging deceptions are what make successful days possible. But even they are sometimes not enough.

One sequence of events makes the arbitrariness of Hours of Service and e-logs painfully obvious. Though I was present at the time, asking questions, and though I had driven a truck previously myself and had a decent sense of how the timing works, I was still mystified. I will try to make the problem clear to readers, but remember that if you're confused, it's because the system is confusing. In order to run legally, truckers have to fit their pickups, drop-offs, inspections, breaks, and sleep into a tight schedule. It often feels like a logic puzzle.

On this occasion, Reba and I get up at 4:00 a.m. in order to deliver her load in Compton, California, and we then drive up to the salad bowl (trucker slang for the produce fields stretching north from Los Angeles) to fill the truck. The first pickup goes well, taking only three and a half hours, which we log as "not driving, in sleeper berth," and then we go to the second distribution center. We get there early (at 11:20 a.m.), knowing that if we make good time, the rest of the return trip will go smoothly. But soon we learn that the distribution center doesn't plan to load Reba's truck until five, and this delay makes the timing of our return trip complicated, almost impossible.

Reba goes in to talk to the customer to try to get loaded sooner, but the customer repeats that her appointment is at five, and when she calls her company, she finds out that dispatch knows that but didn't bother to tell her. She says, *"Well, now we're fucked. The three and a half hours we spent at the first customer logged as 'in sleeper berth' could have been eight if we had stayed there, and my clock would have been reset. But since we came over here we lost those hours, and now we will have to wait eight more hours here so that I can then drive. We need to do that because otherwise 1) no income and 2) no parking. If we leave here at 5:30 loaded, we only have a few hours left on the clock, and we'll run out of hours in the evening in California where there is no available parking. We'll be in violation. So we need to sit here eight hours and then drive eleven hours, because the fruit needs to get there in three days or less by agreement."* Reba does math to determine how many hours she'll need to drive that night to make this possible. Her point is that she needs to manage her schedule and her sleep. The company takes that away — and makes it a huge struggle — by withholding information. Technology is only part of the problem. She calculates: *"I have twenty-three hours left on [my legally allowed] 70. I need thirty-five hours to get to Lansing, which is 2,323 miles away. I can run an average speed of sixty-five miles per hour at gross. Tonight if we drive 400 miles, it will take six hours, from 6:00 p.m. [California time] to midnight central time. Then we'll need ten hours clocked out, so I can't drive again till 10:00 a.m. Then I'll drive from ten to ten, all eleven drive hours, 700 miles, and I will then have only six hours left on the clock. If we run six hours on Friday, we can start at 8:00 a.m. central time, making 400 miles when we reach seventy hours. I started on Friday, so on Friday at midnight EST, my eighth day starts. I get ten hours, plus sixteen minutes, back on eight-day recap. So on Saturday, I can run ten hours, 850 miles. Then I'll be out of hours again and must wait till midnight EST. At midnight EST, I will have been stopped for ten hours — not ten hours and one minute, but ten hours."*

That's the planning Reba does as we sit in California, waiting to get loaded with peacharines. We plan to sit here until 7:20 (exactly eight hours from when we pulled in and switched the e-log to "off duty, in sleeper berth"), when Reba will again be able to drive. During that time we'll load this new fruit, so she can't really sleep and will have to drive most of the night after getting up at four. She does the complicated math above to try to figure out how to get home legally within the three days her company's customer allows. If there were speed limiters holding her speed to sixty-five, it wouldn't be possible.

We sit in the heat, waiting. It's over 100 degrees, and we can't idle the truck to run the air conditioning because California has laws against that, so it's hot. We're in a vehicle parked in the sun on asphalt. Sleep? You try it. Reba finally goes in to check on our load, and they say she has three trucks ahead of her, because you have to sign in at your appointment time (she thought her signing in hours ago counted — go figure). So we may not get out at 7:20 as planned and may be further delayed. But mercifully, they tell her to pull up to a dock soon, and we're ready to roll in ten minutes, which is only ten minutes after our earliest possible departure. Reba gets the paperwork from the customer, pulls forward, closes the trailer doors, and brings the tandems forward. Qualcomm asks for a vehicle inspection report, and we're off.

When we finally pull into a truck stop after about ten driving hours, we've been awake for more than twenty-four hours, being jerked around by scheduling regulations disguised as safety precautions. Reba's only comment is *"My shifting leg hurts."* I am exhausted — drained dry — and say so. Reba rolls her eyes at me and gets out of the truck and just proceeds with her life. Nothing rare here for her. Just for me.

When we talked near Bensalem, I asked Dorothy, who has been driving for over thirty years, if regulations have changed during her career. Her response, in part, is "Holy shit, *girlfriend, they're micromanaging us. They're getting ridiculous. If it's truly safety, then I don't have any problem with it, but a lot if this is not safety, it's management. Insurance companies. Take the on-board lane protectors, and I'm referring to the ones that stop you if you get too close to somebody. One of the ladies that's been driving for about two years had one on her truck, and then every time you hit a rumble strip it sends an email to [the] safety [department], and then they want to know what's going on. But I'm running across [Interstate] 90/80 up there, and they're doing construction, and down to two lanes, and you don't have any choice, all you can do is run those rumble strips. [My friend] said, 'I'm in the construction, and there's a barrel a little close to the line, and my truck's slammin' on the brakes because it detects something,' so insurance equals safety? No, I don't think so. What are you risking and what are you gaining?*

"And some of this stuff they've been coming up with, micromanaging, is robotizing the driver. So now we've got inward-facing cameras. Where do they come up with this shit? You've got some gal that comes out of the college, and never driven a truck before is going to decide that something that's in your truck is hazmat? If the camera records fifteen seconds before and fifteen after

an incident, it has to be on twenty-four hours a day. They say it only sends you to a third party when you have an incident. Well, who's looking at it the other twenty-four hours a day? But now we're not allowed to have a drink. If you smoke you're not allowed to smoke a cigarette. Don't twitch, don't fart, don't sneeze. Well, here's the problem: it's the insurance companies, and they want to dissolve themselves of responsibility, and then anything that's a safety issue can be put on the driver. So they have an incident, OK, maybe they didn't do anything, and it shows that they didn't do anything, but they have ten incidents that they've been called on the carpet for and talked to about, so now we've got past practices. It's all geared to blaming it on the driver."

Rhian blames the increased regulations on truckers' bad behavior: *"Now, the trucking industry could have done a lot of things different. If there weren't a lot of drivers who don't police themselves and regulate themselves, we wouldn't need all these regulations. It's so different, they grouse about it and they don't realize we're all the problem; we did all these different things and so they did all these regulations."* This strategy is not uncommon — truckers often don't blame large structural forces for their struggles. Rather, they blame each other, or themselves. This makes perfect sense, since truckers are part of our culture, which emphasizes personal responsibility especially when it can be directed onto stigmatized, vulnerable populations. Rhian, and other truckers, thus reproduce a rhetoric, and a perspective, that does them harm. (Everyone does, right?) What's surprising is how often truckers escape this rhetorical trap, and in its place a sense of who is doing what to whom and why begins to emerge.

There is nothing rare about these stories — they are the mundane every-day situation of truckers doing their jobs. One trucker posted this on Face-book on September 9, 2016: "This is going to be such a long night . . . been up since 9 here in Cali only to find out I have to start driving to pick up a load at 1030pm and drop it at 9 am tomorrow . . . when I want to go to sleep. I started crying for no reason and can't make it stop . . . WTF is wrong with me?"

Shit rolls downhill. Regulations could be structured to prevent trucking companies, brokers, and shippers and receivers from abusing truck drivers. That's how labor legislation is supposed to work. But truckers are so deval-ued that even basic rules like the eight-hour day or the federal minimum wage are not applied to them. Instead, as Quentina says, *"the risk of trucking is directed at the truck driver,"* and you can succeed in driving truck if nothing ever goes wrong. *"But as soon as there's one little problem, they take the driver down to maximize their profits."* Part of the problem here is that everything can be fine; if the weather, and the driver's health, and all the other drivers on the road all cooperate, trucking can be a good, rewarding, if tiring, job. Truckers are encouraged to believe that since this is theoretically possible, if anything goes wrong, it is the driver's fault. They take full responsibility for any and all delays, often without analysis of the system that made them inevitable, and they commit acts of superhuman courage, endurance, and strength as part of their regular daily routine. They feel justly proud of their ability to do so. And they feel (less justly) willing to maintain this pattern in order to feel the pride that is their reward for its achievement.

Working-Class Heroes

Regulations, then, provide another way for truckers to be the pivot point of the twenty-first-century American paradox. This job is their last best hope for dignity and autonomy, yet while it appears to offer freedom and independence because there is no visible boss or time clock, a less visible but much more demeaning and limiting regulatory system manages truckers' employment and increases their dangers. Further, the rhetoric of competition and personal responsibility encourages them to adopt that risk voluntarily, and their personal strength, built up through generations of fierce class and national pride as rebels and underdogs, lets them survive — and even sometimes thrive anyway. To go back to the trucker who wrote the Facebook post I quoted above, the real problem is that she does it — navigates this perfect storm of scheduling hell. Truckers are people who do the impossible every day at least once, and that's a source of pride for them. It's justified. Government and its endlessly increasing rules consistently make it harder, but they still do it. People who have historically been deprived of access to pride through achievement — people like queers, truckers, immigrants, high-school dropouts — can experience the thrill of overcoming mounting, illogical obstacles. They do that but at the same time wonder why it has to be so hard.

Xena, both a lesbian and an immigrant, expresses her frustration that truckers push themselves to meet unreasonable requests from their companies or brokers. Officially, no one forces the truckers to take these risks, but she describes an unstated yet coercive message: *"The more you do, the more they just push you. No company ever tells us that we have to do what they ask. You don't have to do nothing, but they make you worry. Maybe they're thinking, 'OK, fine, you want to sit. You can sit for a week.' It just makes you feel like, 'If I don't go, what's gonna happen?' But we were never late. Pickups, deliveries, we never miss. It can rain, it can snow, whatever, we are there."* Gabrielle,

Edwina Webb posing to commemorate having driven more than
2 million safe miles. (Used with permission of the subject.)

Xena's life and trucking partner, does all the backing in their truck, while
Xena watches in awe. Xena points out that success eventually becomes the
problem: *"It's hard because, just like I said, you have to back into a dock where
you don't have no head room to position the trailer; you can't do it. But truckers
make it in. So why would they want to improve anything, because everybody
makes it? That's the problem with us."*

Gabrielle explains this from her own perspective: *"What she's referring to
is some of the docks are virtually impossible to get into. And you can see sea-
soned drivers as well as unseasoned drivers try and try and try and try. And it
might take you forty-five minutes, might take you an hour, but you get backed
into the dock. I say, 'My knees are killing me.' Sometime she'd had the Advil
'cause she knew I would be so exhausted, and I'd say, 'Why can't these people
fix it?' And she says, 'Why would they—you're in the dock aren't you?'"*

The loading dock could be designed to make the trucker's job less rig-
orous, and faster. To do that, the customer would need to spend time and
money expanding the docking area and would need to believe that the people
who pick up and deliver their goods merit such treatment. Instead, their
culture follows the pattern set by the federal government and the companies

truckers work for in demanding superhuman achievement from truckers—
and blaming them when they fall short.

One reason this structure doesn't change is that no matter what road-
blocks government, culture, and the physical world erect, truckers usually
find a way to accommodate them. Further, they often derive pride from this
accomplishment, while also feeling irritated that it was necessary in the first
place. Queer, trans, and nonwhite truckers feel this pinch and an added pressure to do whatever is asked of them. Not only does this occur because they
can't get work outside trucking so they need to keep these jobs, but also
because trucking expresses something meaningful about being sexual and
gender outsiders for many of them. Gay and trans truckers, women, and
immigrants are outsiders among outsiders, both rewarded and rejected by
the cowboy community, itself the ultimate oxymoron. The marginalization
and sexualization of trucking culture both calls for and excludes their bodies and viewpoints, and the extra obstacles it erects become part of their
self-definition.

Shane Hamilton historicizes the links between the myth of the trucker
as outlaw, the emerging regulations that shape trucking life, and sexuality. Trucking as a job choice and a national scheme emerged when farming
shifted to a corporate model supporting very few people well. Trucking offered the people stranded by this shift a way to maintain some connection to
their old way of life, even though their work as truckers directly contributed
to its demise. Their incentive to participate in this devil's bargain was the
popular understanding of a truck driver as "a man in control of his time and
possessing an untamed sexuality" (Hamilton, 110). Only about 8 percent of
truckers are unionized, though they are isolated and exploited by increasingly harsh working conditions. In explaining why truckers often are hostile
toward labor unions, Hamilton observes that "working-class manhood, particularly in a rural context, has traditionally been defined less by whether
one owns the means of production than by an ethos shaped by uncertainty
and the pride of overcoming that uncertainty on one's own terms" (108).

Gay and trans bodies, indigenous bodies, disabled bodies are all devalued
and stigmatized for being members of working-class culture—and ostracized within working-class culture as well for their other differences. These
are not the queer people whose rights mainstream gay-rights groups fight
for, and they are not usually seen by or included in gay media or scholarship.
Overcoming obstacles and surviving then becomes a very powerful identity
tool. It's a means to becoming visible and gaining respect. Piled-on regulations and other hardships become a challenge; personal coherence comes

from disdaining both the system and the people thought to uphold it, and from identifying and overcoming the newest roadblock set up to halt your progress.

Billy is a bisexual, disabled, Jewish trucker. He tells me he was born with no toes and only eight fingers, but when we meet, what I see is not what those words had led me to expect. To have four fingers on one hand is to lack one, but his hands are a whole different ball game. His left hand is very small and has four little stubs with some independent movement. His right hand has two almost-half-sized digits and a kind of bifurcation that gives his palm flexibility. He tells me that his DOT physical involves a grip test, and he demonstrates by grabbing my upper arm that he's very capable of that. He goes on to describe an infernal layering of obstacles—medical, legal, regulatory, sexual, cultural—that he must navigate to be able to continue working. *"But I just keep driving down the road,"* he responds.

On the surface, it looks like Billy's mother took thalidomide—he has the stature and the limb anomalies that frequently accompany that condition. Yet he says she denies this and that there is no explanation for his random circumstances. He had many surgeries when he was small, taking his family from financial comfort to severe poverty, since, he tells me, this was in the days before medical insurance. What strikes me most is how nonchalant he is about all this—the customized shoe expenses, the leg tendon and muscle development from shifting with his heel, the sexual and social implications. He's found work-arounds, and developed toughness. For Billy, and for many of my narrators, seizing control of difficult circumstances is a form of resistance to government intrusion, which disproportionately falls on poor and disabled bodies. Seizing control this way is a form of class resistance; ironically, insisting on individual responsibility is a means of asserting collective working-class identity. As J. D. Vance reminds us, the message conveyed to poor and working-class Americans is that their choices don't matter and their effort is futile (177), so insisting on agency is rebellious.

Working-class people's resistance to government intrusion and regulation has a long history, and just as long a history of scholars attempting to analyze and understand it. (J. Blake Perkins's *Hillbilly Hellraisers* and Nancy Isenberg's *White Trash* are excellent recent examples.) Working-class people benefit from government interventions including food stamps, unemployment insurance, the enforcement of fair labor standards, and the Occupational Safety and Health Administration. So why are these very people so ready to say that government has overreached and should back off—that regulations don't work?

I have two answers to this recurring question. First, the people who most benefit from government interventions aren't working-class people but those who profit from their labor. Food stamp benefits are small and go to comparatively few people. Almost no truckers get unemployment, because they count as independent contractors or because their company starves them out, so they're effectively forced to leave rather than get fired. Their companies can also direct all blame onto them for the truck's upkeep or for accidents or DOT overweight violations; any of these can be used as a reason to fire truckers with cause, thus giving them no access to benefits. However, seen from a different perspective, every one of these circumstances draws authority from a federal policy or rule that benefits the employer. Benefits given to individuals via regulatory structures are more visible, but not more sweeping or more lucrative.

Second, the rules imposed on truckers don't fit the imagined contract of government in which you exchange some measure of your freedom for promised support and safety. Regulations like posted speed limits restrict individual freedom for a common good, so that drivers who protest them either don't understand that trade-off or think their own needs and wishes outweigh the common good. People who don't understand the regulations truckers are subject to could easily assume that truckers' complaints fit into one of these categories. To the contrary, I argue based on what I have heard, seen, and read, that the regulations that limit truckers don't benefit the general population but only the megacarriers. Since we all share the road with truckers, it's tempting to argue that regulating their speed, sleep, etc. will keep us safe. But as Hours of Service rules are written now, that's not what happens. Truckers, and everyone who shares roads and highways with them, are put at risk by regulations designed to increase the degree to which megacarrier owners—and the corporations that profit from fast and cheap goods transport—make maximum profit. Shane Hamilton and Steve Viscelli have both argued this point persuasively from a policy perspective; the Owner-Operator Independent Drivers Association endlessly attempts to educate the public about this from the driver's perspective; and literally millions of truckers know it well.

Truckers' response to regulation emerges from this knowledge, from their class position, and from their attitudes as Americans. As the trucking workforce changes, new possibilities for understanding, analysis, and policy emerge.

Take Jodie, for example. She's a lesbian who has worked in the oil fields and in over-the-road trucking. She tells me, *"I'm a big shit talker. I'm one of*

those [people] that very little bothers me, and I can roll with just about any-
thing." She raised two kids in a small, west Texas town. She also supports her
disabled dad and her marginally employed little brother. All this is not rare;
working-class children often funnel care and money up the generational lad-
der rather than expecting supplemental support or inheritance from parents. Lesbians often provide the principal financial support for extended
family, maybe because their ability to get and keep masculine-coded jobs
gives them access to more income than more traditionally feminine jobs
offer. And butch women sometimes buy acceptance from extended family,
who might otherwise be censorious. Christina pre-empts the critique she
assumes her nieces and nephews would direct her way, saying, *"I don't know*
what they'd think if I didn't make more than both their parents put together—
I take turns buying the kids what they need." Class and sexuality are linked
here—the swagger Jodie demonstrates in her opening words is defensive,
and marks her both as working class and as someone claiming the right to
working-class belonging in spite of sexuality-based ostracism.

Jodie goes on to say more about her life choices and how they have been
shaped by her context: *"I had to be one of the guys, and I had to learn real*
quick to suck it up, buttercup. I've had bad experiences, and a lot of bad things
have happened to me, but it was worth it in the long run because I was able to
raise my children and do right by them, and that's the whole reason I started
[trucking]. What I'm saying is, I never want to say anything bad towards moth-
ers that have to be on welfare or do anything like that, that's on them—but
for me, personally, I didn't want to be a welfare mother. I wanted to be able
to give my children whatever they wanted or needed, I didn't want to be in the
system and be stuck there, so that's the whole reason I've worked the way I've
worked. I worked in the oil field as a roustabout for a couple years and I went
to driving a truck. And like I said, when I make that statement, I never want to
say anything bad about welfare mothers; they do what they do to take care of
their children, I just didn't want to be one of them because I knew I could work
and make a whole lot more money than the welfare system could ever give me.
And now I'm very lucky. I own my home, it's paid for, it's not a Ritz mansion
but it's mine."

Much has been said about the white working class and its tendency to,
like Jodie, distance itself from "takers" and welfare recipients. Some of this
analysis is useful for understanding truckers' attitudes about regulations.
But there's nothing white about my study, nothing exclusively white, anyway. Jodie is Mexican. She got married and had children because, when she
came out to her mom as a teen, her mom's response was *"No, no, no,* mija,

you gotta be attracted to men. You got to give me grandkids." She accepted this as her duty.

When she says "I've had bad experiences," Jodie means it. She was raped once, experienced attempted rape again, and didn't report either because it would make her unemployable. Raising her kids is her priority.

The white working-class distaste for welfare and other government social services, combined with the reliance on them and the confusion that this intersection brings, is not what's motivating Jodie. Vance notes in *Hillbilly Elegy* that many working-class whites where he grew up "talk to our children about responsibility, but we never walk the walk" (147). He notes that when working as a bagger in a grocery store as a teen, he saw many people who received government benefits without working. Though he usually locates these assessments outside himself, he explains that though many working-class whites work hard and make good choices, "my mother, and increasingly the whole neighborhood embodied another [ethic]: consumerist, isolated, angry, distrustful" (148). By contrasting Jodie with this view, I'm not trying to situate her in the first half of Vance's overly reductive, victim-blaming binary (she isn't one of the "good whites" who are unlike Vance's mother). Rather, her case and the stories of many truckers, when put within Vance's formulation of who the good guys and bad guys are, begin to explain truckers' antipathy to regulations, and particularly how this gets understood in racial and political terms.

All my narrators are subject to unfair governmental regulation, which mainstream accounts don't know of or understand. Their antipathy to government is, thus, both justified and misdirected. From my perspective as an ethnographer, I understand that regulations would benefit truckers if what was regulated was corporations, rather than individual truckers. Regulation and government are not inherently anti-trucker, but when my narrators attack government and blame people who benefit from it, it's because they see the government's regulatory machinery directed only down. Their stories convey a need for these interventions to be directed at structures that profit both from regulations and from poor people's antipathy getting directed at other poor people.

3

STOPPING

GETTING LOADED

Customers, Shippers, Receivers

"Since I'm in the butt crack of nowhere,
I'm going to be hurt."—Adele

I GOT A CALL ONE EVENING from an unknown number in Oregon, and it turned out to be Kate, a transwoman asking for help. She had her own truck and had been trucking for more than thirty years, so she said she wasn't *"one of those crybabies just out of CDL school: 'Waah, waah, I want to get home.'"* Nope, she was willing to roll. But the company she had been with, though it was owned and managed by a good guy who treated her well, fired her because of lies that shippers and receivers had told her boss. They routinely "sir" her, though as Kate says, *"I'm wearing a skirt, a blouse, I got this long hair. But it's my build as well as my facial features."* Even though her boss, she says, *"was trying to treat me fairly, the client base he was dealing with kept saying I was yelling."* Kate adds that, often, *"on the driver's side of the chain link fence there is only one bathroom, men's, and I'm not going to go in there dressed as a woman. I value my life."* She wanted me to refer her to a trucking company that is LGBT owned and safe for people like her. I could not do that—there aren't any. When they reach shippers and receivers, truckers are alone, and whatever the people who work there say or do goes largely unseen and unregulated. For queers, people of color, and visibly trans bodies, that can be a nightmare.

In the myths and movies about trucking, motion dominates the discourse, but that rolling doesn't make any sense without talking about the stopping that is its justification; your job is to move stuff around, but the goal is getting that stuff somewhere. Though queerness or other types of difference shape how truckers understand and experience the movement, it's the stopping that forces their differences into bold relief. A typical customer expects delivery or pickup within a time window. They may have worked with this trucker or company before and may have spoken to them by phone, or they may not have. In any case, when the truck pulls up and a person gets out, there's potential for shock, surprise, learning, danger, fear. In other words, drama.

Several things are worth noticing here. First, the immediacy of this interaction provides some of the joys of the job. So much of modern life is mediated. I lived fifty years before I started trucking, and I never realized how much I was walking around in a fog until I experienced the trucker life. Just for example, I knew that toilet paper is made from paper and that paper comes from trees. I know that now in a different way because I drove into a paper mill in Mississippi one week and into the distribution center for Kimberly-Clark a few days later. Now when I use toilet paper, I live in the world more—I know what I'm doing. Certainly, one reward of any blue-collar job is the pride of actually *doing* something—acting in the world. Because trucking is essentially the world's circulatory system, truckers feel directly connected to various realms of effective, necessary production. It feels *real*.

Second, that immediate experience of the world gets vulnerable bodies right up there, face-to-face with a not-always-friendly world. Research on gay work and work settings by historians including Allan Bérubé and Miriam Frank argues that some jobs are disproportionately gay because queer job saturation, combined with "gay" features of some jobs, draws an increasing concentration of gay workers. Trucking offers that concentration, but not the associated safety. Truck stops, rest areas, and terminals all contain at least some other people and thus potential reinforcements; someone will hear you if you scream. By contrast, customers are often incredibly isolated; several of my narrators deliver hazardous materials to nuclear facilities or storage locations that don't even register on GPS. Others access distribution centers or freight yards that are in huge facilities in or near cities, but not the parts or places where anyone goes voluntarily. These places get built where land is cheap and plentiful, so they are neither central nor well policed. Imagine being lesbian, trans, Muslim, black, or Mexican (or some combination) in these places. Vulnerability is increased by the anger, resentment, and blame woven into working-class attitudes toward racial and sexual difference. Imagine being this visible and vulnerable in the middle of the night, in winter, when your hours of service have run out, so even if you have somewhere to go, you can't leave without forfeiting your job and very possibly all future jobs.

I say all of this to emphasize the violence that could happen to truckers at customer facilities, and to point out that it usually does not. Typically, lesbians and transwomen get sirred or snarled at, threats are made of something worse, and the potential for violence is constant. Transwomen bear the brunt of this, if only because they often can't (or don't choose to) avoid detection. Almost as often, customers meet queer and trans truckers with disinterest or warm, supportive curiosity. Repeatedly, I was reminded that racism and homophobia get attributed to working-class communities by middle-class audiences, not by their own members.

This is not to say that trucking work settings are hospitable to trans people—they aren't—but neither are white-collar and professional work settings. The 2016 National Transgender Discrimination Survey reports that 90 percent of trans people face discrimination at work (Grant et al.). Kyla Bender-Baird's important survey, *Transgender Employment Experiences*, finds discrimination that "ranged from being outright fired and struggling to secure meaningful and gainful employment to facing harassment from coworkers and inappropriate bathroom and dress code policies" (8). Bender-Baird's participants faced more anxiety than they did overt discrimination, and more harassment than full-on firing, which Bender-Baird postulates may be due to race and class privilege. Bender-Baird had too few low-income respondents to make accurate assessments, which is a gap that these truckers' stories begin to address. Truckers have very few workplace protections, and some are laid off easily or simply not given enough freight to get by. Yet few of my narrators said they have faced such overt discrimination—mostly it stays on the slow-burning anxiety level. Bender-Baird concludes that fear of discrimination at work, combined with actual discrimination in other parts of life and with a lack of coherent legal protections for trans people, makes "anxiety in the anticipation of discrimination . . . pervasive" (103). This describes my narrators' experiences well, as does the climate of harassment and aggression that does not usually rise to the level of dismissal. Truckers, at least, are not significantly more likely to get fired than higher-status trans employees. But in terms of the daily work environment, they often experience bullying and ostracism, and sometimes rape and violence.

When Sisyphus first came out as trans, she was frequently harassed. She adds, *"I still get it. I have people who will not treat me cordially, if at all, because I'm trans. One guy will cuss and swear at me in the parking lot because*

Jennifer Lynn Mcclung living the cowboy ideal.
(Used with permission of the subject.)

he has a problem with me being trans. Whatever. After twenty-two years I'm kinda used to it, and it just rolls off." She adds that shippers and receivers typically don't know she's trans—their interactions are brief and not usually repeated, so they can't establish a history. As a result, she says, "*I get misgendered a lot, that's probably the worst of it. I've never been refused access to any place I needed to pick up or deliver freight because of it.*" Although these fleeting encounters lead to misgendering, they also offer safety. Sisyphus says, "*I keep to myself. When I was over the road, I wouldn't go into the truck stop unless I had to. Just stayed in my truck except for my shower. Just stay in the truck and keep to myself, because yeah, it's dangerous out there. When you're alone in a dark parking lot you could be attacked at any time. It's the same issues for cisgendered women. It's not safe for them, either. They can't cross a parking lot without some male trucker thinking that they're a 'lot lizard.'*

Women are constantly being harassed and expected to perform for the men, and it's like, no, we're just out here working. In some ways my experiences are different, but in a lot of ways it's really no different than for cis women—it's dangerous out here."

Many transwomen use the lack of repetition in customer contacts as a camouflage. When things go wrong, it's typically with people who are familiar. Anonymity and movement offer safety, which becomes a source of pride. Jane (who passes well enough that I initially thought she was a lesbian) says, *"I don't accept different treatment from anyone else out here, and I kind of demand it. I had a supervisor—well, not really a supervisor, but someone in authority—[who] kind of harassed me at work several times about it. I got hurt at work this one time, I fell off my trailer and I got hurt pretty bad, and he didn't say nothing. I was banged up pretty bad. And he spent two minutes saying 'I'm glad you're OK' and then the next forty minutes chewing my ass over it because of who I am. And yet if you look at my record, I have no customer complaints, I've always been on time on my loads unless they've given it to me late, it's just these kinds of things that, y'know, four different times, it really kind of pissed me off. More than anything it pisses me off. I don't take offense—well, I guess that is taking offense if I get pissed off. I've never had any customer say anything to me—most of the time I'm getting compliments about how I do my job. Being who I am, I tend to overachieve anyway. My boss has told me a couple times, 'I wish I could clone you,' and he's told me, 'You're the one driver I don't worry about.'"* The bravado she opens this story with is one of the reasons I read her as a lesbian. That feisty response to harassment is one marker of working-class lesbian style—giving back as good as you get in response to a visible vulnerability. She ends her story by bragging: *"There's a reason I don't get in any accidents, there's a reason I don't have any CSA [Compliance, Safety, Accountability, an insurance metric] points, there's reasons for everything, so I just do it right. I just do my thing, and if people have a problem with who I am, that's on them. I really don't need their help. I really don't. And there are people who I can ask questions of if I need to. It's rare that I ever ask for help, 'cause I don't like to ask for help. If someone offers to help me, I don't turn it down, either, because it makes them feel good that they're helping somebody. So I'm not going to turn it down, but I coulda done it myself."*

Lesbian truckers can also maintain invisibility; in a ball cap and a loose shirt, they interact briefly with customers who often don't know they're women. Like transmen, they can fall back on invisibility. There's a price for this hiding, but since the interactions are brief and superficial, the price feels insignificant. Casey, whose appearance and bearing easily identify her as a lesbian, has been harassed by customers with diatribes about *"taking food out of the mouths of babies and taking jobs away from all the men who need work."* She responds by giving them her employer's contact info, saying they're hiring drivers now, desperate for workers. But she says that's rare: *"I never really felt threatened as a woman in that work environment, because I'm very, very masculine, very butch, so unless you get up real close to me, I think most of the truckers just saw me as another man, didn't take the time to look. But I know a lot of the women that I run into, the nice femmey looking girls, get a lot of shit. They're eating and get harassed, and they're trying to get a shower, and people say things on the way in. A lot of the gals I talk to say you really can't sit and have a peaceful meal because someone will come sit down next to you like you need company, and most of the gals would actually come into the truck stop, get something, and go back out. Or not at all. One gal I spoke to got so disgusted by it that she bought a portable shower thing that she put up in her truck. To feel like she was not going to be treated like female flesh trying to get to a shower. And I get that, I understand what they're saying. There's not a lot of good men out there."* Like Sisyphus, Casey compares her trucking experiences to those of straight cis women, noting that nothing worse happens to her as a means of emphasizing how vulnerable all women are in big-rig culture.

Some lesbians describe tacit acceptance by customers. One lesbian couple, Xena and Gabrielle, drove team and ran a very regular route. Xena says that if she went to a customer alone, *"they'd ask, 'Where's the other one?' That was common."* These women didn't identify themselves as lesbians; Gabrielle says they *"never wore a rainbow flag,"* but she thinks everyone could tell because *"we were almost glued at the hip."* Xena adds that they avoided explicit identification because they felt vulnerable, but Gabrielle provides a counterstatement: *"I call her Deary, and I . . . sometimes I call her Deary, and I might forget, and we're standing at a shipping office and I'll say, 'Oh, here. You're going out to the truck, oh, here's the bills, Deary,' and it would just pop out of my mouth. But at the same token, I'm not saying, 'Hey, I'm a lesbian, you better accept me,' so I'm not—we just live our lives."*

The Risks of Being Visible

At least for some truckers, customers are accepting, but visible racial difference or gender nonconformity sometimes leads to problems with other truckers and with their home companies. Marilu is a perfect example. She told her company that she intended to transition and to present as a woman full-time. She asked her driver manager, *"Do you think it's going to be a problem?"* and the manager said, *"I don't see why, it's nothing to do with us."* Marilu adds, *"But then [the manager] mentioned it to the main office, and the HR woman there went a little bananas and said that I had to stay in uniform. The handbook mandated a uniform shirt that nobody wore. I didn't even have one. I just told them, 'I don't even wear polyester, so you might as well keep it, then I don't have to give it back to you.' But since I was now transitioning, I was warned that I had to be in uniform. Well, that didn't happen.*

"It was about a year later that I was at a pickup and joking around with the girls in the office, and one of them wanted to see what I looked like dressed. At this place, I had some time while they were getting the freight ready, so I went out to my truck and changed, and she came out by the truck and we laughed, talked, and joked around about how fabulous I looked. Then I put the sweatpants back on and went back onto the dock and finished counting and stuff. Before I got in the truck, the phone was ringing off the hook. 'Oh, you gotta come into the office.' Apparently [the girl had] mentioned something . . . and said I was wearing a skirt on the dock, and I got in all kinds of trouble. . . . So anyway, I gave 'em some shit, and they gave me more shit, and I was informed in writing that next time I got caught in drag at work it was going to be grounds to get immediately fired. That was when I started wearing women's clothes on the dock."

As these stories demonstrate, nontraditional truckers elicit a variety of responses from customers with whom they come in contact. Sometimes they use humor and approachability to build a rapport that, given the transitory nature of their interactions, feels welcoming, if only by not being hostile. Others avoid detection by using gendered assumptions to slide under the radar. Neither of these strategies works as well for my nonwhite narrators.

Braiden is a black woman who has driven truck for many years. She doesn't experience face-to-face racism, but often people make comments that they deliberately hope she'll overhear. She just continues to work and refuses to dignify them with her attention. But it can also get dangerous. Once, just a few miles after leaving a customer, she had two tires spark and catch fire, causing her to pull over and call for roadside assistance. Then, she says, *"a truck with a U-Haul pulled in front of me, and two dudes kept getting in and out of the truck, walking around back and forth towards me on the shoulder. Then a white car pulled up facing westbound over the grass area on a dirt road by the woods and just sat there. One guy got out and walked across the grass to the U-Haul truck. Then shortly after that, two small wrecker trucks pulled in behind the U-Haul. But check it, no one did any work to anything, they just sat there waiting, getting in and out, walking towards my truck. I'm terrified. I don't know what these four vehicles in front of me are doing having a swap meet at 1:00 a.m., watching me. Two dudes came towards my truck and stood there, staring up at me. I'm staring down at them with my Taser on my lap. He bangs on my door, I yell, 'Get the fuck away from my truck.' Then police finally came. I told them, 'I've been calling, why did it take them two hours to get to me? I could have been on fire, dead, missing.' Anyhoo, I told the police what the four vehicles and the dudes were doing, and he walks towards them. Check this: how about as the white police was walking to them, they all left."*

Braiden tells this story as evidence of her racial and gender vulnerability. She suspected nefarious intent, though the mechanic didn't find evidence that anyone had tampered with her brakes. But the fire in *two* tires so soon after leaving the dock, followed so quickly by what looked like a planned stakeout of her truck, really scared her. She felt targeted for personal harm or freight theft. She wonders if they chose her because she was a black woman alone outside Dallas, figuring that they could assume the police would respond to her slowly and discredit any story she told. Racism isn't something you prove, but Braiden links this *"precarious situation"* to her race, and she's the one who was there, felt the fear, and now relives it at other truck stops, drop-offs, and pickups — racism's work has been done.

Zoe is very matter of fact about her experiences of racism as a black woman. She says, *"Truthfully people in trucking are pretty racist and sexist, but in terms of personal experiences, it's never had a tremendous impact. I try to handle customers the same way, and in some cases I keep a friendly 'fuck you' for everybody, but it's just gotten to the point where nobody cares. You've still got some men who say you should be at home if you're a woman. As far as the racist thing goes, as I say, collectively, trucking is sexist* and *it's racist. I did construction work for six years before this, then I did office, then I went into trucking, so I did — what do they call? — nontraditional jobs for a while. And you know what, America's racist, so that's just what's out there, you know, that's just what you get. It's something we'd all like to sweep under a rug and not talk about, but with trucking, if you look at some of these loads, these specialty loads, that they haul back and forth that are really paying, you hardly see any black people hauling that stuff, man or woman. You know, these oversize loads that really pay money — you don't see minority drivers do that. That's why I say trucking as a whole is racist, but then America is, so it's not a surprise."*

Wendy, another black woman, says she dresses really feminine. *"I dress every morning as I would for any other job, maybe a little more casual,"* she says. *"I'm a female and I want to dress like one. I think this contributes to the harassment I get from shippers and receivers. It's like they gotta say something.*

A trucker took this selfie while
waiting at a customer.
(Used with permission of the subject.)

But I don't let that bother me any." At the end of our conversation, she emphasizes that she wishes trucking were safer and that she'd leave in a heartbeat
if there were any other viable job options.

Ulrike is a black trucker who has worked in the industry long enough to
experience many layers of racism from both employers and contacts over
the road. When she started driving in the early 1990s, she says racism and
sexism were rampant, especially from customers. The only company that
would hire her was J. B. Hunt, which still has a reputation for being willing to hire black truckers. Even now, with trucking jobs plentiful, African
American drivers have a hard time getting hired. They disproportionately
wind up getting jobs with a few companies known in the business for their
racialized hiring—and are given racist nicknames as a result. Ulrike's firm
is still commonly called "J. B. Hunt a nigger down." In 2018. That's the environment she works in.

Ulrike says, *"I cried all the time. Like I said, being black and a woman. J. B. Hunt had about seven black women working for them, and they used to call us on the CB the J. B. Hunt she-niggers."* She laughs. *"And they did everything they could to make your life miserable. You had to learn how to do everything that the guys had been doing forever, and they're either coming on to you or they were picking on you. So I learned how to do everything that they could do as good or better than they could do it, because when you got to the shipper and receiver, they were worse than the drivers out here. Like I said, with me being black and a woman, it was rough. I'd think, Why am I doing this job?"* I ask what shippers and receivers did specifically, and she replies, *"Calling me the n word, telling me to go out to door five, and there'd be a great big dumpster in front of the door, that kind of thing, or if I asked to use the bathroom, they'd tell me they didn't have one. They made me sit and wait all night to get loaded for the next day. Stuff like that."* When she reports a particularly racist customer to her company, her employer responds that she doesn't have to go there anymore. That's considered responsive and responsible — the possibility of demanding fair or decent treatment is not even raised.

Josephine, a Latina, says, *"FedEx, Amazon, and UPS gave me the most trouble for being female. And FedEx was the worst. Dropping off and picking up at FedEx, they treat me like crap, they were very belligerent, and irate in the line to get my paperwork done. Yeah. And nobody did anything. Nobody said anything; they just turned their heads."* She thinks the mistreatment is partly because she's not butch, so they don't know how to read her. *"I'm not an obvious lesbian, so I try to dress a little bit, um, like, I wear the trucker cargo shorts and T-shirt. But you know, I've been a hair stylist so long, I look female, and I'm not trying to be butchy, and I think they're not sure if I'm lesbian or not. So I've had men, I've had men call me a fucking dyke several times. So they automatically assume, because I'm just, like, comfortable, you know. I honestly can't tell the difference between the female issue or the lesbian issue."* She concludes, *"It's always hanging over your head, and out on the road — oh no, I don't feel safe, ever."* She says customers often *"cut their eyes"* at her, and she longs for harassment training for both drivers and the people they interact with.

Readers may wonder why all the black truckers I'm describing are women. First, I didn't talk to many black male truckers, so I'm hypothesizing based on related evidence. Lesbians often can avoid harassment because, in the man's world of trucking, they can slide into the culture without disturbing people's assumptions too much. White gay men often lie low or find corners of acceptance. That doesn't work well for African American truckers, so if you're multiply, visibly stigmatized, you're likely to leave the business, either voluntarily or because your company is making your work life intolerable. Who I am is also going to skew the data here. In general, men were harder for me to engage in the preliminary conversations, in which I described my research and asked for an interview. In public spaces, especially those occupied by truckers, lone women who engage men in conversation have to manage context and expectations carefully. I often could approach gay men because I'm readable as a lesbian—they knew what our interaction wasn't. But there were still awkward, vaguely threatening moments, and this fraught situation is magnified across racial lines; so I talked to relatively few black gay male truckers, though I think I saw plenty out there. The ones I talked to told pretty grim stories.

For example, Patrick got injured on the job and had to leave, but he had been miserable even before that. He says, *"Being openly gay, I have some stories about that as well, stories of discrimination because of that. What I do instead of filing a report—people will be idiots, so I try to look into the situation with that lifeline, so I try not to let everything get under my skin. I do want it to be known that this is not tolerable, so I would make a mental note and tell the manager 'This happened' and 'I've been noticing this, and noticing that,' so then if an incident did occur where it got out of hand, my supervisor wouldn't be taken off guard by my case. There were a lot of snide comments, sexual innuendos, but I don't believe I have been discriminated [against], because I kind of know what demeanor will let me to persevere, so it's clear I'm not here for that. So it was kind of no big deal."* In addition to being a black gay man, Patrick is also HIV positive, which, he says, he *"always hid from people with my job even though there are laws protecting us. Even though there are rights, doesn't mean people will enforce them."* He adds, *"So, like I said, with me being HIV [positive], I have to take drugs to get my body back to functioning, and I can't allow myself to do that on the job. So there was this day that I had to call off, and they wouldn't let me. They said, 'Anybody can get sick,' and I wound up telling them, 'I have an illness.' I didn't want to do that, but I had to tell them, 'I need to get rest with my body breaking down like that, I need to go take the forms to my doctor so he can fill it out,' and they still didn't let me off even after I did all that. I would have coworkers come to me and tell me little side jokes that other coworkers would say about my sexuality. And I caught a couple jokes on my own."* He overheard racist comments constantly, some of which even appeared in emails, and there was such a hostile work environment on every level that Patrick repeats, *"Trucking was killing me. It was killing me."* Trucking was better than other available alternatives, but doing it, he says, *"I hated my life. I really did."*

Isabella blames truckers themselves for at least some of the poor treatment they get from customers: *"Going back to the customers, I would like to see more respect. But this respect goes two ways. Truckers aren't the most professional people, they also don't have that good of hygiene, so when I see someone walk in slobbish and stinky, I probably won't treat them real well. But some of these customers, it don't matter. I mean, I wear nice jeans every day, treat them real well, boots, a nice shirt, I even do my makeup, 'cause I'm a girl. So I go into one and I took 'em a load, and I have a load coming out—is it ready? 'No, it ain't ready yet, come back in two hours.' So I did, it ain't ready yet. This went on for about twenty-four hours, and finally I said, 'Why is there a holdup?' and she says, 'Well, we don't have an empty trailer.' I said, 'Well, I brought you a trailer, can you use it?' She said, 'Well, we ain't ready for that stuff yet.' So I went back another four times—adds up to another eight hours—and I said, 'OK, I really need to get this load.' She says, 'But we ain't got no empties.' And this is happening at a lot of shippers. You back into a door, and it's three or four hours before they start, and then all of a sudden it's lunchtime and everybody goes to lunch, and they don't understand the driver is missing their next load. 'Cause I've had to turn loads down 'cause I can't get over there to get it. I don't think the shipper or receivers understand that."* Though this starts out as a responsibility narrative, it turns into a victim one—she was kept waiting for no apparent reason and deprived of income.

Dorothy, who is white and feisty, describes getting "the fish eye" from shippers and receivers, and responding in a way that takes control of the situation. Here, she takes what could be a harassment situation and reenvisions it as no big deal; nothing she can't handle. *"At shippers and receivers? Yes, I got the fish eye,"* she says. *"I've gotten, 'You know, we don't have anybody to help you untarp, we don't have anybody to chain that load for you.' And I'm looking at them, and I said, 'I don't remember asking you. I got this, I don't remember saying I needed help.' But were they ugly about it? Most of the time not. When I did grain and feed and stuff going out to the barns, I'd hear, 'Can you back that thing up?' Well, I've heard that shit before, y'know—if you've got to come over and watch, I don't give a damn. They'd grumble. Well, you asked. So have I experienced anything? Yes, I have. And has it been mean or vicious? No, it has not. Years ago when I was younger, and slender and tough, I mean tough like a nail, I pulled a lot of lumber. Did I get hit on? Yes, I did. Did anybody ever really get out of line? No, they didn't."*

Ciara, a smart-mouth white woman, puts it simply: *"If someone gives me a dirty look, I'm more than happy to ask, 'What's your problem? Did you not get enough Wheaties for breakfast or something?'"* And other customers are shocked to see a woman hauling hazardous waste: *"They're so shocked—it's like, what am I? A dog? A cat?"* She reports that many of those customers don't have women's bathrooms and that *"there's nothing you can do to please them but get off their property."*

Loneliness and Fellowship on the Road

When I ask Carolyn whether customers know or care that she is trans, she snaps back, *"Well, they might care but I don't."* She adds that she avoids unnecessary interactions on the road. So does Hanna, who is also trans. She explains, *"I've had people ask questions, but I'm pretty quiet. I keep to myself. I went into trucking for self-security—you don't have to be around a lot of people."* The isolation caused by trucking and increased by visible differences between truckers is an important component of the job. What customer interactions add to that is a sense of being assessed, and then either accepted or interpreted as a threat. There is a wide range of possible reactions, and they make an enormous difference to the trucker quality of life. Curtis, who trucked as a gay man for over a decade before starting a gradual, uneven transition, describes how good being seen can feel: *"I had a trailer full of parts in my truck, and I go to the shipper and check in, and she says, 'Oh, you don't have [long] pants. Here.' And they slide this white zip-up suit that I had to put on over my shorts. . . . And I wear glasses, so I put the plastic glasses over my glasses, and put my earplugs in, and I went to check in at the dock. And she said, 'Oh, I remember you, you're always so nice.' And we talked for a moment, and then she said, 'Freight goes to dock number two,' and I said, 'First may I use the restroom, please?' And she said, 'Well, there's a . . .' She said, 'Well, we have a men's or a women's, which one would you like?'"* Curtis laughs. *"And I said, 'Oh, well, I prefer going to the men's.'"*

Curtis laughs again and continues: *"I thought that was delightful. I thought, wow, she actually could see that, the purple color on my nails, and my earrings, and I had a little bit of makeup on, and my hair was a little special. But other than that, I was in my uniform shirt and, of course, these overalls that they supplied for me. So, sometimes people can just see you for who you are, and sometimes people are just oblivious. But what people always see is just my nature. How I treat people and how I greet people. I'm not real flamboyant, you know, but I love being softer than the average guy."* Curtis attributes this acceptance to geography. Based out of Chicago, Curtis says that the metropolitan context is an advantage and speculates, *"If I was a local driver in, say, another Southern state, or something, it might not be as easy for me."*

Yolanda, a transwoman, also believes that living on the West Coast contributes to her acceptance, especially by customers there. She says, *"There's the initial shocker when they hear your voice, and then they see you and shock a little bit, but they never say anything—there's just that initial jolt. Some kind of look at you weird, some it doesn't even bother them. Most of the young people anymore, you tell them you're transgender, they say, 'Oh, that's pretty cool, that's who you are.' We live right near the border to California, and everything on our side of the world is pretty accepting. We don't put ourselves in situations, like, we won't go to a country and western bar. There is that little thought in the back of your mind all the time, that 'don't put yourself in a compromising situation,' but for the most part it's pretty accepting."* For her, safety exists, but it depends on some measure of self-policing.

Vito echoes that sentiment, and also questions it: *"I found that I am less likely to be open in—it's probably more of a stereotype because I've found that shippers and people at these truck stops out in the middle of nowhere are actually really kind, really nice people. I mean, it was probably worse years and years ago, but when I grew up it was a little more under the radar. So it's kind of engrained in my head whenever I'm out in rural areas [that] I don't present myself openly as gay, because I'm afraid of walking back to my truck and maybe having to confront somebody, or going into a shipper and one of them has a problem with it and therefore not wanting me to come back and do deliveries for them, so I just lie low. I know there's a lot of people out there that's OK with me being gay, but I don't always present myself openly as gay, especially if it's a rural area. So it does suck—it's one of the things where I want to be out and proud, but there's a safety aspect to it too, where if you are out and proud there's a good chance that something could happen to you out there. That's one of the things that has crossed my mind every now and then. I go to the middle of nowhere to pick up various kinds of produce, and you have to think, 'Is this somewhere I can be openly gay without fearing that somebody might come to my truck in the middle of the night and punch a bunch of holes in it?' Or even something mild like keying the truck, or popping the tires, or damage the trailer, you know, they can cause major issues, and the truck is so vulnerable. That's something I think about."*

For nontruckers, there's irony in the statement that when transwomen, black women, gay men, and lesbians are out in blue-collar spaces, what they find vulnerable is their *truck*. Pulling the pin that locks the cab to the trailer is a quick and easy way to end a trucker's run, and possibly the trucker's life. So is interfering with tires, air lines, lug nuts. Therefore, the truck itself is vulnerable, and it takes you to dangerous places, while you work under

A proud, professional driver. (Photo by Yevgeniy Fiks,
used with permission of the subject.)

regulations and circumstances that add to your exposure. Being visibly different, then, adds to, rather than initiates, risk.

The places where truckers collect and drop off their freight (everywhere
from customers to freight yards to dark drop yards to ports) are isolated and
often unsafe. And as Sean points out, even in cities and places that seem
secure, *"there are some places that are so remote — customers and shippers —
and if anybody gets a wild hair up their butt, in some places nobody can hear
you scream."* My narrators add this to the ongoing fear of violence that characterizes modern life, especially for gay, trans, or other targeted groups. Cit-
ing the Pulse nightclub shooting in Orlando as motivation, Sean is investi-
gating the option of concealed carry for a firearm.

An ongoing sense of living in fear—without being able to pinpoint the
danger or its harm, yet feeling its effects—becomes part of my narrators'
lives everywhere, but especially at customers. Ingrid, a gentle, shy transwoman, says she gets put on the back burner at shippers and receivers. This
means waiting longer and earning less. This is not something that she can
prove, but it makes for an unpleasant work environment with practical consequences. She adds, *"People I speak to tend to be more curt than courteous*

with me, regardless of how much I smile and try to be friendly." She also says she would be terrified at loading docks if she weren't armed at all times. She doesn't carry a gun since that's against company policy, but she has what she calls *"an odd self-defense-oriented manicure"* of custom-sharpened steel fingernails. She shows me. It's a heart-stopping symbol of physical terror transformed onto a personal frame, where femininity, the origin of targeting, becomes simultaneously the only available defense. She sheepishly explains that she makes them herself: *"I do a little metalwork as a hobby."*

Eliza can use her butch appearance and mannerisms to avoid harassment and possible violence. This works especially well because she doesn't see the same people in the same places; constantly shifting surroundings help her pass. She says, *"I been driving a year and a month now, and as far as heckling at truck stops, the first couple months in, I was still not very confident at parking and backing, so some of the guys would be like, 'Trucking ain't for women.' You know, just stuff like that. Once I got more confident, the heckling kind of stopped. I try not to be feminine out here because I don't want the harassment from the guys, so I wear comfortable clothes, you know, jeans and a T-shirt, T-shirt and basketball shorts, and I wear a ball cap. At truck stops I walk more confident, I'm not slouching and looking scared, I keep aware of my surroundings, and that tends to keep the guys away, as far as them heckling me at the truck stops or harassing me in any way. As far as at shippers and receivers, I do wear a ball cap, and I wear, like, T-shirts and shorts. Sometimes they don't realize I'm a woman until I speak. They just kind of glance up, see a ball cap, say, 'How can I help you, sir?'"* Eliza isn't consciously passing as a man, she's just choosing "comfortable clothes," but she registers that these also help her avoid harassment at truck stops, so she carries that look into shippers and receivers as a shield.

Being in "the butt crack of nowhere" makes you vulnerable. But it's at shippers and receivers—where truckers repeatedly tell me "no one can hear you scream," where workers are transient and often untraceable, and where the culture is thus lawless and marginal—that my narrators feel most isolated and scared. When their trucks are getting loaded or emptied they can't leave, they often have to enter other people's workspaces and worlds, and they are often in remote corners of the country, alone.

4

ROLLING

DRAG AND FLY

Race, Racism, and Trucking

A TRUCKER WHO RETIRED after twenty-three years of driving posted an impassioned sign-off on Facebook on August 12, 2016. I quote it at length here because it glosses so many of the issues I take up in this book, and especially in this chapter: "Trucking has been good to me. It bought me a beautiful home, lots of toys and the ability to look after family and friends. But it took my life and wrecked my body. I've pulled dry box, reefer, livestock, grain wagon, flat bed, stainless and compressed gas tankers. I've seen everything from the Mexican border to Grand Prairie, Alberta and coast to coast. I've seen this industry go from proud people who loved their jobs and helped each other no matter race, creed or color to a bunch of self-centered camera-wielding picture-shaming children who think they're better than anyone. We used to be looked up to and now we are treated like criminals and we have only ourselves to blame."

Truckers, whether they're white, black, or otherwise, talk about race often, and many have attitudes that can be called racist. I'm not trying to be an apologist for racism and racists. At the same time, talking to a wide variety of gay and trans truckers about antiblack, anti-Muslim, and anti-Mexican attitudes has taught me that we need to understand where these ideas come from and what they mean to the people who profess them. That's my goal for this chapter.

The story I opened with imagines past truckers as unconcerned about "race, creed, or color." The invocation of a preracist utopia in the 1970s and 80s is clearly a white fantasy—an imaginary time when truckers just did their jobs unimpeded by politics or people advancing their special rights. A black woman like Ulrike, who has driven truck for longer than the twenty-three years of the retiring driver, has an entirely different perspective on the past: racist hiring, dispatching, job assignment, pay, and harassment existed alongside real, visceral danger for black bodies sent alone into threatening, "whites only" spaces.

I began my research believing that truckers were predominantly white people, but the long drives I did as an observer in Reba's semi proved otherwise. Reba's analysis of changing trucker attitudes about race helps make sense of these different experiences. I ask her about what's changing, and she says, *"There's an influx of Indians from India who live in Fresno, Oklahoma City, and Canada. You can hire immigrants for less and they share the story that they can get hired by word of mouth."* I ask about black people and she replies, *"KLLM [a trucking company] is almost all black people; they recruit in Alabama. Panther Trucking is related to the Black Panthers. It's still a minority-owned business. J. B. Hunt has a nickname: 'J. B. Hunt that nigger down.' If you go up into the valley, over the hill [into California], white people are the minority. I guarantee it—you won't see but a handful of us. If a new business starts up here, they have seven years before they have to pay taxes, and lots of immigrants take advantage of that. They have nice equipment, the magic-carpet drivers. They don't have CBs, they don't have our customs, like using flashers on the side of the road. There's plenty of jobs in our career, so it's not like they're taking jobs from us, but people have such a boner about them being here that they won't help them."* Notable here are her admiration for immigrant drivers' equipment, her free use of racist and ethnic epithets, and finally her linking of all this to male sexual function: "People have *such a boner* about them being here." White American truckers feel threatened and get angry, and Reba figures their response as sexualized, with maybe a veiled threat of rape. Racism among truckers is, I will argue, about masculinity and sexuality. It displaces anger about loss in these realms onto more visible, safer targets.

Intersectionality: Race, Sex, and Class at Work

Reba's reference to immigrants and the complex underlying tensions of her statements are echoed or expanded on by many of my narrators. For example, Maci is an owner-operator who has driven for more than twenty years and says pay has plummeted in the past few years. She adds, *"A lot of it does have to do with the immigrants, because a lot of the immigrants, they ride four and five deep, maybe only two of them have CDLs and the other ones don't but they'll still drive, and they'll go out and buy a truck, and they* will *undercut, you know, and that hurts us. That's what happened with the produce. When I used to haul produce we got paid very well, and then the immigrants started buying trucks and trailers and started driving for half of what we were getting on produce. Say we picked up a load for $6,000 in Florida to take to Hunt's Point. They cut it down where they were making $2,000 and eventually started kicking us out of hauling produce, because we were making $6,000, and they were willing to do it for two."* Ciara observes that although *"truckers could shut this country down within a week, if you walk off the job you're going to get Pedro and Rafael and a bunch of those guys that will work for less money."*

This undercutting of freight rates was reported by many of my narrators and verified (without the racist implications, of course) by research. Michael Belzer's groundbreaking *Sweatshops on Wheels* spends most of a chapter describing how the deregulated bidding process drives freight rates down. Belzer explains how truckload carriers respond to deregulation by setting up communication networks, yet "anyone willing to work for less can make a low bid and take the freight" (40). Truckers can calculate how much it costs to move freight per mile, adding in fuel, tolls, vehicle depreciation, and a fair wage for their time. But megacarriers staffed with new drivers often underbid that rate and will often move freight at a net loss, which drives freight rates even lower. Because deregulation gained steam during the Reagan years, unions could not mount effective resistance, and trucking became "an occupation of last resort" (Belzer, 43). This, I would argue, is why so many queer, trans, minority, and indigenous people wind up there. My narrators and I shared the experience of sliding very quickly down the slope between career trajectory to job of last resort in part because the climate in which we labor offers no meaningful federal protections.

Maci adds that truckers *"had everything lined up, but then when a lot of immigrants came in, like I said, they started undercutting us and now nobody wants to haul produce anymore. Because to get up into New York it can cost $300, $400 just to get up through the tolls in and out of New York. With the fuel and all that, you can't afford to haul it for that. But all these guys they live together, two, three, four families in a house, they pool together and they do this. But us as American people, we try not to live three, four families in a house. But people are moving back in with their families with their wives and their children, because they're not making enough money to keep their own place. And I've been homeless in my truck. I did that three, four years ago, because I couldn't afford anything else."* As with Reba, what begins as a racial point

The truck becomes a source of pride.
Here, Keaira poses with the rig she customized.
(Used with permission of the subject.)

for Maci becomes a familial and sexual one. Maci's imaginary trucker is the breadwinning male who can no longer fulfill his mandate, but instead must move his "wife and children" back in with his parents, even though he works ridiculously hard. This failed masculinity is caused, in her logic, by foreign truckers who "pool together," thereby driving freight rates down because they can survive on lower incomes. Racism then derives from a slippage in masculinity—its failure to maintain its internal logics. Belzer explains why the masculine ideal slid, and the truckers I spoke with repeatedly assign the blame for this slide to immigrant truckers; my goal is to explain their logic.

Arlie Hochschild's research on the emotional roots of the Tea Party movement and Trump's popularity in Louisiana argues that working-class whites feel they have been waiting in line for their chance at success. Hochschild interviewed seventy people and, though none are truckers, all share much with my narrators in terms of feeling invisible, stigmatized, and underpaid. They think that liberals and racial minorities are cutting in line—using their prior victimization to justify getting in front of the rule-following waiters.

Natalia repeats this familiar lament, adding a new twist. She describes the precipitous pay decreases in certain trucking jobs: *"That job that was paying $60,000, it's now paying $30,000. And that's the game. When the grandfather opened that company, you had to have five years of experience to work for them. Right now, they'll damn near take you out of school. There's no way that me, with a mortgage to pay and kids to support and all—there's no way that I can work for what the immigrant brothers that are living out of that truck and sending the money back to Mexico can pull it for. They have no overhead. For them, a dollar a mile is great fucking money. So to them it all looks great, but when they do it for that, it cuts my throat, because I can't do it for that. I got to pay taxes on that, I've got a family to support. I have repairs that I've got to make. I can't do that."* The assumptions here are racist: she has a mortgage, repairs, and children, but immigrants don't. It is the performance of her familial obligations and her gendered sexuality, both seen as private and normative, that she holds in contrast to immigrants, whose lives, families, and sexualities are thereby seen as more porous.

The concept of intersectionality was introduced by Kimberle Crenshaw in 1989. I use it in two ways: first, to emphasize that no person has a single or simple identity, and second, to show that different strands of the ways people understand themselves pull them in different, competing directions. So, it's not just that people identify with several groups simultaneously, but that these groups disagree about what thoughts or actions are valid. My narrators, for example, are working-class people who belong to various racial categories and fit within a complicated sex and gender system. How do they navigate the often-contradictory needs of each aspect of their being in their day-to-day working lives?

Dean Spade's work can help answer this question. Spade is a lawyer, writer, and law professor who founded the Sylvia Rivera Law Project, which extends respectful and affirming support to low-income people of color who are trans or gender nonconforming. He draws on the discipline of critical race studies to argue that trans lives won't be improved by working to increase the rights available to trans folks, partly because even when rights-based employment claims work (which is unusual), they only protect "the least marginalized of the marginalized" ("What's Wrong," 189). Rights language, Spade shows, depends on an inaccurate understanding of human behavior. Namely, prejudice isn't the malicious acts of bigoted individuals; it is in and shapes everyone. You can't find perpetrators to punish, and even if you could, that wouldn't change how the violence of discrimination, in all its forms, works. Spade draws on legal analysis by Alan David Freeman to argue that instead of focusing on law reforms, we should "turn our attention to other systems in law that produce structured insecurity and shortened life spans for people and consider alternatives of intervention" (Spade, "What's Wrong," 193). My goal here is to unpack the structure of violence that truckers' rhetorical strategies both analyze and perpetuate. One question is how sexual and gender violence get displaced onto racialized situations. Another is how the public, hypersurveilled culture of big-rig drivers imagines changing norms around race, sex, and gender.

How Sexual and Gender Violence Get Displaced onto Racialized Situations

An African American narrator I'll call Enid was pressured to drive as part of a team, even though she had years of successful solo driving experience. Her codriver was a white man, while she is a black woman. Unbeknownst to her, the company stored a "black box" on the truck that recorded its miles driven. When they brought the truck in for a safety inspection, they were told that their miles driven divided by time driven indicated they had been speeding, and she (but not her male codriver) was fired. They had divided their driving time evenly and no logic was advanced about why only she was culpable. Enid didn't fight it, realizing how utterly hopeless that was. She needed to support her kids, so she just went and got a different job. Most black truckers have similar stories of blatant racist hiring and firing, which the companies don't even attempt to conceal, knowing that truckers have no legal recourse in this "at will" employment structure.

African American women face sexual discrimination and heightened levels of harassment in addition to racism. Black women often respond to racist behaviors differently than immigrant or Muslim women do, seeing themselves as truckers first, and people of color second. Intersectional feminism derives from conflicting, divided alliances like these. Gwynneth tells me, *"I've met racists. I've met people that will say, 'I like you, but the rest of them?' And for me, I don't know, I just feel like, well, don't put me in any category. Don't put me in a woman category, don't put me in a black category. I'm so much more than that. You want people to know that or you don't. I don't care."* She relates this to her commitment to responsibility; her abhorrence of victim language makes her unwilling to own racial identity and eager to be evaluated on individual terms. She tells me stories of being mistaken for a prostitute at truck stops and of a pattern of treatment that some people would label harassment. Her response is to say to the perpetrators, *"That's OK, but you should just be careful about that,"* she says. *"So that's how I*

*handled that, but there's a lot of people who would say, 'That's so offensive'
and 'How dare you' and 'Oh, you dirty dog.' So for all intents and purposes, no,
I do not look like a prostitute, but I'm empathetic in a way, and apparently he
could come up with no better way to express that."* Gwynneth is suggesting
not only that "a lot of people" — by which I take her to mean spoiled white
women — would respond with outrage, but also that her race equips her to
manage the situation more effectively.

All female truckers are sexualized at work, and their responses vary based
on racial categories, age, and other factors. The best proof is the ironic comments made in some form by many transwoman narrators. As Hanna puts
it, *"I first knew other truckers read me as female when I got propositioned and
then harassed. It's been an everyday part of my job since."* Black woman narrators often respond to this predatory work culture by deflecting, rather
than directly engaging with, harassers. Presumably they've learned that
they won't find the needed backup if they fight, so they handle the situation
themselves. Enid laughs at me when I ask why she doesn't report offend-
ers. Her response is simply *"I need my job."* This strategy is, as Gwynneth
says, *"cultural, or I should say, subcultural."* It's also the safest and most self-
respecting response to a structure that combines racial and sexual tropes
during moments of crisis.

Felicity, a white transwoman from Texas, brings structural violence into
bold relief on several fronts. I spoke with Felicity for several hours one night.
Or rather, she spoke to me. I squeezed in the occasional question, but Felicity did not need much encouragement: her experiences had made her angry,
and copious amounts of "windshield time" had shaped these experiences
into impassioned monologues. A few months after our formal interview, Felicity got into a minor accident (not her fault), and the company used that as
grounds to dismiss her. Fired for cause, however illegitimate, she could not
get another trucking job, wound up trying other options, and then decided
to return to the Middle East, where she had worked previously for Blackwa-
ter. Though she had returned home to Texas to work when her truck was hit
for the twentieth time by artillery, she tells me that there are parts of the
Middle East where globalization has created lucrative, easy-to-get jobs for
truckers who are willing to risk death and dismemberment.

While Felicity's experience in the Middle East subjected her to wartime violence, most striking in her monologues was her relentless logic of blaming
racial minorities for her vulnerability to sexual violence and her repeated victimization. Following the patterns discussed in this chapter, Felicity doesn't
own or acknowledge the sexual violence, because her class and sex position

are so precarious that it would be intolerably scary, so she displaces it onto racialized bodies. While still employed at the trucking company, she says the company tells her that if you experience discrimination on the job, *"you have to report it, but then you have to prove it,"* but then the company might turn around and say, *"But we're not going to let you come talk to a manager of the Pilot [a truck stop chain] about bathroom legislation. We'll just tell you that as long as your attire is legal, you're OK."* Felicity adds, *"But then they basically tell me that if Donald Trump or Ted Cruz is president, and they decide to kill me, there's nothing they can do about it. And if Donald Trump or Ted Cruz is president, and they decide to send me to forced gender conversion therapy camp, there's nothing I can do about it. And they tell me that if [I] use the women's bathroom they can send [me] to prison; there's nothing they can do about it. And if [I] use the men's bathroom when I'm presenting female for ten years, and I'm in the men's room and I get beaten up and arrested for following the law, there's nothing I can do about it.*

"Now, I wrote a letter because I sat there pounding on them. I told them three months in a row: we have a problem here. I'm not trying to be political. It's the political system that has waged war on me, but I have to function in Interstate 35. I have to keep going to the same truck stops and not use the men's room. And I'm not going to the men's room. I don't care if Jesus becomes president. I don't care if Hitler rises from the grave in an H. P. Lovecraft parallel universe, I don't care if we're all worshipping Satan, eating ramen, devouring children, and having sex with birds — I'm not using the men's room."

She goes on to describe her gender transition — all the medical and bureaucratic hoops she has jumped through and the complete lack of social and political support they have earned her. But each iteration of this righteous injustice includes at least one appearance of racial blame: Felicity traces each source of harm done to her back to vengeful black people. Here are some examples: *"When Trump defrauded the government of $80 million in tax fraud, he didn't have to deal, like I did, with a black woman that told me I was legally tax exempt in Afghanistan. And then I had to borrow $3,000 for a tax penalty to the IRS, because they didn't honor an exemption that they had already agreed to on their own tax form using their [own] IRS agent."*

And: *"If the navy and the Marine Corps, which are part of the armed forces of the government of the United States, which is predominantly Judeo-Christian, doesn't care that I transition male to female, how come black students who hate me and beat me up and J. B. Hunt are going to give me shit about it? How come the Buddhists in my GLBT group are going to automatically tell me, 'We can understand a gay black schoolteacher around white kids in the D.C. school district, but we can't understand a white girl that's transgender and used to be a man'? And I told them, 'I'm not giving you shit for Shinola.'"*

What interests me in these stories is how Felicity, like so many other truckers I know, experiences daily difficulty and struggle, which she then understands via a racialized narrative. When these setbacks orbit around sexual or gender nonconformity or racial othering, that heightens, rather than diffuses, the blame projection. In a context of feeling profoundly beleaguered, my narrators are angry and hungry for justice. Felicity ends our conversation on a more hopeful note: *"Maybe I can keep one more woman from being murdered by telling this story. If you can talk to people, you need to remind them that a whole lot of us are in the NRA and that we're very well armed. If they come at us, we're going to turn on them, and we'll fire first and ask questions later."* She is here identifying herself with a group (women? transwomen?) placed in contrast with other "people," whom she threatens with violence in self-defense. Who does she mean by "them"? First, note that she doesn't name them: rhetorically, she leaves that for her audience. The information she gives is that she imagines that I have access to these people, and that they plan to "come at us." Maybe they're liberals who oppose gun rights and working-class rebelliousness. Maybe they're racial minorities with whom these liberals make common cause. Felicity doesn't name her enemies, but she does name their threat: the murder of her and her people. Her understanding of violence, and of rights including the right to retaliate, is channeled through a (sometimes unspoken) language of race.

Gay men who drive truck conflate racial and sexual tropes in different but parallel ways. Vito has worked for large and small trucking companies, and he experiences the least discrimination he's ever had from the small outfit he drives for now, which is why he chooses to stay with it. He connects the company's acceptance to its immigrant status. Vito says, *"These people are foreigners. They get that same attitude presented towards them, where they're not the typical or normal truck driver from, like, the 60s and 70s, of white straight male, like, 'you're the rock' and 'jam it out,' and 'cruise it in' and 'roll' and everything else. And these aren't those type of people, so naturally not being one of those people either, I feel a little bit better. I'm not a stereotypically over-the-top gay man, but there are little things that I do. For instance, I have a massive shoe collection on my truck; there are quite a couple of drivers who are like, 'Hey, can we check this out? What's your fascination with shoes?'"* Though he feels loyalty to his first company and loved working for them, Vito says, *"I just never felt that I could be comfortable any time I was at a terminal, any time I was dealing with dispatchers or anything else about my needs, so . . ."*

How the Public, Hypersurveilled Culture of Big-Rig Drivers
Imagines Changing Norms around Race, Sex, and Gender

Often, conversation about race and change in the trucking industry is described as a contest between old-school and new-school drivers and driving styles. Vito's comment invokes this debate by linking trucker slang like "jam it out and cruise it in" to an anti-immigrant, white-male, traditional driving culture. In another example of race, change, and trucker slang, Reba told me that when old-school truckers complain about truckers wearing flip-flops, they don't mean her (though she never wears anything else)—they mean Muslim immigrants. (Memes honoring the time before truckers wore turbans and flip-flops abound.) "Flip-flops," then, serves as a coded racial slur to describe a Muslim of Middle Eastern descent, subbed in for other terms such as "towelhead" or "hadji." The reference to footwear is less apparently racist but carries the same meaning.

In a somewhat different approach to characterizing old-school and new-school drivers, Bridget explains truckers' attitudes toward Mexicans and Muslims by using language that links racist views to the loss of a gendered social order. She says, *"There's kind of, like, a gulf between the old school and the new school. You'll have these other drivers—and I hate to say this, but you'll see it in a lot of foreigners—that drive like bats out of hell. They take a lot more risks. Some of it I think is cultural; some of it is that they have this massive sense of their vehicle and what they can and cannot do, whereas I don't. I've got a good sense of my vehicle, but I'll be damned if I'm going to take out [a] little car with three kids in it. But most of the old-schoolers that are surviving are the owner-operators, and they're ungoverned, and they'll take curves that are marked at forty-five at sixty miles per hour. The risks are taken by old-school owner-operators, for the most part, and by new-school foreigners. If there's another truck that's passing me, and they know the length of their truck exactly, and they're going to come over soon and they don't indicate—that's not a very well-trained truck driver. If I'm passing them and they decide that they're going to keep me over in the left lane for ten minutes because they don't want me to pass them—what's their problem?*

"But I think there's a lot less respect in the new-school drivers. Specifically, I've had men and women drivers tell me, 'Men don't hold the door for women anymore.' Men just look at you like you're another man. They cut you off, they're not polite, they don't say hello. It's losing the polite, mannerly things that bothers the old-school truck drivers. But I had an old-school truck driver who told me one day, 'I will always hold the door for a woman, because I'm

from the South and I was raised proper. And if a woman opens the door in front of me, I will slap her hand and hold the door for her.' I'm like, 'Oh, so you don't think that a woman can open a door, and you'll go all the way to abuse because you're such a proud southerner?' What an idiot." Here, old-school truckers are asserting a gendered order as a response to immigrant pressure — asserting that order to illogical lengths. The absurdity of this trucker's insistence indicates a hidden meaning: a reassertion of sexual access and male centrality and an enforced female helplessness.

Risk is another sexually coded construct here. Bridget says she has "a good sense" of her vehicle, but not to the level of old-school owner-operators who take curves too fast but know what they're doing, or to that of new-school immigrant truckers whose something "cultural" gives them "this massive sense of their vehicle." Bridget experiences these as risks and avoids them, but she believes that other truckers' senses of virility, danger, scale, and knowledge of and oneness with the truck gives them access to behavior that she codes as masculine and links to immigrants.

Not all narrators describe the new school of drivers in the language of risk; truckers' attitudes about race and their analyses of racism are just as varied as intersectionality would lead us to expect. Some truckers, both people of color and white people, observe the way that their industry scapegoats immigrants and marginalizes African Americans, and they try to disrupt that pattern. Donovan says she plans to get a Black Lives Matter decal and attach it to her truck. She knows that she'll be asked to remove it because other truckers will complain that it makes them uncomfortable, as happened with her "This Machine Kills Fascists" sticker that she chose in tribute to her hero Woody Guthrie. Her strategy for the Black Lives Matter decal is to have it made huge and consist of many tiny dots, which will take hours to remove. I have other narrators who identify as liberals and are appalled at the racist and anti-Muslim comments they overhear, especially on the CB, where anonymity works as a shield and people get provocative just to pass the time.

Other narrators take a middle path to describe new truckers. Sisyphus, for example, says the trucker population is changing rapidly. She observes, *"There's a lot of Sikhs out on the road, a lot of Hispanics, a lot of Muslims. I was at one customer, and while [a driver] was waiting to get unloaded he pulled out his prayer rug and was doing his prayer, which he has to do at a certain time every day. Just right there in the parking lot. He was taking quite a risk doing that, knowing how people feel about Muslims today. Guy had a lot of guts. There's a lot more immigrants out here now. Lot of eastern European people, too. I think part of that is that trucking companies know they can take*

Photos give a sense of both who does the
work and how seriously they take it.
(Used with permission of the subject.)

*advantage of groups like trans people and east European immigrants and Sikhs
and Muslims, because they know that we have limited opportunity to go elsewhere. Some of these trucking companies that are solely based on hiring Sikhs
or eastern Europeans are the worst companies out there, because of how they
force their drivers to drive illegally."* Reba, when she sees a truck over on the
shoulder, often assumes it's *"a hadji doing required prayer."* She says there's
nothing wrong with that and, like Sisyphus, has a grudging respect for
people willing to take that kind of risk for their faith, but she emphasizes the
danger they cause other truckers when they rejoin traffic.

But maybe Nate's rhetoric best represents the cleaving of forces that occurs
when truckers consider old-school versus new-school drivers. When he tells
me that trucker safety and pay are both rapidly deteriorating, I ask whether
the people doing the work are changing as well. He replies: *"I think so; guys
are more disrespectful. One trucker shot another there in Jessup County the
other day. The story goes that the little Oriental guy shot the white guy out of
pure mistake. He thought it was someone else, and he went up to him and shot*

him, and then he jumped out in front of a train later that day, killed himself. So it was a case of mistaken identity.

"They're also letting the ruling that you must be able to write, and read, and comprehend English go to the curb. CVSA [Commercial Vehicle Safety Alliance] just wrote something last month, or two months ago, that says it doesn't matter if you can read, write, or speak English, that should not be a thing that should prohibit you from getting a driver's license. The thing of it is, these guys that don't speak English, they don't understand what they're getting paid. And it's so much more than they were getting wherever they were before, that they really don't care. It's all about cheap labor."

When Nate tells me about the mistaken identity shooting, it reminds him of his anger that truckers don't need to speak English anymore. Thus, what begins as a story of random violence — presented as evidence of a changing workforce and the loss of the feeling of belonging and camaraderie — becomes instantly racialized. First, the shooter is described as a "little Oriental guy" and his victim is "the white guy." The terms, particulars, articles, and additional adjectives are all telling. Then comes the twist: he shot the wrong guy by mistake and, apparently related, killed himself. Was this from remorse, or to avoid a prison sentence, or for some other reason? The storyteller doesn't specify and probably doesn't know. Nevertheless, his thoughts go from this brief tragedy to the relaxed language requirements for truckers. The race of the shooter apparently suggests other observations about race. Again, immigrant truckers are seen as dangerous to other truckers. Nate goes on to say that they lack experience driving on *"back roads with lots of different terrain,"* so they're prone to accidents. He notes that immigrant drivers depress wages for everyone, because even low pay is better than what they would get back home.

Nate is white and native-born. His attitudes about immigrant truckers serve two functions. First, they motivate an understanding of labor and wage systems. The mythology of the "American dream" is echoed by truckers' independence myths so that, when combined, the two rhetorics make it very hard for truckers to notice and critique how their individualist striving and hard work, rather than advancing them individually, destroys them collectively. Immigrant behavior is more visible as *group* behavior, and seeing its causes and effects can raise consciousness about labor issues more generally. Second, denigrating Mexican and Muslim or Arab truckers can generate solidarity between black and white drivers on the grounds of "Americanness" — a solidarity powerful enough to encompass different genders, significant sexual and gender variance, and racial differences. Because immigrants are understood to cut freight rates by hauling for less, truckers' organizing around slogans like "Say no to cheap freight" has racist overtones. They can imagine a solidarity that enables them to turn down loads without fearing that other truckers will snap them up only to the extent that they can envision an "us" against a "them," which consists of Mexicans and Muslims.

There are enough minority truckers out there that groups have formed, such as the National Minority Trucking Association. Its CEO, Kevin Reed, was interviewed for a 2016 article in *Pacific Standard*, in which he describes covert and overt racism on the road. He says his group and its Facebook page exist to share stories and work against the "lone wolf" attitude among black truckers (Rojas), yet the article about his experiences doesn't mention queer or trans truckers. Nothing rare about that, of course. Even though no one believes the assumptions that all working-class people are white, that African American and Latinx folks aren't gay, and that queer people are financially comfortable, each assumption does keep getting reinscribed in discourse. The economist M. V. Lee Badgett demonstrates how the "myth of gay affluence" makes antigay discrimination seem illogical. She then crunches numbers to tell the real story of a pervasive earnings gap for gay and lesbian workers, and demonstrates the economic, social, and psychological structures that underpin this discrimination. It takes many dense, particular narratives (like Badgett's and mine) to begin to dislodge assumptions like gay affluence and working-class whiteness, since they mostly remain unconscious.

Most of the stories in this section describe changing trucker mores: with a pool of new drivers comes a new culture—and new attitudes. Although we can reiterate that the U.S. working class contains enormous racial and ethnic diversity—and that we imagine the white working class to be racist and homophobic as part of a rhetorical and political project that attributes "progress" to cities, the coasts, and liberals—it's also true that gay, trans, and black truckers can and do project racist attitudes. However, regardless of trucker color, gender, and sexuality, perhaps the most violent examples of racism involve Islamophobia. Social media is one location where truckers can express their anti-Muslim sentiments, though you have to be vigilant to catch them. A trucker posted two photos to a Facebook trucker page on November 1, 2015. One photo depicts two turbaned men from behind; in the next photo, these men are praying on mats placed between the fuel pumps and the truck.

Photo downloaded from the "Truckers Had
Enough" open Facebook group, November 1, 2015.

The accompanying post reads: "OK . . . SO Muslims are now dictating what freight they want to haul in America. . . . NOW you pull up to FUEL and do YOUR JOB . . . and see this!! What's next?? Pray to Muhammad on a restaurant buffet line FLOOR?? Maybe at a busy intersection?? How about in PRIVATE. . . . NO COMMON SENSE OR COURTESY WILL EVER BE EXERCISED BY A MUSLIM . . . EVER!!" Comments from truckers proliferated, suggesting that the poster piss on the men's rug or throw a pork sandwich on it. After six minutes, Facebook pulled the post, I assume because of a complaint or because its algorithm detected hate speech. Both the ranting and the post removal are recurring patterns.

I'm not here to understand, explain, or justify racism among American truckers. Nor do I hope to explain how the language of race gets mobilized by and through the American working class. These are both important projects, and significant work is being done on the second one by sociologists and people working in the field of critical race studies. Their work goes far toward addressing the first question too. My research contributes to these projects by observing and analyzing a pattern: a unifying regime of racism and anti-Muslim vitriol gets activated in response to challenges to sexual and gender certainty. It addresses the image of the trucker, of whatever gender, who gets read as and given the status of masculinity by virtue of being an outsider—a rebel outlaw.

Corporate Underpinnings of the Cowboy Myth

Truck stop sex is one sphere in which masculine behaviors and norms (tropes of the cowboy, maverick, and bad boy) get mobilized and then challenged. Reba assures me that sex on the road is just as rampant as ever, and my eyewitness testimony combined with countless hints and conversations confirms this. One way that truckers feel free, "male," and in control is by proud and frequent access to sex, of any and all types, in public space. Queers know this, truckers know this, people who live near truck stops or work in them know this. However, it's also true that as more and more truck stops get swallowed up by the big franchises (Love's, TA, Petro, etc.), the sex becomes more hidden. Increasingly, it's a culture only visible to truckers and other insiders, because companies like TA and Pilot don't want to acknowledge this component of the industry.

Sexually rebellious culture continues at these truck stops, but it's now marked by shame and secrecy. That shift contributes to a feeling of emasculation that carries a class- and race-marked charge. Truckers are being pressured not to conform to middle-class, tame sexual norms, but also to act like they do conform by at least publicly disavowing an important component of their identity. Arlie Hochschild describes how her interlocutors—white Tea Party supporters from Louisiana—are subject to "feeling rules." After both the Civil War and the civil rights movement, their viewpoint was on the losing side, not just in the military sense but also in the ethical sense. The North effectively got to decide what feelings were allowed, and what feelings would now be labeled racist and forbidden. This feeling hegemony, where one attitude prevails and invalidates another, still-occurring attitude, can result in resentment and backlash. Hochschild reads Trump's popularity as an expression of this, and it's how I understand instances of racism in truckers. For example, remember Felicity's comment about those "people": she avoids saying words I might consider racist, suppressing the words but not the thoughts they express. Truckers are supposed to be sexually wild and dominant, yet they are denied any real power or reward, and the frustration caused by this contradiction sometimes finds a scapegoat in black Americans, and occasionally in Mexicans and Muslims. Racist attitudes and scapegoats are not organic excretions of working-class life, but rather effects of corporate and governmental policymaking that tap into historical tensions. To say the working class is often racist gets us nowhere. To understand why, to whose benefit, and at what cost can enable and motivate change.

Certainly, there are historical and sociocultural explanations, and working-class racialized interactions have been studied thoroughly. But my narrators, because they are sexual as well as class outsiders, enable another level of understanding. Structural changes in the trucking industry (including corporate consolidation of trucker spaces and the accompanying erasure of various kinds of difference) call forth new understandings of trucker sex. Though sex still occurs, it becomes more covert. Further, certain types of sex are now culturally identified as gay, which makes anyone who indulges in them suspect. Since truckers are mostly men, they share a pattern of engaging in male-male casual sex. The historian George Chauncey documented this practice in early twentieth-century New York, and scholars like John Howard and me, in my first book, establish that these patterns persist in the present in certain blue-collar workplaces. In the past, truckers frequently engaged in male-male sex acts without accruing any taint of gay identity. Though these practices stay substantially the same, culture has changed around them, and there's now a lifestyle and a stigma attached to them. While getting a blow job at a truck stop from another man was once read as masculine and innocent, it might now be read as gay. Since truckers have no control over this shift, they might feel angry and resentful. To understand why these feelings frequently find a racial target, we need to understand risk as a part of big-rig culture, especially as it relates to masculinity and sex.

A group of researchers published a paper in 2015 that discusses the methodological challenges of gathering data on truckers, sex, and HIV. They note that "the trucking subculture, occupational stressors, and broad trucking milieu in inner-city neighborhoods create unique work and living conditions for long-haul truckers and their social networks that elevate their risk susceptibility" (Sonmez et al., 113). Their goal is to learn how network structures affect behavior, and therefore data, and they choose to focus on the "risk-taking behaviors of a transgressive minority" (114) whose effects can be widespread, since mobility distributes their reach. The researchers began with indexers, many of whom were female sex workers, because truckers were unwilling to discuss sexual experiences, fearing that they would get fired.

These indexers then became go-betweens so truckers could talk confidentially with researchers. Further, they began with a field team comprised of female, white, middle-class graduate students who were uncomfortable at truck stops, not surprisingly. They replaced these with two fortysomething, male, African American interviewers. These replacements weren't truckers, but they could access the networks and weren't frightened off by trucker settings or culture.

Risk, at least in this study, is seen as something outside of the research relationship—something truckers do and interviewers hope to find and understand. In ethnography, particularly as it overlaps with queer studies, risk is more dialectically produced, and shapes the data, as well as all of the people involved. In doing my interviews, I shared some risk with my narrators, hanging out in sketchy, even dangerous places, driving and riding in semis as truckers did their jobs, and talking to strangers in often very intimate ways. Feminist and queer ethnographic methodology aims to be reflexive about both meaning and risk, partly by emphasizing the unnatural circumstances of advancing to a very high level of interpersonal exchange very quickly, and partly by remaining aware of how that intimacy shapes the data generated. Around the socially charged tropes of sex, race, and religion, these risks are as important to understand as the truckers' behaviors over the road themselves.

For example, when truckers told me stories about Muslims or Mexicans, they knew they would be read as racists and they accounted for this in their words and affect. The risk for them is of being misunderstood—reduced to a culturally devalued stereotype. Yet for them these statements offered explanatory value—allowed them to analyze changes in their condition and identify a responsible party. For me, the risks included having narrators keep their real feelings and beliefs to themselves in order to avoid my presumed censure, and allowing racist words and opinions to go unchallenged, thus tacitly consenting to them and adding to their authority.

Often, when engaging with a socially "forbidden" topic, a subculture develops a coded language that allows insiders to know what's being discussed, but sidesteps censure from outsiders. I believe that the "driver shortage" is one such code.

Reba believes that there is actually no driver shortage; rather, she thinks that megacarriers perpetuate the driver shortage myth as a strategy that allows them to (import and then) hire immigrant workers, chiefly Mexicans and Muslims. When I was training with a megacarrier, I made friends with a fellow student named Ayub who was from Somalia. He told me that he had immigrated to Columbus, Ohio, because a trucking company had agreed to pay for his airfare if he came to train there. He says this recruitment is very common, and certainly I met many Somali truckers out on the road. None of them, including Ayub, became my narrators because none identified (at least to me) as queer, gay, or trans. I had brief conversations with many, but they were always itching to get rolling and make money. In addition, none of the many Sikhs I saw driving truck would really look at me, let alone enter into conversation, and the social networking sites I used to start conversations with truckers didn't have any Sikh presence that I could see. Both Sikhs and Muslims are large trucking populations that need to be studied by people who have the cultural capital to get conversations started. My data is anecdotal, combined with the fuller story I got from Ayub. However, there is ample data in my narrators' stories about how Somali and Muslim truckers are seen and treated by other (white and minority) truckers once they have immigrated.

Putting these stories together, I conclude that megacarriers recruit from certain ethnic and national enclaves where they have established contacts, and they claim this recruitment is justified by a lack of qualified truck drivers already present in the United States. They pay the immigrants less, push them to break rules that they don't fully understand, and mobilize racism and Islamophobia against them to distract native-born truckers from protesting this wage undercutting. I would go so far as to speculate that they target for recruitment populations that are easily recognizable—that have a visible ethnic look, language, behavior, or head covering. The easy-recognition factor of the new immigrants facilitates the redirection of truckers' frustration about wage depletion onto the population of truckers on its front lines, rather than onto the corporate decision-makers.

Predictably, this racial scapegoating pattern is a consequence of the loss of status previously accorded to the working-class male breadwinner, or whoever (of whatever gender) occupies that role and thus benefits from its status. Reba lays this all out when I ask her whether switching to hourly pay, rather than piecework or mileage pay, would alleviate some of the problems with the current system.

She says: *"Hourly work won't work for truckers because there's no direct supervision. People complain that you have to work seventy hours, when I'd like to work eighty. What's in it for me if I do it in less time? Less pay. More pay if I deliver late. You'd have to go to a percentage system instead. That's an incentive. That lack of direct supervision is half the draw of the job—be your own boss. The e-log is an attempt to supervise truckers. There could be mileage pay with hourly starting as soon as you arrive at a facility. This is a last-chance job — so those people aren't good candidates for hourly pay. People who have done the job don't think that it's easy. That attitude is demeaning. It's physically easier than it's ever been, it's mentally harder than I ever thought it would be. Twice as many cars on the road, you have immigrants in trucks and cars. You have old people. If they keep the mileage pay but add detention pay from the minute you get there, shippers and receivers will get moving. The trucker has zero influence. Even though I work for a really good company, all that bullshit [of a recent, frustrating scheduling glitch] was on me. Just me. But in return I get really good miles and a good living. And I earned it. You shouldn't expect this money coming right out of school. You need to establish a record and then use that to negotiate with an employer. The government subsidizes megacarriers in various ways, like write-offs for training people off the unemployment rolls, or immigrants that the government needs to find jobs for — like refugees — which means they can lowball freight and still make a profit. So they harm companies trying to treat employees as an investment. [The government] should only subsidize training if it leads to retention — percentage doled out over two years. This is exactly the middle class losing their ass. This is it right here."*

The Problems Truckers Know but Won't Name

While Reba's observations illustrate the way racial scapegoating patterns adhere to issues of pay and status, additional forms of racism and racist violence continue to pervade trucking space. Wendy, a black woman, laughed out loud when I asked if she felt safe exercising on the road. She closed down the conversation by saying she never leaves her truck after dark, and only leaves it for necessary work tasks otherwise. *"I keep a treadmill in there,"* she reported in a tone that informed me of the stupidity of my question. Violence, racism, sexism, rape, and fear structure the lives of all my narrators, and they seem to experience all of it as background noise — always there, but not worth calling attention to, since that acknowledges its intractability.

An almost casual racism directed at Mexicans and Muslims is separate from this and shared by a diverse range of my narrators. On I-40, crossing New Mexico, Reba comments offhand, *"Here we go with the hadji race"* when a trucker passes her. That night, we're parked at a Little America truck stop outside Flagstaff after a long day's driving, Reba leaning back with her bare feet crossed on the steering wheel, smoking and talking. A truck backs in next to us with a decorated fringe draped across the top of the windshield. Little dangling balls. Reba calls this truck a magic carpet, the scorn in her voice only slightly undercut by humor.

Though I couldn't interview any Muslim truckers, six of my narrators identify as Mexican. They resisted seeing themselves as victims and reported few,
if any, negative interactions with other truckers. When I ask Gloria about
being Mexican in a truck, she responds, *"It's good money, and Mexicans, we
don't have cultural education, we don't have a degree, and trucking is easy to
get into."* Her kids worried about the risk more than she did—she likes the
adventure, likes to be in control, and adds that her kids know they couldn't
stop her from doing something once she's set her mind to it. She stays in
the truck at night, packs food and water with her, and doesn't let anyone
steal her joy.

Felicity, a white transwoman, spends more time than my other narrators
explicitly engaging with race as it effects trucking and transness. She tells
me that she often gets challenged at truck stops: *"When I got up to Dallas,
I got to another truck stop, and the same story, it's always a black woman.
Eighty percent of the transphobia in Texas and Louisiana is at the hands of
black Americans because they've decided, 'We figured out you're trans, and
we're going to punk you, and punk you, and punk you until you react.' And
I always push back, I don't give anybody an inch. And all I've noticed is that
Americans are selfish, psychotic, transphobic, ignorant, and they're bullies,
and they hide behind religion, they hide behind the Bible. And nobody gave a
shit about which bathroom we went to until Ted Cruz and Donald Trump ran
for president, because—I'm going to tell you the brutal truth. The brutal truth
is [Americans] don't want a nigger president, and they don't want to let a bunch
of fags gay-marry. [Obama] is not a nigger, I'm not racist, and I don't think of
gay people as fags, but I'm using the language of the enemy because I grew up
in a household that was Southern Baptist, and I'm telling you, they don't give
a damn about it, they don't give a damn about our rights. They know we have
gender dysphoria, they're just scapegoating us, and the trans community does
a terrible job of fighting back, because all they do is sit around and whine about
it and sing 'Kumbaya.' So you got an interview from a transgender who's Repub-
lican, in the NRA, and is voting for Hillary, so I hope you've learned something."*

Felicity's trans identity is saturated with logics of blaming black people
for violence and for feeling victimized as an attempt to understand her low
status and the sea of harassment and hate in which she lives. She doesn't
want protection—doesn't see herself as a victim. Like the African American truckers I interviewed, her difficult circumstances lead her to embrace
personal responsibility rather than look for structural explanations. She
then looks for someone to blame—some way to blame, and some means by
which to understand violence. In the United States, certainly, and globally

as well, the language used to name and manage violence is the language of race and of blackness. Carol Anderson historicizes this link in the United States, explaining how "crime and blackness . . . became synonymous" in the 1950s (104). This link, Anderson explains, enables continued inequality: by saying that black people are criminals, the United States can distract its citizens from policies that criminalize blackness. The crime, then, is not what black people do, but what twentieth-century American society does to black people.

Often, when my narrators feel visible and vulnerable owing to their sex and/or gender, they use the language of race to express that fear. They live in the world Anderson describes: a world where violence and criminality adhere easily to black bodies. Discussing bathrooms as unsafe places for transwomen, where violence often happens, Thelma says, *"As far as other truckers go, in the truck stop, nobody gives us any trouble. We haven't had any trouble. It's when they have busses, travelers, we hear a code orange or a code 152. I'll say, 'A bus is coming, let's go. Time to leave, let's go.' And that's it. Some Mexican lady yelled at [Louise, Thelma's partner]. I was sick. I have an abscessed tooth and it flares up from time to time. So she went into the ladies' room by herself, which I don't like to let happen—I try not to, but sometimes she's got to go alone—and she went in, and this Mexican lady was washing her hands while my wife was applying her lipstick. And the lady said, 'You don't belong in here,' and my wife said, 'I have the common courtesy to shave my facial hair, at least you could do the same.' I'm like, 'Oh goddamn, that's funny as hell.'"*

Fear caused by vulnerability and disempowerment can lead to humor, to racism, or to both. Occasionally, it leads to paranoid beliefs. A transwoman trucker whom I interviewed for a previous project posted a Facebook update on October 30, 2015 that said: "You know what is weird, today I have seen several semis with the word ISIS on them and the symbol for the ISIS terrorist group, on I-80 today, wonder how they were allowed into the U. S., must be the foreign driver policy that our government has in place and that's why our freight is dropping down, because they allow them to come over here and take our jobs and freight away from the American driver, now we are the minority in the U.S."

Reba showed me this "ISIS" symbol at a truck stop. She told me that she had heard it described as an ISIS symbol but had done her own research and determined it was actually crossed Arabic swords symbolizing acceptance of the American way of life. Either way, many truckers understand it as proof that Muslim truckers are increasingly common, that they drive down freight

Cheryl drives in Hawaii. This image expresses both pride and longing.
(Used with permission of the subject.)

rates and take American truckers' jobs, and that the trucking lifestyle is thereby under serious threat.

On the one hand, this imagined idea that the working class is vulnerable to a leftist-supported minority incursion and the loss of a traditional way of life needs to be critiqued as nostalgic and racist. On the other hand, liberal-led policies that generate increased governmental micromanagement (ironically labeled "deregulation") have radically disempowered truckers over the past thirty years, and the language they find to name and condemn this pattern is that of gender, sex, and race. Truckers who find themselves marginalized within the industry (and often physically vulnerable, and often poor) participate in these logics.

My point here is that gay, trans, and black truckers share patterns of racist scapegoating with other truckers, and with disenfranchised people generally. But the extra layers of visibility and vulnerability they experience as truckers, combined with the continuing (though empty) myth of the "lone wolf" trucker, also add to their frustration. Studs Terkel's *Working*, from 1972, includes an account of a truck driver named Frank Decker, who transported steel from mills in Gary, Indiana, to plants in Wisconsin on "about

25 hundred trips" (206). When he started, all he needed was a chauffer's license, and the only regulations concerned load weight. "The minute you climb into that truck, the adrenaline starts pumping. If you want to have a thrill there's no comparison, not even a jet plane, to climbing on a steel truck and going out there on the Dan Ryan Expressway" (209). Decker recounts the family and health problems truckers face, but concludes: "There's this mystique about driving. The trucker has a sense of power. . . . You feel like your day's work is well done when you're coming back" (213–4). Decker's comments, and Terkel's framing of them, are not about race or about gender or sex. And thus, they are. With race not mentioned, whiteness is assumed, and with gender implied by glossing family problems as problems "with the wife in particular" (210), straight maleness is assumed. This sense of power — of importance — happens because it's male and because it doesn't know that. As soon as power is forced to acknowledge the structures that uphold it, by concurrent but unrelated social and political shifts since the early 80s, it deflects that anger onto racial targets.

5

STOPPING

JESUS, TAKE THE WHEEL

Road Accidents, PTSD, and Fear

GRACE LEE BOGGS, the late Marxist activist and working-class warrior, reminds us that capitalism is what makes people compete with each other; it structures our experience so that we think each one of us is best able to meet our own individual needs, and that we're fighting for rank with others. When truckers are in dangerous situations they often respond with "Jesus, take the wheel." Though they still hold the steering wheel themselves, I read this response as coded acknowledgment that they feel overwhelmed by the responsibility perched on their shoulders and seek structural support. Even though they're encouraged by their companies, American culture, capitalism, and their psyches to believe that they can handle whatever arises, they also need help. Road accidents are a part of the driving experience that helps force truck drivers out of the typical American individualist mentality and into the community that's created by sharing tragedy. It thereby offers both revolutionary potential and daily trauma: a potent mixture.

One thing that makes trucking, and blue-collar work in general, special is the physical engagement of the body of the worker. Often, we think of this feature negatively: that all that workers have to offer on the labor market are their bodies, which they will sacrifice until they are literally used up. But work that depends on and uses the worker's body also confers power—it means that your body is *for* something, and it and you are needed. Agency is then more embodied, more lively, more organic.

Let me pause here to observe that I've started this chapter about road accidents indirectly, because they're hard to talk about. Accidents are the leading cause of death among truckers, but usually the trucker isn't the one to die when the accident involves a car. Consequently, most truckers see, or participate in, many accidents involving a fatality to someone else. These accidents are almost always caused by cars. The FMCSA studied 6,131 fatal crashes involving a car and a truck and found that 83 percent were caused by the car. Most automobile drivers have no understanding of how trucks work: no idea how much space they need to stop, how much visibility they have down their sides, or how their load affects their ability to maneuver. So, often without even realizing it, four-wheelers (car drivers) make choices that truckers must respond to—sometimes fatally. From the truckers' point of view, it isn't relevant who or what caused an accident, because seeing someone die, whether or not that person caused it, changes you. Unlike military service members, law enforcement officers, or medical personnel, truckers receive no training in how to handle this.

A woman I trained with called me from the highway shoulder, sobbing. She had just seen an accident, been able to avoid it, pulled over, and stopped. But from the shoulder, she had witnessed the emergency crews arrive and pull two bodies, one clearly dead, from the wreckage. She was a new driver and this was her first experience seeing that happen. In a truck, you're seated high up and have a very good view down onto the road. She saw the whole process: from driving, to the grinding crash, to death. She phoned her dispatcher to say that she was too shaken up to drive right then and would need an hour or two to recover before she could continue. He responded that her load was due and she needed to keep on schedule. She called me because she knew that I would understand the gendered nature of the veiled threat in those words: feelings have no place in this job—if you can compartmentalize them you'll do fine, but if you let them leak into the workplace, we have other people standing by ready to pull your freight. She made her delivery on schedule.

Isabella describes the mental process truckers go through when they balance the need to drive, so they can get paid, regardless of the circumstances, with the fear that unsafe conditions increase their likelihood of putting people's lives at risk. She says, *"I go back to what I always told my students: trust your gut. Push the envelope a little bit, that's how you get experience; but when your gut tells you no, there is nothing in that trailer that is worth your life. The other thing I used to tell them is if you're tired, pull over. It is much easier to explain your load being late because you needed to take a nap than a dead family of five."*

This chapter includes accounts of the road accidents and near misses experienced by my narrators, research on crashes and their causes, and reflec-

Julie Murphy returning to her truck after a thirty-minute break,
beverage in hand. (Used with permission of the subject.)

tions on the mental and physical effects of collisions on truckers. Finally,
it also includes thoughts about crashing as a type of stopping that fuels a
critique of the stopping/running binary and of the capitalist system that
animates it. Ulrich Beck is a German sociologist who (starting in 1984) has
shaped how scholars understand risk. He sketches a past where risk was
personal and people who chose to engage in it might thereby profit. Then,
he describes a present in which risk distribution replaces wealth distribution
as the mechanism of modernity. He argues that we need to stop assuming
that technology and industrialization *cause* risk, because social and political
forces also contribute. Though "wealth accumulates at the top, risks at the
bottom" (35), risk also contaminates upward and internationally (44). Impor-
tantly, while wealth is visible, risk is not. Its consequences are elusive and difficult to mobilize politically, and the quality of a community changes to one
based not on need but on anxiety (49). These changes certainly describe and
contextualize the psychic world, the stress, and the loneliness of truckers.

Being in the Room Where Death Happens

Only a few narrators related stories of their own accidents. One reason might
be that once truckers get in an accident, their employment is typically ter-
minated and they have a hard time finding new trucking work. Thus, they

didn't wind up in my narrator pool. Another factor might be that many Americans scrupulously avoid getting labeled as victims and prefer to see themselves as survivors. However, many truckers did tell me about being the first to arrive on the scene after an accident, witnessing an accident in which they were not involved, or acting to prevent an accident from occurring.

Sean describes an incident: *"Just a few days ago, I was one of the first responders on the scene of an accident, and I never thought that would happen. To be honest with you, this woman must have had an angel up her butt. About 2,000 feet up the road from me, I think it was I-55 in Kentucky, she veered towards the left side of the highway into a very steep ravine with trees, and then veered right, in between two cars, off the highway, just missing a copse of trees, turned left again, and went up this very steep hill that brought her to a slow and safe stop. She was unconscious that whole time, so I don't know what turned that wheel. It was crazy!*

"I jumped out and went to check on her, and she was unresponsive. I thought it was diabetic shock or something like that. Other drivers arrived, and we had to break a window open to get to her. We were searching the car for medications, anything that would give us a clue what was wrong with her. The EMT shows up, and she finally starts to come around a little bit, and when she opens her mouth a little bit, we could instantly smell alcohol. I was concerned about this woman but also very, very pissed off at her. She could have taken us all out. The other people that stopped with me were a family with just the cutest little boy, and she could have killed us all. The way she was acting, it was alcohol. I've seen my grandmother in the same state. Oh my goodness, she had Illinois plates, I don't know where she stopped to tie one on, enough to pass out. That was my first accident. My biggest fear is a fatality accident and being one of the first responders." Sean makes connections between what he witnessed and his intimate family circle, thinks about who could have been hurt, with particular emphasis on a young child, and directs his anger at the individual driver — all recurring tropes.

Reba tells many stories about near misses. For example: *"One time I was really heavy and I was climbing out of the Hoover Dam bridge. It's ten miles per hour because you have to wind up and down and there's a sharp turn onto the bridge, and so it's already hard. And one time I was driving that, and I turned and there were two big mountain goats right there."* She almost went off the road and down the cliff. Relaying another example, she says, *"You can drive through a cloud in Cabbage, Oregon, but the cloud is windy. It's different than driving in fog because it swirls around, like when you put your hand in dry ice. It can play with your mind — spook you."*

These stories testify to Reba's ability to avoid danger and to the thrill provided by its routine presence. These two are natural events, but she gets similar satisfaction, though less thrill, from eluding danger with more human causes. For example: *"A while back, a truck was on the shoulder and it pulled into traffic unexpectedly, and a Danfreight truck rear-ended it. I was coming down the hill and saw a big plume of black smoke. Both trucks caught on fire. I and a few others pulled off onto a side road, and we got by but had to see the wreckage."* She tells me that there's a road to Cincinnati called the "celestial highway" in trucker slang, because it's lined with white crosses. She describes driving this road as being "spooky," which is language I hear often around the topic of crashing: drivers are haunted by the fear and the memory of death.

As I rode through Arizona with Reba, we saw an accident. We had seen dust devils (swirling winds that pick up dust and create a funnel cloud) increasingly often, and the head wind she was driving into decreased Reba's miles per gallon to six from the usual nine, but she said that was still preferable to battling crosswinds. Visibility got worse, with dust storm warnings on road alert signs and on the Qualcomm. Then Reba remarked that there was no traffic in the oncoming lanes (a change I hadn't even noticed), and she slowed down and went into high alert. Almost immediately there were brake lights ahead, and we crawled down the road, eventually seeing an accident in the oncoming lanes. A Con-way double (two shorter trailers attached to one tractor) was stretched across two lanes, and a white semitruck was perpendicular to it, with a car compressed between them. Air bags had deployed. It seemed like a guaranteed fatality. Traffic was backed up to a standstill for miles and miles. We didn't see any bodies, but it's still an intense emotional experience. Traffic hazards in our direction at that point consisted of a stopped semi in the right lane, with shattered glass sprayed under it, and two cars on the shoulder. Probably no one hurt there, but the rubble offered quiet testimony to what it was like to see the accident unfold.

All truckers live with a fair amount of fear, though they usually downplay it as part of their tough and competent persona, or maybe just in self-defense. Alys tells me: *"Always expect the unexpected. I've driven in a lot of heavy snow where you could hardly see the front of the hood, let alone out half a mile ahead of you. As far as pulling single trailers, I never worry too much, because I've always prided myself on being a safe driver. And when weather conditions got too bad, I always remember what my father said: if it gets too bad, get someplace and go to bed. And that was something I was never afraid to do. If it got to the point where I got nervous and couldn't handle, like, snow conditions, I would just get in a rest area or in a truck stop and go to bed. Pulling these doubles up and down the thruway now, it gets a little white-knuckle driving out there. With a single trailer, you leave yourself, like, five to six seconds between you and the vehicle ahead of you. Pulling these doubles, you want to be leaving somewhere between eleven and thirteen seconds between you, and it's a lot of room, and those people that are pressing you on a slippery road, they go, 'Wow, I can get right in there.' Well, they just cut your time right in half, you know, and then when they make that move, then they feel their car start going sideways, and they step on the brakes, and you gotta worry about two trailers trying to get by you instead of one. I've had a good, clean driving experience, but the older I get, the more the weather does bother me. Especially in the wintertime, the weather driving is really beginning to get to me."* If the cab stops but the trailers don't, their momentum as they "get by you" can easily lead to a fatal crash.

Vito drives mostly at night, when it's less busy. He loves the quiet, and the empty roads, but, he says, *"nights are when most of your really bad storms happen. Right outside of Salt Lake City is the pass named Three Sisters, and I've been on top of that in the dead set of winter in a complete whiteout, because it caught me so off guard. At the bottom of the mountain, you're completely fine. It's dry, it's warm, but when you get to the top of the mountain, it's snowing so you can't see anything. There's nothing you can do if you stop because you can't see the lines in the road, so you can't tell if you're stopping on the side of the road or if you're stopping in the middle of the lane. You can't tell if you're stopping a couple miles from a truck stop or if you're stopping in the middle of nowhere. Once, I saw a truck just parked on the side of the mountain, where there was so much snow that those people had to be rescued off the side of the mountain. But their truck was just left there, because they couldn't get to it—they had just driven off the road completely.*

"One time, I was so new that I let one of my dispatchers tell me what to do. I was running up on 49 in Missouri, and the wind was really bad, and I think I might have had like 10,000 pounds in the box, so my trailer is getting pushed from the slow lane over to the hammer lane. I rode like that for, like, ten miles or so, till I wrote into my dispatch that I had to pull over to the side of the road—the wind is freaking bad here. But they said, 'No, this load has to be there. In a couple hours, you have to get there.' So I put it in drive, I drove another five miles, and it got so bad that I had my steering wheel cocked halfway to the right, and the trailer was all the way to the left-hand lane. So I found a truck stop, I pulled over, and I parked, and I told my dispatcher, 'This is not safe, I'm not driving like this.' And when I used the word 'unsafe,' dispatch had to auto-

matically back off, which they did and I was thankful for. But because I didn't know that beforehand, you know, I went an extra five miles that could have killed a person in a four-wheeler, or it could have killed another truck driver or anyone else. I went that additional five miles because I thought I had to do it."

Josephine explains that her company doesn't pressure her to drive when weather conditions get bad; it actually encourages her to stop and wait. Though she experiences this as care and is grateful, I'm more cynical and interpret it as insurance for the company at the trucker's expense, because any parked time isn't paid time. That makes deciding when to stop challenging. She says, *"Snow and ice. You know, both companies I've worked for have been really, really good about saying, 'Don't drive on ice. Just pull over, don't drive on it.' Finding parking during those times is a little harder, but I can do it. I just suffer through it. I was in a storm in Pennsylvania the other day, where all the road construction signs were flying around the highway. I had to pull over. That—yeah, that I don't care for. And as I'm just sitting there, the truck is, like, swaying."* She laughs. *"I was on the side of the interstate. Yeah."*

Liam confides, *"Every winter I tell myself I'm going to find a real job, I'm done with this, it's not worth it."* But then summer comes, and he doesn't.

Daryl, who was out driving with his son when we talked, thinks about how truckers handle all this risk. He brings his son along on some summer runs to give them time together and give the preteen some life skills, though it can get awkward, since his son doesn't know Daryl is trans. But it's through his role as a parent that Daryl comes to understand the risk of the job. He tells me: *"The bad out there . . . the bad is really bad. I had one incident that actually scared me enough where we actually pulled over, and I physically wasn't driving; one of my students was. We were traveling on a four-lane highway, and we topped the hill at five miles an hour, and when we got to the bottom there was a crossroads that was not marked prior to the hill. And there was a car stopped at the stop sign, and he let us get within twenty feet, and he pulled out in front of us. Luckily enough, [the trainee] had time to react to it, pulled out smashing the front brake, didn't hit him or anything. But it scared him, and it scared me. I ended up having him pull over and taking control of the truck. 'Cause he couldn't drive anymore. He was so shook up, 'cause after the car had got across the front of us, we realized there was small children in that car. One split-second decision on that driver's part could have cost us four lives. My son's now thirteen, but he was seven or eight when I started out here. But that car saw us going downhill, going down that grade, you know, and the four-wheeler just thought [disparagingly]: trucks."*

Perhaps in response to this disparagement, truckers develop a macho sensibility. Daryl goes on to say, *"Out here, you'll hear it referred to as the trucker mentality: 'Oh, I've got this, I've got this.' You know, you see them running down hills, and they have no control, they've lost their brakes, the brakes are on fire, sparking, they can't stop. There's nothing else you can do besides watch them go. And hope, and pray with everything you've got that they're gonna make it to the bottom safely, you know. Nothing else is sure. You have to watch, you know, helplessly, at what could possibly be their last ride."*

The "trucker mentality" he refers to is confidence born of years of experience mixed with sheer desperation. In order to make money, you have to keep rolling. Sure, you want to stay alive, and you fear killing someone with your truck, but the grim reality is that you often keep going and hope for the best because you have to. This structure forces responsibility onto the truckers — if truckers "choose" to keep driving rather than pull over and wait out a storm, they are shouldering blame if something goes wrong and adopting a mantle of anxiety that is personalized, and therefore doubly insidious.

Billy tells me he's seen lots of accidents, but *"most of the stuff I seen is at sixty-five miles an hour,"* which allows for some distancing. One incident shook him up both because it was so grisly and because he felt it could have been prevented. His usually voluble style shifts to short, choppy sentences for this story: *"I've seen a lot. Saw a guy lose his head — got there seconds after it. Guy was riding on the wrong side of the road, we were all on the CB, everybody got out of the way, but this church bus didn't have the CB on, and he comes flying by. It's a church bus, and the hood of the bus just sliced his head off. We'd been talking about this guy on the CB for twenty miles, everybody's getting over. I left. I was so mad at the bus driver. Why didn't he have the CB on?"*

I could keep telling stories about wrecks: every trucker has these stories, and they are important and instructive. Readers who share the road with truckers should spend some time looking into this and educating themselves about road safety (for example, by reading the FMCSA blogpost "Driving Safely around Trucks"). Here, rather, my goal is to try to understand how truckers, especially queer truckers, trans truckers, and truckers of color, live with this trauma. Culturally marginalized, often rejected by their families, living with the stress of large and small acts of hatred, contempt, and anger, these truckers experience PTSD — and also resilience. But if just hearing and retelling these stories makes it hard for me to hold myself together, how do these people get back behind the wheel and keep driving?

Billy with the author in his home.
(Used with permission of the subject.)

The Psychic Cost of Living So Close to Death

When I ask Gwynneth whether snow driving is scary, she responds, *"No, it's pretty."* I laugh and say, "You might be a little tough — just saying." I use this open-ended, admiring response to encourage her to elaborate without influencing how. And indeed she does continue: *"Well, see, I'm from Chicago, so I'm familiar with snow driving. Granted, it's a little different in the truck, but you just slow down, you know? Driving in the snow is beautiful — it looks like this weird, screen-saver video game, depending on how it's falling, it's coming at you, it's so cool. I'm not a fearful person because I do believe in predestination, and everything happens for a reason, and I can't control my death. I have no choice in the matter. What will be will be, so I have to listen to my intuition. I don't have a whole lot of fear. I remember the turning point: there was an incident where a car spun out in front of me, crossed the median, and just came to a complete stop. And I was fine. I remembered having a panic reaction — sweating palms, difficult breathing — but I didn't get that then. Now*

I'm able to think through things more because I'm not in panic mode. I have people who think you have to slam on the brakes or wiggle out of it. But I stay real calm. I'm resigned to my fate. I don't try to bring it on but . . . it's a great fit in terms of a job for me."

Her account shows that one way truckers handle the risk and the fear is by getting habituated to trauma. Gwynneth reports learning to revoke control and accept her fate, and this choice explains her belief that trucking is "a great fit in terms of a job" for her.

Zoe has a similar response: *"I've seen the weather, I've seen the mountains, I've seen the fog where I couldn't see at all. I've done the whiteouts in upstate New York where you can't even see the road. By now it's just part of the job. Hell, like I said, it just becomes part of the job. When I first started driving, I thought the truck turned over every time you went around a curve, so I would go around a curve so slowly I was almost backing up. But after a while, eventually, you kind of get into a groove, like any other job. You think, 'I got to be careful here, but I can drive like a bat outta hell here.' And on the ice and fog, driving on a wing and a prayer, that's just where it's at. I mean hell, if the cars don't kill us, and the weather don't kill us, you're doing good. And now you got to watch out for the new truckers, too. I mean, I've had scary situations with trucks where they have a problem keeping their truck to their lane—these are things you just got to watch out for."*

Both Gwynneth and Zoe are black women with years of experience in trucking. Both of them describe a strategy for managing the fear of being in an accident without letting that fear paralyze them, which arises from their driving skills and professionalism, as well as from their attitude. Zoe ends by drawing a distinction between beginning truckers' and veteran truckers' skills regarding avoiding and managing trauma—a perspective Donovan backs up. A month or two after our formal interview, Donovan witnessed her first fatality; she reached out to me and posted on social media about this experience. This is from her Facebook post of September 30, 2016:

> I watched a man die today right in front of me in one of the most terrible ways imaginable. It's an image and sounds I don't know if I'll ever be able to erase from my memory. My heart aches and goes out to the family that lost their kid. Words can't express what I'm feeling. I think to myself "God, what if he was like me? 1000s of miles from his family?" Considering how transient this city is . . . I also watched a truck driver in the last moments of his career realize the weight of what just happened. I think "what if I'm like him someday?"

This job has pushed me to fantasize about death and dying. I saw death for the first time today. I don't want to die.

This job has pushed me to deep depression leading to complacency. I saw that too. I don't want to be complacent.

Donovan is specifically stating that she fears complacency—the detached manner she identifies in veteran truckers. She has just seen someone killed in a road accident—seen him die—and she is holding onto her horror, worried that if she were to see this repeatedly, that feeling would fade. Truckers get no training in how to live with this trauma and fear, and Donovan is worrying here about what that would mean for her psychically.

Odette says that driving, even in snow and ice, doesn't make her scared. She says, *"Nervous, maybe. But not scared. What scares me is some of these dimwit supertruckers blowing past me at sixty miles per hour, when I'm struggling to keep traction at twenty-five. On one trip alone I saw four fatalities, and I lost count of how many jackknifes I saw—but I saw four fatalities, and one of those, the driver was thrown from his truck. That was really upsetting. I really try not to internalize it. It makes you anxious, but you can't let it stop you. Yes, there's the reality that every day I might not make it home to my wife and my daughter. But I do the best I can every day; I'm as cautious as I can be. If there's going to be an accident, it's important that I be as safe as possible and be as safe for other people around me, because I don't want someone hit on the road because of a mistake that I made. But it's one of those things— you can't internalize it because it would destroy you. It would absolutely destroy you."* Odette is an intersex trucker who values the anonymity the job provides, which allows her to escape gender-related employment challenges. She is respected and liked at her company, where the other drivers know her only as a woman. She values that regard, because her previous jobs have not afforded it to her; she knows it's at least partially premised on infrequent interactions because, she says, *"we're all running different schedules and different routes."* Thus, it's the relative anonymity of the job that makes it safe for gender-variant workers, but which also contributes to the risk and feeling of vulnerability. Odette doesn't connect the fear of road accidents with being intersex, but I hear a connection in her and other truckers' stories, in the language of *internalizing*. Intersex truckers know the cost of living with trauma.

Carolyn, another intersex trucker, explains that she was not informed of her condition but rather operated on as a baby, given hormones, and left to sort it out later. She adds, *"Most of the people like me that that was done to committed suicide between their teens and thirty years old."* Suicide rates among trans and intersex populations are both high and underreported, and suicide is also a common cause of death among truckers overall. Carolyn links these here and elsewhere, and she points out that when you're on the margins sexually, trucking may be a place you can find a home. But even then social exclusion compounds with the anxiety and loneliness of trucking and leads to depression. Anxiety caused by being a sexual outsider, with all the familial and social challenges that implies, multiplies when combined with the trauma and stress of trucking. Seeing and fearing death so much adds to this mental stress.

Carolyn points out that truckers are *"being forced to work fourteen-hour days with just a half-an-hour break."* She adds, *"They're getting tired even quicker, and they don't have the stamina, and they're making mistakes. They're making fatal mistakes. For instance, about three weeks ago, I was going down Illinois Route 130; there was a one-lane bridge because they were doing construction on it, and about halfway over I look at taillights sticking up in the air—truck taillights. I get off the bridge and go running back there, and the poor man is in there screaming like a banshee. And the truck's teetering, and the wheels [are] hanging off the ground. I call 911, ask if he's hurt; he says his neck and back hurt. He asks me to call his wife; I call his wife and let her talk to him, and then later on I called her up and talked to her. He'd only been on the road by himself for two weeks. He'd spent twenty-eight days out with a trainer beforehand, and the trainer really seldom even let him drive. He got into a tight situation, didn't know to handle it, and went off the side."* Carolyn blames poor training and long hours for this near tragedy, but she and I go on to acknowledge that this trucker will be blamed and fired for it. So truckers fear getting killed, killing someone else, and making mistakes that inevitably lead to termination. All this stress makes the job, and the life, more dangerous.

Gabrielle and Xena describe fear as a constant. Xena reminds me, *"Don't ever . . . don't ever let go of the fear, because if you have no more fear, you get cocky. I never got over the fear, and I felt that we should not, when you see [an] accident or something like that. When you get to driving, you just got to be ready. That's how I start my shift, by asking myself, 'Are you ready to die?' You drive all night knowing it can happen."* Gabrielle remarks quietly, *"We counted 153 accidents one night."* Xena says you just learn to live with the fear.

Fear of death, fear of causing death, fear of job loss, and fear of financial setbacks or ruin all overlap. Brad says that on the day we talked, a distracted four-wheeler made a last-minute lane change in front of him, and he almost hit her, *"braking and swearing and sweating. But if I hit her, I'm at fault."* He then describes an incident involving a friend who *"was driving in West Virginia on curving two-lane roads."* Brad continues: *"He was an owner-operator, so the truck was his, and he was solely responsible for everything in the van. So he came up over a hill and there was this lady driver* in his lane, *coming fast towards him. He had to dive off the road and bury that trailer. She was drunk, clearly, but if he hadn't done that and hit her, he would have been charged with manslaughter for not moving over. And he was out for the repairs, the tow, and the contents of his trailer."* It's a truism that "shit rolls downhill." These truckers' stories illustrate that risk is carefully managed within trucking so that each individual trucker bears the cost of a wide array of circumstances, many far beyond their control. A trucker involved in an accident becomes prohibitively expensive to insure, so even well-intentioned companies can't offer them work. Truckers wind up feeling disposable, as they are dismissed as soon as anything goes wrong.

Accidents Don't Happen by Accident

Even when they're telling me stories about accidents and their causes, the truckers circle back remorselessly to the theme of overregulation and unfair micromanagement. You can hear this in Brad's account, where he states that no matter who causes a crash, the trucker gets blamed. This perception is certainly borne out by experience, and it's used to increase the micromanagement of truckers through additional technology like drive cams (typically, video cameras installed on truck dashboards that record the road or, increasingly, the road and the inside of the truck's cab). Yet footage from the truck rarely saves the trucker's job, because after any accident, insurance gets too pricey. That knowledge is what convinces truckers that they work in a rigged system and adds to their stress. If anything goes wrong, whether or not they could have prevented it, the trucker's job will be forfeit.

Regulatory structures increase the odds that something will go wrong. Nate says, *"A driver starts his day at six o'clock in the morning, so he has fourteen hours to finish his day, and he gets jammed up somewhere. And he's going to a place where the DOT posts a mandatory brake check. Nine out of ten times, they're going to go right past that checkpoint 'cause that takes time out of their driving. See, under the new regulations you can't split your sleep up, so you have to drive all fourteen hours straight, and then sleep all eight. We used to do eight sleep hours and ten nondriving hours, but we could split the sleeper-berth time any way we wanted to. Now truckers have to push themselves. I've never seen so many tired guys in all my life. These guys just look worn slap out, they look like zombies. We're not being able to stop."* His ending plea — "we're not being able to stop" — is both about the drive clock and about the truck — an unintended, unfunny pun.

Bridget agrees that there's a link between regulations and accidents, which gets manifested in a driver's affect. She says, *"The ways the laws are written, the ways the responsibilities fall, everything's your fault. I mean, I may not be ticketed, I may not be at fault, but I get nailed. And that's totally misunderstood by the driving public. They don't understand that my CDL is at risk every time I hit the brake; every time I change lanes, my license is at risk. And if I don't have a license, I don't have an income.*

"They don't understand the dynamics of the vehicle, they don't understand the life — that it really is very isolationist. It is very frustrating unless you've got many, many years at it, and that frustration either is going to play out in the driver's responses, or it leads to accidents — because there is a frustration that is expressed through aggressive driving. And the aggressive driving is usually triggered by a four-wheeler doing something stupid. The four-wheeler's idea is 'I'm faster than you. You're in my way. I'm quicker than you. I can't see past you.' But as a trucker, I'm not in a race with you. I'm delivering the stuff; you wouldn't have your car if it wasn't for a truck driver. You wouldn't have your shoes if it wasn't for a truck driver. You wouldn't have nothing if it wasn't for a truck driver. When four-wheelers show off their capacity for speed and agility, all they're doing is putting everybody at risk. But again, it's that sense of competitiveness that is so promoted in this culture — American culture. Understand that you just put yourself, me, everybody to the sides of us, everybody behind us — you just put potentially so many people at risk. And I'll see you at the next stoplight, at the next off-ramp, I'll be right behind you."

Bridget makes several interlocking claims here: That too many impossible-to-follow rules frustrate truckers, who express their anger via erratic driving, causing increased risk of accidents. That truckers' invisibility and isolation — the way that trucks are huge and everywhere and indispensable, yet simply not seen — causes resentment that leads to reckless driving and maybe accidents. Finally, that automobile drivers acting stupidly and jockeying for position leads to accidents. All these are narratives used to make sense of trauma and of the conflicting needs to be human (always) and to deaden, be professional, not react, and not emote in some pretty harrowing situations. They are narratives that understand the underlying structures, psychological reactions, and the political and social technologies of stigma.

Narrative and trauma are linked; narrating it helps to both identify (create) and survive (manage) it. The emerging field of critical trauma studies explores what counts as trauma and how we process it. Within this field, Maurice Stevens thinks about trauma not as a descriptive term for events or experiences, but rather as "a cultural object whose function produces particular types of subjects, and predisposes specific affect flows" (20). As I describe and quote truckers responding to frequent road accidents, the words and images I use evoke PTSD; trauma and its aftermath shape the lives of truckers and shape how I discuss and describe them.

Trauma and Mental Health

There's plenty of research about trucker mental health and its relation to accidents and trauma. One researcher, Mona Shattell, is a public health nurse with whom I've collaborated on a number of occasions. When we met, she convinced me that more research on trucker mental health is needed and that truckers' working conditions and mental states need to be understood and addressed as a public health issue. The point in Shattell's research, and in our collaborations, is not to blame truckers for working through mental health issues that endanger them and other drivers, but rather to understand how their jobs contribute to their compromised mental conditions, offer too little support, and in fact coerce silence about mental health altogether as a condition of employment (Shattell et al., 564).

My narrators contribute powerful examples that illustrate their attempts to understand trauma as both cause and effect; trucking, and particularly trucking while queer, trans, and/or brown, causes stress and even damage, which must be beaten back or hidden to keep working, meaning it often surfaces at the most dangerous moments. These are hard stories: hard to hear and hard to write about, let alone hard to live. They make me angry, but even more they make me want change; nobody should have to live through this.

Donovan signed a lease on her truck and has been struggling to make money since. Her total net earnings the year before we spoke came to $37,000 for a year in which she was home four days. She says, *"Like I said, especially as an owner-operator, they get you and they fuck you and they fuck you and they fuck you—and they don't give a rat's ass about whether or not you can pay your bills. There's weeks where I'll get just 700 miles or 1,200 miles, and then that puts me in the hole. . . . I had run out of my medication, my hormones, which puts me through emotional swings, and I had been begging them for a month to get me home. Well, finally I was on my way home—and when I have those emotional swings, I get panic attacks, because it makes my anxiety a lot more forefront. The hormones help my anxiety a lot. I was driving down*

Brandi, ready to roll.
(Used with permission of the subject.)

the road and I had a panic attack, so I pulled over to the side of the road. In the midst of my panic attack, I forgot to pull the emergency brake and rolled forward into the truck in front of me. Those repairs took me off the road for two weeks, and that was January 29. Before that I was only getting like $300, $400 settlements [i.e., weekly pay], that was all I was getting paid a week. And then I got in that accident—that put me off the road for two weeks—so obviously that put me behind in my payments, and I didn't see another settlement, another positive balance settlement, from January 29 to April 29."

Listening to this trucker describe her earnings and her working conditions shocked me anew. I thought I knew how bad it was out there, but this beat all. When I asked Donovan what she ate during those negative settlement months, she replied that the company gives her (that is, loans her) $100 per week when she gets negative settlements to stay alive on the road. She's gained weight, because obviously all she can afford on the road for that kind of money is junk, which in turn affects her mood and anxiety, and the whole cycle continues.

The mental health consequences of trucking are a recurring theme for Terell, who has been driving for about ten years and is a talker. He describes himself as an introvert and says that most truckers are *"your loners or your social outcasts."* Many *"talk a blue streak,"* but only because they have all that time behind the wheel to recover. Terell clearly uses his windshield time to think and to analyze trucking situations. He tells me that truckers' *"outlets of stress are so dramatically different from a normal person."* He adds, *"It's very difficult to go see a movie—most truck stops are not near movie theaters, [and] most movie theaters do not allow truck parking. Getting out of the truck and doing things that most people would take for granted is a challenge; it requires a lot of planning and organizing. In my case, I can't smoke—I'm allergic to tobacco. I've never been one to pick up random women or guys to sleep around with. A lot of these quote-unquote vices, we don't have, and our stress release is food. I find, talking to a lot of drivers, a lot of people start judging drivers because they're fat, and they don't understand the reason behind it.*

"A lot of drivers are actually terrified to go and get counseling. And the reason is when you go to your DOT physical and say that you are seeing a counselor, getting therapy, they might say, 'Hey, why are you on this antidepressant?' or 'Why do you think you need an antidepressant?' or 'Why did you need counseling?' They use this to determine whether you're fit to be behind the wheel. There's a real fear that if we admit to having a mental health issue—and it may just be a short-term case of, maybe not depression, say, but you're stressed, you're overwhelmed, you're feeling a little blue, it's nothing major, you're not suicidal, you just need to get out of this slump—there's a real stigma in the trucking industry that if you admit to this problem, it could cost you money or your driving career. And how true that is a good question, but there are certain companies that, how they look at it is, if you have to be on an antidepressant, they really don't want you. Because their concern is if you're in an accident, that could come up in court, and the attorney will sue the company, alleging that it was a suicide attempt by the driver. Truckers have a high rate of PTSD for a variety of reasons. Witnessing accidents. In my ten years I've been very blessed: I have witnessed very few traffic accidents. I have seen the aftermath of some nasty accidents, some of which you knew people were deceased. But I know several drivers that were there, holding somebody's hand as they breathe their last breath. PTSD is really the biggest problem with driver health."

Sarah is a transwoman who served in Vietnam before her transition. She shares a story of parachuting into the jungle and inadvertently shooting a civilian. She was dishonorably discharged, which made finding work difficult. Especially because of her PTSD, which she attributes both to this and other traumatic combat events and to the VA's bumbling and malicious treatment of her transition. She had just been kicked out of the women's room in a truck stop and told never to return because another patron was frightened of her. This even though she had used that same restroom bi-weekly for more than a decade. In both of these narratives, a challenging event is then intensified by an instance of trans phobic violence, increasing the likelihood of incapacitating PTSD.

I'll end with a final story that combines highway accidents, health concerns, and sexuality in profoundly troubling ways. I won't be quoting here, because this narrator didn't wish to be recorded. Her trial was pending at the time of our interview, but she told me she would release the general outline of her story if I kept it anonymous and didn't publish it until after her trial (which took place in early 2017).

Quentina entered trucking in middle age, loved the independence, and did very well for nine years. But one day she sank into mud in a parking spot and had to call a tow truck to come haul her out. Her company responded by telling her she needed to retrain, and they would only keep her if she agreed to team (i.e., ride with another driver) for a while. That's when her problems began, because the only team drivers available were men with whom she was uncomfortable.

But she needed the job, and the company reassured her that it had a harassment policy and training, and all would be fine. It wasn't. Her team drove slip seat, meaning they handed the truck over to another team often, as part of a tightly scheduled dance that keeps a truck rolling by subbing in fresh drivers as necessary. They were supposed to hand off the trailer near her codriver's house and do a reset there, and the company had agreed to get her a hotel. However, instead of letting her bobtail to her hotel, the codriver held on to the keys and her phone, keeping her prisoner in his house for hours and pressuring her to have sex. Finally he drove her to a dirty motel where no one spoke English. Shaken and isolated, she went up to her room and had a panic attack, in which she relived her childhood sexual abuse. Just hearing about these flashbacks was horrible.

Then, after the reset, she had to get back in the truck with this guy and finish their run. When they got back to the terminal, she was fired and he wasn't.

Not rare.

She took some time off from trucking, did other work, was in therapy, and ultimately returned to trucking, since the only other work available in her area paid minimum wage. On her new job, she was driving a relay load, which she had collected in the middle of the night from another driver, as instructed by dispatch. She got in an accident and spent four days in the ICU. She learned that her load had contained six unsecured steel coils sitting on pallets in the trailer. The reason she got into the accident was that the coils shifted forward when she stopped. So she filed for workman's comp, which the company denied her, and in the hearing, her employer brought in the files of the therapist whom she had consulted after her attempted rape. The company made two claims: that she could have had another flashback, causing the accident, and that she was obliged to reveal PTSD to employers. Her employers said that if she sought a trial, they would challenge her to prove that her accident wasn't caused by a flashback to her childhood sexual abuse and to her mother's failure to protect her. They would accuse her of this publicly, on the witness stand, and give her the burden of proving that this isn't what caused the accident.

She says that she never should have accepted the load without breaking the seal and opening the trailer to verify that the load was secure. But she knew that if she broke the seal, the customer could reject the load, saying she or someone else had tampered with it, so she took the company's word for it. Instead, she should have waited until someone in authority showed up, knowing that any waiting time, at night on a weekend, would be unpaid. She felt that she shouldn't have just assumed the load was properly secured and driven off with it. She was disabled by the accident, but she settled out of court because she didn't want to discuss her childhood sexual abuse publicly, and she was intimidated by the trucking company's lawyers. She took $13,000 in settlement. Her accident left her too disabled to work for a while. She asked me whether there are support groups for people with PTSD. She also pointed out that she had worked her entire adult life (she's now in her sixties) with the childhood sexual abuse in her past, and it never interfered with her work. She had flashed back only at that moment in the hotel, where she had feared for her life.

She is clear about several things. First, the risk of trucking is directed at the driver. She had been doing fine, and it's possible to make trucking work if nothing *ever* goes wrong. But as soon as there's one little problem, the companies take the driver down to maximize their profits. They don't care how that affects the driver. At all. Drivers who are women get this treatment often.

She thinks that women are not safe out there and should be allowed to carry a gun to protect themselves.

She doesn't want to be living like this. She wants to be a positive person, working and enjoying her grandchildren. She plans to resist settling out of court when her appeal makes it to trial, since that would involve agreeing to remain silent about what happened. She wants to be able to describe what trucking companies can get away with; how vulnerable women and truckers are to arbitrary, punitive firings. If companies hire workers who will take anything in order to avoid getting fired, then they will subject them to ghastly treatment, and no one will challenge that. She objects, wants to write a book, wants some different result than that.

This story broke my heart. I can't analyze it. I can only put it here as told to me. I can do that for her. I can add that maybe four months after we spoke and before she authorized me to tell her story, she wrote me to report that she'd gotten rehired and would start trucking again. She was overjoyed, and I wanted to share that feeling with her. But honestly, I was devastated and still am. Quentina deserves something infinitely better: safety, comfort, justice, peace. Rest.

6

ROLLING

GRABBING GEARS

*The Appeal of Constant Motion, Especially
to Gay, Black, and Trans Drivers*

TRUCKING IS NOT JUST A JOB, but a lifestyle. Truckers say that all the time, and it makes me wonder what the term "lifestyle" means in this context. This chapter explores that question by thinking about how gay, trans, and minority truckers describe their transitoriness as an identity, as a way of being in the world. Not coincidentally, the same term is often used to describe gay identity formations, especially in right-wing or unfriendly discourse, in which "the gay lifestyle" is accusation enough. Ulrike reflects, *"I basically don't have a life except for this job. This is my life, this is all I do. You're not out—you're never in one place."* Where stability and heteronormativity are valued, perpetual motion is an affront, however unintentional, and it's one that marginalized truckers often embrace and identify with. When truckers describe their work as "grabbing gears," I believe they mean both manipulating the transmission and seizing authority (personal and sexual). The rolling of the truck provides truckers with a way to tell the story of their life in a way that gives them some measure of control; this is especially true for truckers dealing with racism, economic hardship, or sexual or gender policing.

Motion is the reward offered by trucking, not only literal motion through space—the call of the open road—but also social motion. Trucking offers the potential of a way out of poverty, an alternative to work situations rife with harassment, and a chance to remake oneself. The two parallel myths of the frontier and of pursuit of a personal dream define trucking and the American imagination within which it fits. Sean links these tropes when he says, *"I've seen so much of our country, and it is gorgeous and it has inspired*

In this photo, I tried to capture the view from the driver's seat.
(Photo by the author, used with permission of the subject.)

a sense of patriotism and at the same time sadness, because I know where this country is heading." Sean's statement, which he gives in response to a question from me about the rewards of trucking, gets at a central paradox of both this chapter and of twenty-first-century American life: the fantasy of geographic and class mobility is profoundly unavailable to the people who exemplify it. Freedom contrasts with micromanagement; independence with regulations; movement with waiting, accidents, forced brakes; the American dream of escape, open limitless space, and new beginnings with the fear of change and the fact of class rigidity; the emphasis on personal responsibility with the absence of any real choice. How these paradoxes play out in the lives of America's marginalized truckers, how truckers work through and understand them, and what they say about our culture are this chapter's concerns.

Nate sums up many truckers' attitudes like this: *"It was a good time on the road . . . met a lot of people . . . seen a lot of places."* These words sounds simple, but they hide a complex reality. The road offered Nate an escape from a challenging home life and an opportunity to find and express himself. Gwynneth gets at this feeling when I ask if it's hard for her to be away from home and her kids. She says, *"No. No. I mean, everything happens for a reason. I wish I had discovered trucking earlier in my life, because this is my thing. I have a very wandering spirit; I like driving and kind of being out. The only reason I ever became as sedentary as I was is because I had kids, and you hear all of these wonderful, kind of predetermined status quo things like 'You can't raise your kids like. . . . You have to raise them like. . . . Be sure they have. . . .' And on the one hand, I think that's total bullshit; as long as you love them, and you're not raising them in some weird cult where they're sexually molested or whatever, they'll be good. They're going to live how you live, and they'll be all right. But having to provide for them, and being the sole provider for them, and all of that, I couldn't just be wandering around. But if it weren't for the kids, there's no telling where I would be."* She has raised her kids to be independent and responsible, and they are now old enough to weather her long absences. For Gwynneth, responsibility is a source of great pride. She worked hard to give her kids that virtue, and then it was her turn to spread her wings—to embrace the joy of movement and freedom.

It's not, Gwynneth explains very explicitly, about escaping responsibility. She tells me, *"I have a very high level of personal responsibility. Even in situations where it seems like I have no responsibility, I'll find something to take responsibility for, you know?"* What the truck does is take an individual's actions and magnify them, both practically on the level of scale (the truck operates as an enormous exoskeleton) and symbolically, by tapping into the trope of freedom and escape. I hear echoes of the truck's impact in the identity narratives truckers tell: not only are they escaping from some aspect of their lives or selves, but the truck's size and significance also turn that escape into a powerful reclamation story.

Tammy, for example, narrates her decision to transition by using a trucking symbol: *"I remember looking at myself in the mirror, and I could see [Tammy]. I could see me in there, and I could hear her screaming 'Let me out, let me out, let me out.' I would look in the mirror and all I would see is a boy. I would want to see [Tammy], and I had to make that happen. I've been in the middle of nowhere in this big truck at a T intersection, and there's no road signs. Do you go left or right? You kind of have to just figure it out, just in that moment; you don't know where to go. There was a driver I met over the road once, who told me, 'Follow your gut instinct. It will never lead you the wrong way.' So that's what I did, took his advice. I thought, 'Taking a left seems pretty good,' so that's what I did. And eventually I found my way to [Tammy]."* The logic here is crucial: because she learned to trust her instincts when driving her truck through unfamiliar territory, she can now make the leap to gender transition. Metaphor has power. Trucking leads, identity follows.

Identifying with the Truck

Trucking is rolling . . . motion . . . change and resistance . . . brakes . . . and breaks. The personal stories reveal how the truck, as a physical object, and the process by which it moves through space both instigate and resist change. Gracie, who requested I use they/them pronouns, exemplifies transition. Within the past few years, they've left the Jehovah's Witnesses, come out as intersex, begun a transition toward male identity, and started driving truck. I asked them to reflect on all this change and how it might be connected. Though they start by pointing out that their partner, George (who is present during our interview), denies any connection, Gracie adds, *"Yeah, but to put it crassly, I do feel kind of like a badass in the truck. So no, it wasn't that I chose trucking because of that background, I think, but I do just feel like I can do anything now."* The truck, as an object to which Gracie feels a visceral, even corporeal, bond, somehow authorized their transition.

These accounts are examples of a pervasive tendency among my narrators to link the rhetoric of trucking culture to manifestations of queerness, transition, indigenousness, or disability in their lives. The truck's size, scale, power, and motion speak to their bodies and make being an outsider something meaningful and chosen and visible — and something American.

Yolanda, a transwoman whose partner, another transwoman, is a policewoman, explains that *"you do very manly jobs to try to cover up what you are truly at heart."* She started with gas delivery driving, which tends to be local, short-run work. She says, *"But then I kinda had an itching to drive over the road. I wanted to go and see places, so I started driving for another company that was in town. This was when I lived in Prescott, Arizona. So this company would run loads of dog food out of Flagstaff and take it over to mostly LA, and then reload Budweiser or Miller beer and bring it back over in Arizona. I did that, and I got to start seeing the country; I got this itch for driving. It's kind of addicting — once you start doing it, it's really hard to stop doing it. It's almost like a drug. You just kinda get this feeling — you kind of have a freedom to go different places and see different things. You get caught up in the excitement, and you can feel yourself change, and nothing feels impossible. So that's pretty much been my downfall, and I've been doing that, driving, for quite a few years."* She chose trucking to distract from her gender dysphoria, to sell her masculinity to herself and others, but it gave her a "freedom to go different places," which then enabled transition.

Jodie has driven over the road for years, interspersed with gigs driving in the Texas oil fields. She'd recently had some stressful experiences in which

Both Keaira's hair and her cowboy hat represent rebellion and joy.
(Used with permission of the subject.)

her truck was delayed and vandalized during street rioting, and she was hoping to retire when we spoke. She reflects: *"I've had some knocks here and there, but not like it used to be. The road has been a lot of fun; it's scary, it's damn sure exciting, and it's a learning experience — and I wouldn't change any of it. It's been frustrating at times, it's been heartbreaking — every emotion that you can imagine, I've had out here. In the oil field it's the same thing. Every emotion. I'm used to pretty much being the only woman, I'm used to being one of the guys. Has it changed me? Oh yeah, it's changed me a lot. But I like who I am now. And I'm ok with that."* The truck's motion became her own personal motion — became herself.

Terell had worked in sales for many years, when he wound up realizing that he would either strangle a customer or quit. He says, *"I didn't want to have to deal with people anymore, so I did some research and thought, 'Let me try truck driving.' And in a lot of ways, truck driving, for me, saved my sanity, and it was actually very fulfilling. One, it gave me a lot of time to work through some problems, anger management issues that came from Radio Shack and things of that nature. But two, it allowed me to be social, but when I started getting tired and burned out, I could get inside my truck, pull the curtain, and not have to deal with people for as long as I chose. I have come to realize that the older I'm getting, the more introverted I'm becoming."* Movement, time to think, and the ability to control social interactions have made trucking a good fit for him, and many truckers make similar claims.

I've included several examples, because the language the truckers use is important. They link their self-concept — their vision of themselves as actors in the world — to the movement of the truck. But it's not reducible to the trucker truism that "if your wheels ain't rollin', you ain't earnin'." True, but not enough. The truck's motion — its refusal to be stuck — can be mobilized as a form of personal resistance. To an outsider, this freedom might seem small or even stifling, but the trucker telling the story recasts that limitation as liberation. For example, Sean says that he was closeted and cautious during trucking school, because there were rumors about a gay kid in the previous class who got roughed up and left. I ask if he still felt that vulnerability after being out on the road for a while, and he responds, *"Honestly, no, but I guess then again, I'm not quite as obvious as some. I'm open and I'm very friendly, but I'm a little concerned about how people perceive me and what that could mean for me. If I wanted to cut loose and queen out, it wouldn't be OK. I would get a lot of reactions and probably not favorable ones, right? But again, that's everywhere. I pretty much keep to myself and stay in my truck, and if anything does get weird, I'm gone before they can do anything, right? Honestly, I think it's a little more freeing, because I don't have to be around people so much, and I can be my crazy self all by myself."* This response alternates. Sean starts by denying that he feels fear but adds that he curtails his public identifiability, which he then acknowledges is because he's afraid of negative reactions if he is queeny. But then the twist: he can be more open in the truck and as a trucker *because* he is in motion. We can understand that shift as a defense mechanism or as a rhetorical strategy, but either way, Sean is using the truck to enable his freedom — his "crazy self."

Dorothy, probably the oldest trucker I interviewed and the one with the strongest southern accent, says she has always had an aptitude for engines and no lack of confidence. When she started, she says, *"I don't think I knew what gear I was in half the time, but back then I wasn't afraid to try, and I guess I'm still not scared. If it would crank, I could run it."* Even now, Dorothy tells me about another trucker who decided to refuse a load because she had a tanker endorsement [her CDL indicated that she had passed the additional test for tanker driving] but no tanker experience. Dorothy scoffs at this: *"Well, I'd have jumped right in the middle of that because I've got a lot of common sense. I wouldn't have hesitated a minute, I get right in the middle of it. But like I've said time and time again, big equipment, outdoor moving equipment, forklifts, semis — if it's got a key, I can run it. Might take me a while, but I can run it."* When she wants to identify as a risk taker and a renegade, Dorothy does so by describing her aptitude for moving anything: for getting stuff to run. Her self-confidence derives from her comfort with engines and her ability to make anything go.

For women, queers, immigrants, and people with disabilities, the truck is the best prosthesis ever. Like Gracie says, *"I feel like a badass when I'm driving that."* This comment is poignant, because Gracie has had so few forums in which to feel effective. The ability to leave their limiting circumstances and fuse their new self with a large and powerful machine whose motion they control changes literally everything for them.

Ciara describes this confidence as something learned because, she says, *"in the beginning you constantly think, 'I'm going to quit, I'm going to go back to my other job.' But you're traveling down the highway, and you see this little kid looking up at you in just awe, and you realize that you're dealing with something that they can only dream of. Especially for the women — years ago you didn't see women in trucks, and they just look at you and think, 'This is cool.' You don't get that perspective until you look down and see people think* wow, *and you realize 'I am doing something pretty cool.' It's also changed me: I've become more outspoken, I've learned how to express myself without going off the handle, basically I learned a little more self-control. And it's made me stronger mentally, too, because you spend a lot of time with yourself. You definitely learn how strong you are. There are customers you want to scream at, and there's nothing you can do to please them but get off their property. I'm definitely a lot more comfortable with myself, because every day is a challenge, figuring out how each day you're going to get from point A to point B. So much can go wrong. So much can go right, but it's definitely mental empowerment, and again you're doing some things that, in my case, most women could never do. I want to be that trailblazer and prove to myself that I can keep up with the guys. It's really important for me, and it builds your character up as well, as a person. I don't see myself doing anything else. I get such enjoyment out of it. I couldn't imagine myself anywhere else, and it took me this long to figure out what I want to do, and hopefully I'll stick with driving trucks, because that's where I'm the happiest."* The truck enables personal growth and feminist confidence.

To nontruckers, windshield time looks like loneliness and isolation, but to these narrators, it allows for a freedom they couldn't find at home. Most truck drivers I've met have echoed that sentiment. Some are on the brink of retirement, and they say they have time to think when they're out in the truck—and they would miss that.

Does this identification happen with other jobs? To some extent, sure. Working-class men have a well-documented tendency to anchor their sense of self and masculine presentation in their jobs. The sociologist E. E. LeMasters studied working-class men who hung out at a bar, and claims that though work may be less central to the lives of men in general, "the world of work has retained its basic significance for the blue-collar aristocrats in this study" (20). LeMasters attributes this difference to the type of work her interlocutors do and the pride they take in its material manifestations. I would add that these men, like truckers, have limited access to the social and material capital that professionals, for example, can draw on, which increases their incentive to derive meaning from the work itself. But what my truckers describe goes beyond the claims of pride and solidarity associated with steelworkers or construction workers. Because the truck is perpetually in motion, and their group identity is fluid—there's no local bar, familiar work crew, or union hall, but rather an endlessly rotating series of people and places—embracing an identity via attachment to a job involves change rather than conservation. I see plenty of nostalgia associated with trucking as a bygone way of life (for example, tourism to the Iowa 80 truck stop or trucks printed on clothing for little boys), but truckers themselves tend to mock this rather than participate in it. As the trucking workforce changes, new-school truckers combine the myth of the rebel bad boy with the job's refusal of stasis to reimagine themselves—to begin again. They reimagine themselves as something not permanent and mutable—as queers, trannies, and other people defined by movement rather than fixed identity.

Take the case of Alix, a transman. Originally, Alix's husband was the trucker. They both believed that *"even starting out, truckers make good money,"* Alix says, and that his husband would be able to support the family from the road. Not only was that not true and Alix had to keep working—meaning they had to live with Alix's in-laws for childcare assistance—but also Alix was essentially doing the driving from home. He says, *"So I was managing the house, and I did everything for him. I learned real quick about Hours of Service and trip planning and all of that. All he had to do was get up, he'd shower, shave, drive the truck. And I told him, 'You are stopping at this truck stop for fuel, this is how much fuel is, you're taking this many gallons, you will be stopping for the night at this location at approximately this time.' If he had a shower credit, I told him, 'When you fuel here, you have forty-five minutes for a shower.' All he really had to do was drive the truck."* Alix's level of involvement in someone else's job tasks demonstrates how much he wanted access to what that job offered: freedom both on the road and from a gender prison. He says, *"Even though I have days where I just want to beat my head against the wall, I love . . . I love driving a truck because it's liberating. And out here on the road I can just — it' s liberating — I can be who I am without feeling pressured to be who people assume that I am. I am a transman. I am not completely out to my family, though it's something I started discovering about myself really when I was twenty-one, before I had met [my husband]. It's only been in the last two years where I thought, I cannot live in this closet. [My husband] is accepting of me, but I'm not fully out to my family. I am out to my friends, and out here on the road I live authentically, and that's part of what I like about it. I am kind of leading a double life because when I go home, I'm kind of mom to the kids. Unfortunately, right now we're still living with my in-laws, so I kind of have to backpedal into the closet. So when I get back into the truck, it's liberating, because I don't have anyone's expectations to live up to. People might see me once and then they won't see me again for a couple months, if ever. So I'm just another face in the crowd. It's a lot less pressure and a lot less anxiety. I love doing this job. I haul reefer — refrigerator product — and except for bananas, it's a blast."* I later got the lowdown on what's wrong with banana loads (unpredictable wait times at ports), but here what matters is how the truck's movement allows gender movement. Alix's confidence comes from not seeing anyone again soon or ever, and from rolling away from his house and keeping that movement going.

A Truck Is the Best Prosthesis Ever

Carolyn is intersex — she was very reluctant to talk to me, worried that I would sensationalize her body or her experience. I worked hard to persuade her, but what really helped was passage of the "bathroom bill" in North Carolina. That made her angry, and willing to talk. She finds safety in the loneliness of the job. After leaving the military, she says, *"I needed money, and so, truck driving is for the most part an anonymous job, so as long as I wasn't around the terminal I could be me. So I was, and been doing it for a long time. I went back into truck driving full-time in the mid-90s and been at it ever since."* She believes there is power in visibility, but when describing that, she uses the language of movement: "be out there." She says, *"A long time ago, once I accepted who I am, I chose to not hide who I am. And the only way it's going to get better for myself and people who will come later is to be out there. Something that I learned in the military is you lead, you follow, or you get the hell out of the way. And I'm trying to be more of a leader type, trying to set an example. Let the trucking industry know, 'Hey, we put the trans back in transportation.'"* She laughs after making this joke and tells me I have my book title right there.

Carolyn goes on to tell a story about truck stop violence that links her self-presentation as a marginalized, queer trucker to the national imaginary: *"I've never had trouble — if you want to call it — passing, but I'm not worried about passing; I want to be me. I assume everybody knows the difference, but that's a safety thing. If you assume that everybody knows you're different, then you're keeping an eye out, and when you're transgender you have to keep an eye out. It's just like if a person is gay or lesbian. If there are people around, you have to keep an eye out, because there's plenty of ignorant people in the world. A lot of the viewpoints of guys — it's not as bad as it used to be, but guys out here would think if a woman is driving a truck, she must be a dyke. That's their words: 'Yeah, she must be a dyke, she's driving a truck. She just hasn't got somebody with the right penis yet.' That's their super mindset. Yeah, yeah, hate those. My retort to them was always 'You're just jealous because you know they're getting more than you are.' And most of those clowns couldn't get laid in a whorehouse with a fistful of money, they really couldn't. I ran into a few of them over at the I-80 truck stop. This was years ago. I was listening to the [CB] radio; there was a gay guy there, and these guys were talking about going over and beating up on the gay guy. I won't use the language they were using, but I got on the radio in a really low voice and said, 'Where is this fag you're going to go beat up?' And I said, 'I'll be right there.' And I showed up with my ratchet bar; I'm like, 'Now it's a fair fight, asshole.' We made a bunch of big old boys go running from a queen and a trannie. I'm kind of like America: these colors don't run. That's the one thing, that if you talk to a lot of transgender people, you'll find out most transgender people are more than capable of sticking up for themselves."*

This connection between trucking and Americanness enlarges queer and trans truckers' identification with their trucks to an identification with and through the country, but it also comes with a full measure of racist baggage. Felicity is a transwoman from Texas who talks a blue streak. I can hardly get a word in edgewise, but it doesn't seem to matter. She talks about legislation around bathroom use and references a case where a shooter was acquitted because he saw a trans person and claims he shot the person out of panic. Felicity says, *"All these psychos had decided that they're going to pass laws in Mississippi where I can be murdered at gunpoint because of religious liberty* *with no legal impunity. I can be sent to a men's prison for five years because I'm legally transgender in the bathroom, and I can be fined $5,000. Now how the hell do I operate a truck as a woman who's transgender and then go to the bathroom with black people standing at the counter, and they tell me, 'We have anonymous reports that you're soliciting for prostitution'? And I say, 'I have anonymous reports that you're a big black transphobic bitch, but I didn't call the police.' So then the police show up, and they grab me by the arm, and they look at my ID, look at my truck, and they just tell me, 'Well, we just think that you should move on, you don't need to fuel here.' And I say, 'I think I'm going to fuel here, and I'm going to sue you, and I'm going to bankrupt your little Po-dunk police department. You don't tell me where to buy fuel.' And he tells me, 'If you don't comply, I'll cite you for resistance to arrest,' and I told him, 'If you arrest me, I'll sue you for violating my EEOC [Equal Employment Opportunity Commission] rights, my constitutional right to free assembly, and violating my corporate policy. We're a $12 billion trucking company, and we don't have to stop at your little rat-ass Flying J truck stop at rat-ass Lake Charles, Louisi-ana, so don't push me, and I'm not going to take your crap.' And then I found out if I hadn't complied they were going to arrest me as a sexual predator, and I would have been banned from employment, and I would have been put on a list as a pedophile. That's because he's transphobic, and he thinks he can get away with something."* Felicity feels vulnerable in public space both because of transphobic interventions from strangers and because of bigoted police involvement. In her account, police side with African American people over trans ones. Her strategies for managing these feelings include using the size of her truck and of her company as armor to protect herself, even as she is forced to acknowledge that if she didn't comply, her vulnerability would es-calate to unlivable levels.

Minority Truckers Access Americanness through Their Truck and Its Motion

There's something about driving, about seeing the road and the world laid out before you and moving through space purposively, that gives you a lived, embodied connection to the country. To both meanings of the word "country." To the empty, the rural, the "purple mountain majesties" and "amber waves of grain," the intense variety of landscape, the vast distances between things. And to the United States — feeling and experiencing the glue that makes the nation cohere — and the associated sense of pride and agency.

Because my research began with participant observation and because I live and work east of the Mississippi and am a white person, I thought for at least a year that truckers are predominantly white. In the East and the Midwest, that's what a casual observer would conclude. My CDL class included three black guys out of eight total, but very few of the people who get CDLs actually wind up driving truck, so that didn't shake my assumptions. My trucking school was a class of nine, with only one black student. Ayub is a recent Somali immigrant living in Columbus who was attracted to trucking because many of his family and friends did it. I felt a special bond with him because he was the only student worse than me. Of course, his struggle was attributable to language barriers and racism, but still it felt good to have someone getting a little more negative feedback than I was. At least for a while. Then it crossed a line and started to feel slimy — and then he was sent home. I'm sure the teachers and the school patted themselves on the back for giving him a chance and were "disappointed" that he didn't make it. I don't mean those scare quotes to mock their implicit racism. Or at least not to do only that. That's valid. But I want to think seriously about what makes big-rig culture so white *in some places* and how that fits within the rhetoric of personal discovery through motion that I've been unpacking here.

Reba drives a regular run from the Midwest to California and back. She observes that her company is trying to hire truckers and can't get enough qualified applicants. The reasons are, first, because you need to live in a particular geographic area to make the schedule work (within an easy drive of the terminal), and second, because you need two years' safe driving experience, ideally in produce. These factors significantly narrow the pool. At present, she represents the company's only diversity; everyone else is a middle-aged white guy — the stereotype. And there's another possibility. The company is exploring hiring drivers in Los Angeles who would do the exact thing Reba does but in reverse, adding even more efficiency to this firm's business model. But the company complains that it can't find any qualified drivers there either; as Reba points out, *"That's because they're only looking for white ones."*

It's easy to critique (and be patronizing about) the racism of truckers and trucking companies for their unfair employment practices and general ignorant close-mindedness. In addition, though, I hope to understand how truckers understand race and racism and deploy it in their own complicated lives. Many truckers are not white. In western states, white truckers will probably be a minority by the time you read this, since the trucking workforce turns over, and thus changes, very quickly. I interviewed many nonwhite truckers and met others during participant observation. Whom I did not meet or interview were Arab, South Asian, or Middle Eastern truckers, all of whom are quite common. I passed a billboard advertising a Punjabi truck wash, and every trucker space that I entered contained at least one Sikh. Even as the demographics of trucking change, many of my narrators express concern about "immigrant" truckers, especially those they call "towelheads" or "hadjis." These new truckers interfere with the self-making symbolism that trucking motivates, according to several narrators.

Amie McLean writes about long-haul truckers in Canada, and her ethnographic data often agrees with my own. She asserts that white Canadian truckers perpetuate the story that South Asian truckers drive three or four to a truck and cut a hole in their floor through which they defecate onto the roadway. McLean links this story to truckers' attachment to a rhetoric of mobility connected to their national imaginary. White truckers, she argues, wrongly believe immigrant truckers crash disproportionately often, which the white truckers attribute to a culture that teaches different driving styles. They also believe that immigrant truckers' personal hygiene habits are bad and that this stigmatizes all truckers. First, let me add that my data agrees with hers. Several of my narrators remind me that *"you don't know how many there are in there until they start to pile out,"* in Maci's words, and Reba showed me where "they" cut open the accordion fitting between the gear shift and the floor to insert a tube through which to urinate while driving.

Further, McLean's thoughtful analysis of why truckers tell this particular racist story rings true for me. With infrastructure providing insufficient bathrooms and schedules that make stopping financial suicide anyway, truckers are reminded daily that "men—and especially working class men—may urinate in public" (53). They are not entitled to privacy or dignity yet are required to hide the cost of that prioritization from other citizens who don't experience it. This anger gets projected onto a racialized scapegoat. Humiliation and bathroom access are very racialized in U.S. history and life, and that's now linked to gender transgression as well, given emerging legislation around bathroom access, beginning with H.B. 2 in North Carolina.

What I would add to McLean's argument is that in the context of pressure placed on gay and trans truckers in the United States, their conceptualization of the road—as movement—allows access to Americanness and approval. To a feeling of national belonging. For truckers, this comes from some complicated combination of movement through space, bodily sacrifice (involving both vulnerability and toughness), and outsiderness: being everywhere but settling nowhere.

Edwina's eyes say so much about life on the road.
(Used with permission of the subject.)

Truckers are always somewhere new—most never get the experience of sinking into a place and developing history. In some racial and identity contexts, community means safety; that's why we have ethnic enclaves and hometown bars. Queer and trans populations experience this differently from each other and from racial minority groups. Movement for truckers of all races brings freedom, because home is not a site of safety but of tension. Many of my narrators are estranged from their family and experience home as a space of rejection and emotional pain. While this is common for all trans and queer folks, working-class and rural ones may experience it more frequently, and more hauntingly since many lack the communities and families of choice that queer folks can find in cities. Yet at the same time, working-class community is often deeply rooted in a geographic and regional home. Most truckers live where they grew up, surrounded by people they grew up with, and have a fierce pride in family, hometown, and country, and queer, trans, and black truckers are usually fully part of this identification. Sense of self and purpose draws from this complex web of mythology and imagination, and my narrators navigate this in various interesting ways.

In a world where everyone feels attacked and victimized, how does sense of self map onto space? Truck drivers are people for whom movement defines identity; they belong nowhere and usually find that freeing. But not always.

Donovan is a transwoman trucker who works under a very predatory lease contract. After I interviewed her, we kept in touch, and on several occasions had email and social media exchanges. For example, in fall of 2016 she was in Ohio and posted on Facebook that she was throwing out all of her remaining hormones and didn't care anymore. I worried. The next day she posted just this, from New Trenton, Indiana: "I have no place in this world." These words sounded like a cry for help, and I reached out to her hoping human contact would keep her, at the least, from suicide. I found her language choices instructive. For background, Donovan is homeless in her truck, having lost both her apartment and her storage locker because she wasn't earning enough to make the payments. She was home five days during 2015, so her friends, though well meaning, have built lives that don't include her. When she does get home, it's to see doctors for hormone therapy checkups, and even then she continues to live in the truck, because there is nowhere else for her to sleep. When she says "I have no place in this world," she literally means nowhere to go — no chance to feel anchored. Further, especially given the previous day's hormone comment, it means she has no safe space from harassment, uncertainty, and the experience of permanent, unmonitored, puberty-like emotionality. Sometimes, truckers experience this as freedom, and other times it reads as panic. Both have much to say about movement, choice, race, and the American imaginary.

Sean connects his choice to truck to his sexuality and to his family commitments and belonging: *"I got kicked out as a teenager for being gay. [When I was] thirty-two, my mom had a stroke and I was one of the only ones around. My family basically begged me to go look after her. I was still in the area, even though I had been kind of disassociated from my family for thirteen years. I agreed, 'cause I'm a good son. I went to live with her. She couldn't get a job after the stroke. My sister agreed to get her a job up here in West Virginia, but she wouldn't move without me; now that she had me back, I guess she really wanted to keep hold of me, I don't know. My sister begged me to come back, so I ended up stuck, at thirty-four years old, living with my mother. Technically I still do. Um, it was more of a desperation move to find a job that would not*

only give me the financial assistance I needed to start my own life again—
I was divorced, or married to a guy and then divorced, and that kind of screwed
everything up. I wasn't sure if I wanted to do it, but I knew I had to get out of
that house. I have enjoyed it. Honestly, I do enjoy the life on the road." Sean
connects his exile for coming out to his willingness to return as a caretaker.
Similarly he thinks his mother held onto him fiercely because she had ostracized him before. That tension between extremes motivates his choice to
truck, which forces him to leave her in order to work, and which she's motivated to cooperate with because it's such manly work. Therefore, he feels
attracted to trucking because it drags him away from home, though not into
a safe, accepting alternative that would make home suffer in comparison.

When I ask Christina about what it's like being a lesbian out on the road,
she responds laconically, *"Well, I met one of my girlfriends out here, so there's*
that." And that's not just a joke or a flirtatious remark (though it is both,
certainly); it's also a reflection about home, mobility, confidence, and the
connections between them. During our conversation, she's parked at a loading dock, trapped and waiting. She says, *"I deliberately got here last night so*
I wouldn't be starting my log and then filling it waiting for a load. I want to be
able to drive when I'm full, so really there's nowhere for me to go unless I want
to drive to that little truck stop right over there, which . . . why? I've got every-
thing I need in the truck. I think of this as camping. That's another reason—
because I like to camp. So I have what I need in the truck, same as people do
in their little campers. I'm fine, this is my house, itty-bitty that it is. This is my
house. The best part is being able to do that and being confident enough to do
that, because a lot of people go, 'But that means seeing all that stuff by yourself.
Don't you want to wait and see it with somebody?' Well, if I waited until that
happened, I may never see it, so I see it now when I can."

Christina, Sean, and Donovan are all white people using trucking as a
metaphor to understand how they experience change, choice, and control.
Black truckers use similar rhetoric, as Gwynneth's insistence on finding a
way to take responsibility indicates. Her description of harassment is that
understanding yourself as a victim is an attitude, and one that you can
choose not to mobilize, although she reminds me that she doesn't blame
black or female truckers who experience harassment or discrimination. She
explains to me the steps she has taken to prevent racism from affecting her.
Other black narrators acknowledge and give examples of bigotry and immediate physical risk leading to curtailed behavior, diminished income, and
even termination. But they also tend to focus on how the truck has allowed

them to escape — to transcend their circumstances. It puts them back in control: puts them in the driver's seat.

The motion of trucking, then, facilitates a process of personal discovery and freedom for my narrators, but at the same time it restricts them. They are relentlessly reminded that they are not in control and not valued. Their narratives emphasize the freedom aspect partly in response to its darker side, especially those already disenfranchised by racism, transphobia, etc. Casey is an indigenous/Latina lesbian who trucked for over thirty years, until disability forced her to retire in 2013. She would go back to it willingly, and her reasons for saying so contribute to an understanding of truckers' attitudes about race and mobility. She says, *"I can tell you, I've been out since 2013, and I was — if I was not disabled, I'd go back in a heartbeat. I miss that. It's crazy — you don't have much of a life, but that's okay. But I had everything else out there that the guy that works in the factory doesn't. To me, I enjoyed traveling, I enjoy — people say, 'Don't you get bored out there?' I say, 'I've never been bored out there. I've been bored waiting for the next load, waiting to go get the load, or waiting to unload it or whatever, but out on the road, that was my happiest time.'"*

Alyson M. Cole, in her 2007 book *The Cult of True Victimhood*, argues that contemporary Americans have only two choices: we can make a case for "true victimhood" based only on concrete, individual circumstances, or we can repudiate victimhood altogether (5). Emerging at the close of the twentieth century and gaining steam since, there's an ethic that "categorically denies systemic inequalities and delegitimizes collective action. . . . It displaces or translates issues of institutional power and social inequity into matters of character" (19). The structure of trucking feeds right into this ethic. Because truckers are isolated from an even trucker community, let alone meaningful contact with other humans, they understand themselves as individual actors, making solitary choices that have meaning only in their personal context. The job humbles you and removes any sense that your actions are shaped by, and have ramifications in, larger political and social contexts.

Gabrielle puts it succinctly: *"It gets you off your high horse, really."*

Adele has the chance to experiment with and reimagine her sexuality because of self-reflective windshield time. She says, *"But even though my sexuality is different than some of my fellow lady drivers', we appreciate the fact that we are women, you know — we're doing a tough job, we're not letting it beat us down. Then you have the indecisive ones — they are still learning about themselves, especially because you have a lot of time to think. And therefore there is a lot of self-exploration and analyzing and trying to find one's way, and it helps them identify and redefine themselves. Their past life sucked. You can create a new image for yourself. Your whole new everything. It's like going and getting a new identity from the license bureau. The corner store."*

Bette exemplifies many trucker stereotypes: she's a gun-toting, Trump-supporting, angry white person. And she's trans. In popular media representations of the white working class, these two identities are portrayed as contradictory, yet for Bette they are two sides of the same coin; transness requires gun-rights advocacy, and in turn Second Amendment support derives organically from gender transition. Both are motivated and fueled by the truck's motion. She says: *"I do enjoy the road. I don't enjoy it 100 percent, but I like to get away from society. I hate governments. All of 'em. If you do your research, you realize that every government fails. It's just like our government now — our government's not working. If you don't enjoy trucking, I'll be honest, you're not cut out for it. I raced [NASCAR] in my younger days — the whole nine yards. I'm going to tell you something that I learned early on in my transition: even if you're living a female life, you still have that male side in you. If you don't keep that male side up, you will quite simply go crazy. So guns are my thing. Don't ask me why, but trust me, I've got lots of guns and I have lots of ammunition. I could hurt a lot of stuff, but I'm not going to do it 'cause I'm not stupid. Right now I carry a Smith & Wesson with me wherever I go, pretty much. I ain't gonna be in danger. I've hurt a lot of people, but I have no regrets."* Transition is what taught Bette to "keep that male side up" via the potent symbol of a firearm.

A more complete understanding of truckers' identification with their vehicle in motion and what that means, both for individual truckers and for the culture and the country they belong to, emerges from these stories. The motion intrinsic to trucking affords freedom and fluid identifications, inhibits community, and incubates resistance.

7

STOPPING

THE PICKLE PARK

Truck Stops and Rest Areas

LORI HAS BEEN TRUCKING for five months. She turned to it after basically a lifetime of running from dangerous or threatening situations, starting with *"running away probably ten times as a juvenile,"* she says. She served seventeen years in prison, and she says, *"When I got out of prison, I knew how to do one thing well, and that was have sex and lots of it. So I went directly into prostitution after I got out of prison and supported myself for a couple of years doing that."* At some point in there, she began to transition and worked off and on as a lot lizard (truck stop sex worker), as what she calls a "trans sexual escort," and then as a dominatrix. Proud to now draw a regular paycheck for what she calls "honest work," Lori also challenges the neat border between truck stop sex workers and the truckers who support them. Some people move from one job to the other, some do both simultaneously. What's key is that truck stop culture links movement—running, escape, freedom— with sex, and that the sex is not contained by or understood through the languages of sexual orientation, identity politics, or queer studies as we know them.

Truckers greet each other on the road with the honorific "driver." It's a gender-neutral and profession-unifying form of address: "You been here before, driver?" Just this casual term creates a sense of insiderness—of being seen and understood. You hear it at terminals and at customers (the drop-offs and pickups of goods and trailers), but most of all, you hear it at truck stops, since almost all trucker interactions happen there. Truckers use truck stops and rest areas to refuel, to take thirty-minute and eight-hour breaks, to eat, to shower, to secure and weigh their loads, to do laundry and truck maintenance, and to spend time with other humans. Some truck stops are huge and provide seemingly limitless options. One has a dentist, and almost all have a chapel. Many have a trucker's lounge, with a TV and some chairs. Because most truckers spend the vast majority of their time alone, the community they find at truck stops is very important to the culture, and to truckers individually.

Truck stops may seem like familiar spaces to nontruckers, but that is only because they do not really experience the life of a truck stop, also known as a "pickle park." They are part of the public space and not physically separate from the gas stations used by many commuters and road trippers, but they nonetheless feel different. Though few automobile drivers circulate in sections indicated as those where only truckers are welcome, or enter spaces less clearly marked "truckers only" like diesel fuel desks or laundry and shower areas, the driving public certainly has a set of beliefs about what goes on in truck stops, especially as it relates to sex.

Nadine Hubbs often refers to truck stop lore in her book *Rednecks, Queers, and Country Music*. Hubbs constructs a detailed historical and cultural argument unseating the stereotype that rednecks are and have always been homophobic. She designates instead "the inscriptions and erasures that frame the white working class as a discrete bigot class responsible for America's social and political ills" (5). Often, Hubbs's evidence includes truckers. For example, she analyzes at length a music video for the 2011 Foo Fighters song called "Hot Buns," which depicts the band members as parodies of truckers enmeshed in group gay sex at a truck stop. Hubbs uses this example to argue that "it is impossible to untangle redneck, trucker, poor white, hillbilly, cowboy, and country music images" (25). Though the band presumably intended to mock truckers by playing to the implausibility of gay acceptance and sex at a truck stop, it also generates and calls on a sense of superiority in the audience. Viewers can feel good about their tolerance by comparing it to the presumed horror of actual truckers, yet the video also works because we know that there's lots of sex at truck stops and that often this sex occurs between men.

Many people will resist what is common knowledge and say, "I didn't know there was tons of sex at truck stops!" But that's OK. Conversations I've had with a wide variety of people from all over the United States convince me that most of us do know that sex of all sorts goes on at truck stops. Some truck stops are more saturated with sex than others, and they have all cleaned up their acts somewhat as franchises like TA, Love's, Petro, etc. take over.

Samuel, ready to start the day.
(Used with permission of the subject.)

In fall of 2016, I drove to New York City to visit friends. I stopped at the Grover Cleveland rest area on the New Jersey Turnpike maybe thirty minutes from New York, and sat at a table in the food court near the trucker entrance, eating pizza. A man of about my age, who was thin, white, and wearing jeans and a slate-gray zip-up Eisenhower jacket, walked in. He perused the food court offerings and wandered aimlessly for just a few minutes. Another man came toward him, who was instantly identifiable as a truck chaser (a man who seeks out sex with truckers, a category coherent enough to have conventions). Each garment he wore looked like he had selected it to announce "I like sex with truckers." He had tight, worn Wrangler jeans with a cigarette pack indent in the back pocket, boots, and a black leather cowboy hat. They wandered over to the candy counter together, the second guy selected a candy bar, and they bought it and left together. I don't know whether the candy selection was a coded message similar to the hankie codes of past decades or if that operated just as a conversational pretext. Either way, there was no question what was going on, where, or why.

Adele says truck stop sex is rampant. She adds that when she identified as bi, it was easier for her to hook up on the road than it is now that she seeks only women. When I ask if sex on the road is as widespread as the rumors suggest, she replies, *"Oh, yes. Yes, you know they chase each other around on the CB, and I tried to encourage those drivers to please be careful."* She tells me that she worries about the safety of the gay men she knows out there. *"I mean, let somebody know before you go to hang out with trucker Bob over here, who you talked to on the CB. Message your friend—message me: 'Hey, I'm parked at such and such, at such and such a time, will be meeting up with so and so.' It would be really helpful if you were able to shoot me a picture of ya with Bob, sitting in a restaurant, or can you give me a description of Bob? Hopefully come up with a time—'I might hook up and go to his truck tonight.' Keep in touch with somebody. And if you don't hear back, then you can start putting out the alerts. It goes unnoticed, because I think a lot of the cops aren't willing to put out reports, I don't know. I wonder how many drivers have actually been killed due to being gay and trying to hook up."* One reason for Adele's concern is that she had a gay friend who committed suicide *"about six years ago,"* she says. *"He was a trucker. Him and his partner were on the road and had been together for a while, but he dealt with a lot of depression and self-hate and those different issues, and he is one of the people who had been gang-raped by fellow drivers. There's a lot of fear there, and on one hand I was mad that he killed himself, but on another I was happy for him, because he was finally free."*

Truckers are frequently disparaging about "lot lizards," the name given to sex workers who frequent truck stops, but at the same time they provide enough work to keep them there. Transwomen and visibly gay men frequently are asked to provide sex, and their consent is presumed. Patrick says, *"Everybody just kind of assumed that I would blow them—like they were doing me a favor."* Many transwomen confide, off the record, that they are most likely to be raped or attacked after having sex with another trucker.

Casey describes a climate of overt sex trade at truck stops and then condemns the predatory behavior of the men who manage and profit from it: *"We know it happens, you were out there, you saw it. I hate the disgusting part. Out near Nashville once I saw this truck, and they had already chattered—he dropped this girl off in front of that truck, and then when she was done, they get on the mike, 'Driver, come back and get your girl.' So he'd drive back into the truck stop to drive her to the next spot where she needed to be, which I thought was pretty disgusting. I've known more than one man who defines getting a blow job on the highway as not cheating on their wife. Or whatever else they might want to do. I also know if you're a woman, you can get on that same radio and say something about you want some other kinda company, and that'll get arranged very, very quickly. Near Nashville once, I said, 'I like women a lot, but I like special women.' 'Oh, that can be arranged.' I said, 'That's curious, I never heard that one before.' They say, 'If you ask for something, it can be arranged.'"*

Reba has driven long enough to see things and hear stories. She says, *"Now, I know there's danger everywhere, but really I'm not taking a gun into the truck stop with me. Now, a transwoman is different. People will force them to give them a blow job and then feel guilty, so [they] beat them up or worse. People can spot vulnerable people, so I don't walk across the parking lot like I'm scared."* Though she has considered keeping a weapon, she feels confident enough not to go there. For transwomen, she suggests that a gun would be justifiable protection.

Lesbians handle the sexualized environment of truck stops with brusque affect, often just laughing it off. I didn't hear stories about lots of hookups between women, though a number of narrators had met lovers while trucking, suggesting that at least some degree of flirtation or sex between women goes on out there. More often, they keep a casual, nonconfrontational distance from the climate of easy sex at truck stops. Ciara can be friendly and relaxed without feeling vulnerable because she looks and acts butch and closed off. She adds, *"There are some truck stops I don't go to. A lot of people say that's just hearsay — well, it might just be hearsay, but it's enough to keep me out of there. I don't want to get involved in that. You get what you're looking for, and me, I don't remain a stranger, but at the same time I'm going to keep my guard. If you say hello to me, I'll respond with, 'Hi, how are you?' Just be cordial, not frigid and looking like I hate the world. And if I don't like what I'm seeing, I'll say, 'Excuse me, I need to use the facilities' or 'I need to go get something,' and I'll disappear. So lots of ladies that get in trouble out there, they don't know any better. They don't know what to expect from the guys, and they end up in a lot of trouble. Because they haven't really done the research; they think it's going to be a good time, we can do what we want, but that's not how it works. If you don't want that extra attention, don't look like you stepped off* America's Next Top Model. *Every female gets looked at out here, let's face it. And we [look at] the guys, too, but not for the same reasons as they do. We're gauging how safe we are right now, we're looking over the environment, and if some guy is giving us the heebie-jeebies, we don't want nothing to do with him. I get asked a lot, 'Are you scared?' And I say, 'Scared of what?' As far as someone doing stuff to me, I'm not, but I know how to approach situations. I actually sit at the bar at a restaurant and have a conversation with seven different guys, and I'm totally comfortable with it. But I've been around guys most of my life; I know how they work, I can gauge people and read people. If you walk around truck stops as a female, most guys are buttheads—don't take it personally.*" Ciara takes on responsibility for her own safety, using butch self-presentation and constant vigilance as armor in truck stops and elsewhere.

Odette is usually read as female, but that only helps so much, since then she gets the harassment women face, rather than that directed at people perceived as trans. She says, *"I'm a bit of an extroverted person, but because of a lot of bad experiences, I don't tend to go in and socialize with other truckers at truck stops, because it so often winds up being an experience where I'm ignored, or worse. And talking to other women that drive, that often becomes a common experience that we wind up sharing. We get demeaned, talked down to, harassed, considered not a real driver. It's a pretty demeaning experience, so I've just come to avoid it."*

Gracie, one of surprisingly many intersex truckers I interviewed, says they don't feel comfortable in truck stops. They have a porta-potty in the truck and stay in the truck with the doors locked at all times. Gracie says, *"My thing is, the restrooms are uncomfortable. I don't want to go in the men's restroom because I don't want to upset anybody. But what I do is I wear my binder, and when I have to go to the men's restroom, that's what I do. Actually I really like family restrooms. Rest areas have them. The ones that we stay at on the turnpike, they do have showers. Typically I just try not to worry about it, I guess, I just want to feel comfortable. The bathrooms are another thing, I guess, and I do get out of the truck sometimes and people stare at me. And obviously I look feminine, but I don't really know what I am, and I just don't feel comfortable in women's restrooms. And truck stops are not notorious for safety."* Certainly the understatement of the century.

Reba wears a wedding ring. Though to me she looks, and certainly moves, like a lesbian, the ring can maybe help her pass as just another tough trucking woman. She says it was *"a present from my grandma and grandpa when I went out on the road, so everyone would know I was married and leave me alone."* She adds, *"If they knew what happened out here, they'd be horrified."* And what happens "out here" is everything: harassment, rape, sexual exchanges of all kinds. It's a culture and an attitude. Writing about transwoman truckers in particular, I've described "sex as a strategy of informal resistance to these regimes [which can] replace the independence and excitement the job used to offer" (Balay, "Sex," 97). My focus here is on the way that the movement and ungroundedness of trucker life—combined with abject desperation and lack of control, and with longstanding working-class sexual attitudes and practices—shape the culture of truck stops.

"Blowing in the wind" is a phrase truckers use to facetiously describe a typical night in a crowded truck stop with only a few lot lizards doing the rounds. I stayed at a truck stop with Reba in Ontario, California, that simply oozed despair. As we were parking, a woman got on the CB and said she didn't have panties on. She wasn't even trying; just going through the motions. I'm glad I didn't see her, because I've never heard such weary resignation in a voice before. Truck stops feel sad and desperate and lonely, but hearing that in the voice of a human was almost too visceral to bear.

Dirt

Reba had allowed me to ride along with her on one of her runs to California, and we had reserved and paid for parking at this dispiriting truck stop in Ontario. This in itself is noteworthy, because we had a delivery in Compton, which Ontario is not close to. However, truck parking is very limited in California, especially truck parking that Reba (with twenty-nine years of experience as a badass trucker) considers safe. So she had decided that afternoon, while we were still several hundred miles away, that it was worth it to park this far from our delivery spot and to pay for a reserved parking spot, so that we didn't wind up with nowhere to park when her hours ran out, in violation of Hours of Service, in imminent danger, fucked. Because of her experience and ability to plan, she wasn't going to let that happen to us, and though the cost of parking (a cash-only payment) would be deducted from her take-home pay, I falsely assumed we'd experience comfort in exchange.

There was a film of slime on everything—a layer of grease and diesel exhaust in the air and on all the surfaces, with dust and grit adhering to it. I'm guessing there were over 800 trucks there, and only three women's toilets, one of which had a black plastic garbage bag covering it. Illustrations on the insides of the other stalls indicated, in pictograms, that one should toss used toilet paper wads in the toilet and not on the floor. By the end of the night I saw why this sign was needed. We ate at the Popeyes chicken restaurant, the healthiest option, and I hope someday to forget the texture of that "meat."

This all makes me sound, and feel, pretty whiney. After all, I had not been the one to drive eleven hours and work countless more. I was not facing years of this life—countless future nights in this hellhole. But the people who live this life are brave and stoic beyond my capacity, and I want to convey the flavor of the physical location, because the environment, though ghastly, was only a fraction of what felt bad about that place. The air was so heavy with human desperation. I learned later that many megacarriers strand newbie truckers there for days — even weeks — waiting for loads to get them north or east. These truckers pay out of pocket for parking and food while no money comes in. Freight is unpredictable, and large companies station people there, ready to go, but maybe without anything to take. This ties up the companies' tractors but otherwise doesn't cost them, and it gives corporate headquarters flexibility, which the current freight market demands. The cost, both personal and financial, falls directly on the head of the driver. You can feel it — anger, hunger, fear — in Ontario.

Reba paid fifty dollars for this: twenty-five dollars per night, starting at midnight, which adds insult to injury. Given delivery schedules and Hours of Service rules, 99 percent of truckers have to park all night, so they all get charged for two full days. Fine — at least we got to leave, while all the workers who trailed in, many carrying wrinkled plastic grocery bags, to work at the windowless fast-food spots there, faced a whole day (a whole life?) mired in that sticky despair. Gloria Gaynor's "I Will Survive" played as I was buying my morning's coffee. I cried.

While at the Ontario truck stop, I saw plenty of sex, loneliness, and boredom. It all felt leaden and lifeless. Also, I've never seen so many racial minority truckers in one place. When megacarriers choose whom to send out west with no preplanned return, they choose new, thinly resourced drivers, many of whom are African American. As we pulled away, I relearned lessons of how hope — and how rage — is racialized in America.

Talking this experience over with Reba, because certainly that's something that trucking leaves time for, she linked the despair to sex as well. She described the feeling of loss of control: you feel that you're the puppet of actors far away, even though the culture is telling you that you're your own boss. And then you have shit tons of windshield time to contemplate that situation, and your frustration builds, and you're away from home — where they have that vision of your freedom and your cash — so you feel blamed and responsible and pissy and isolated. This frustration gets tied to sex, or to conversations about sex. Reba had a trainee who thought she would give him blow jobs, who responded to her refusal by jerking off in the bunk. She says that truck stop sex is rampant, especially in places like Ontario, if only because there's not much else to do.

Transmen are, not surprisingly, more comfortable at truck stops. Liam has been driving for twenty years and has never had a problem. When I ask him whether he feels safe at truck stops, given that he's trans, he says, *"It doesn't even really cross my mind. It doesn't come up every day. Every day I'm really just more worried about the money and where I'm going to get the freight than being a man."* For him, truck stops offer more community than fear, though that's fading. *"We were down in Laredo, Texas, and there was a hurricane. The dispatcher was pretty worried. But we went into a truck stop, and we watched the hurricane come in on a big-screen TV. They brought out pizza and beer for everybody—it was really kinda cool. A lot of that community is gone now. It used to be, if you were pulled over to the side of the road, other truckers would stop and ask, 'What can I do to help?' or 'Is there anything I can do?' Now you don't really have time. I always stopped at mom-and-pop truck stops—I just loved them, and now they're few and far between. But there used to be community out here—everybody watched out for everybody else, and it's just not like that anymore. Now it's just a job."* He's a white guy who passes for a traditional trucker, and that works for him as long as truck stop bathrooms have stalls available, though he acknowledges that some don't, or if they do, they might not have doors. In these cases, he uses an emergency system in the truck, but his confidence appears unshaken—he has access to ease and safety.

Daryl, another transman, gets around even this problem, saying, *"You know, I don't get cornered by anybody. Like I said, you can't look at me and say, 'Oh, I think. . . .' This is gonna sound crazy, but I had done absolutely 100 percent of what's necessary, to a point where I can literally walk out behind my trailer and take a leak. That sounds kind of derogative, you know, I don't mean it that way—but I can walk into a man's restroom, walk right up to a urinal and use the bathroom and the urinal, and walk right back out, and nobody would ever notice. So, because I've taken the time to do the research, to be able to properly pass as I need to, I live my life day to day like a man."*

Hernando, a gay man who went into trucking when his long-term job as a maître d' ended and he couldn't find another job, is not out at work, though he says he finds "people to flirt with" at truck stops. Mainly, he describes the truck stops as dirty. When I ask what has been the hardest change to get used to, he laughs and points to being physically dirty. He adds, *"My hair. I always had perfect hair when I was at the club. At the club, I taught etiquette to the staff. I was in charge of a dining room and I trained new hires, and I taught them all the refineries of dining etiquette. And I've gone from that to being an animal on the road."* I laugh at that, but he continues: *"It's OK. I'm OK with that, though. The truck is quite luxurious, I can't complain about it. I have air conditioning, stereo, microwave, disc player, clothes, food, I'm good. I love it. But oh yeah, [truck stops] are filthy. Filthy. Just the pee that everybody dumps, throws their bottles in the parking lot. When it's ninety-five degrees out there, the smell is not very pleasant."*

Transwomen like Alys are proud that they don't get clocked. She says she's never hassled in bathrooms or other trucker spaces, but hearing horror stories from other drivers makes her wonder. She says, *"I don't know if I should feel fortunate, or rather, I should just, you know—maybe I'm doing things right, and [I should] look at myself and go, 'I'm doing things right.' I don't know."* She's self-congratulatory here, takes being hit on as a compliment, and doesn't share any instances where that got scary. Lesbians often do, though. Josephine has been hassled constantly by trainers and other truckers who solicit sex from her and respond with hostility when she refuses. She caught one guy, whose advances she had rejected, *"trying to unhook my trailer, and he tried to pull a pin out on me, just at a fuel stop,"* she says. The tractor and trailer are attached via a kingpin through the fifth wheel (a seat and connecting mechanism), and there's a safety pin that locks them together. Vindictive truckers can release the pin on a truck, and if a driver doesn't check it and drives off, the trailer falls off and sustains damage of varying degrees. Any trucker rejecting a sexual advance from another trucker fears, and checks for, this retaliation. Josephine says, *"I don't feel safe in truck stops. I mean, whenever you talk to a man very long, you're his now."* Given that men are practically all you see in truck stops, this leads to a pretty lonely life.

Most women I did see in truck stops never met my eye, and it was very hard to initiate a conversation. Bridget says, *"[At] truck stops we don't stop and talk to each other; we just keep going doing what we have to do."* I saw two black women walking toward their truck who I swear were gay, and I couldn't, even with a significant glance and my obvious lesbian presentation, so much as slow their stride. Typically, there's an eye-contact acknowledgment between queers, and certainly between gay women, in public space. We notice each other and quietly mark what we've seen. This practice generates community and allows for some sense of support, should that become necessary. Women in truck stops don't make eye contact with anyone, and so can't participate in this acknowledgment. I speculate that this is because they work in a predatory, male-dominated environment where, as Josephine says, any communication is read as sexual consent. But even in women's restrooms the practice continues, probably because once people learn to remain perpetually alert, they almost can't let their guard down—they forget how. Maybe this tendency helps make it hard for truckers to sustain romantic relationships. This increases the chance that they will seek casual contact on the road, which in turn triggers these self-protective walls—a self-perpetuating cycle.

Daryl is one of the few narrators to raise the issue of sexual safety. He notes that *"wives at home often find it hard to trust somebody, when you know that somebody's not being safe out here."* Research on truck stop sex typically focuses on HIV/AIDS transmission as a metric of risky behavior. Jacobo Schifter writes about this in *Latino Truck Driver Trade: Sex and HIV in Central America*. His findings are very detailed and not surprising to anyone who has spent time in a truck stop. His book documents how (male) truckers are expected to be sexually voracious and not too picky—that's part of big-rig culture. Though they are explicitly homophobic, sex between men is common; it's embracing a gay identity that's precluded.

Understanding the sexual pleasures and possibilities of working-class people like truckers should expand and challenge queer studies scholarship. Cultural presumptions are that gender and sexual experimenting is largely a middle- or upper-class phenomenon, but scholarship shows that same-sex intimate exchange and gender-role violations have been continuously practiced in blue-collar worlds, across lines of race and enabled by geographic mobility. George Chauncey's pioneering research demonstrates that in early twentieth-century New York, men found pleasure and partners across lines of class, and working-class men didn't bother to conceal this behavior. Nadine Hubbs adds that homosexual behavior, which is now embraced in middle-class life, was not long ago firmly excluded there but welcome in working-class worlds (48). Drawing from these and other histories, and from my previous work on gay steelworkers, I contend that there is a continuous thread of fun and free gay sex that happens in public and that is fully acknowledged, if officially repudiated, in blue-collar work worlds. If queer studies seeks a vision of queer life less colonized by nuclear family structures and capitalist regimes, it could start by looking in blue-collar workspaces.

In addition to sex, truck stop stories often revert to themes of guns and beer. Maci, a Latina lesbian trucker, ties these together. As part of a conversation about health insurance (she has none) and pay (it's too low), I ask Maci if she's scared out there. She replies: *"Now more so than ever, with the way everybody is at each other, and the racism is really bad. I am—I really watch myself. I always watch myself; I try not to get out of my truck after dark, if I have to do anything I try to do it in broad daylight. A lot of truckers have been getting robbed in rest areas, some of them in broad daylight. So people say, 'I need help with my tandems,' and it's not that I don't want to, but I can't help them, because that's how they're getting them. They'll walk around, and there's two or three other people waiting to jump on 'em. In Ohio, Illinois, and Mississippi a lot of truckers have gotten killed. I have to watch my back, and I'm at the point now where I think that we should be able to carry pistols across state lines. I worry when I take my ten at shippers and receivers, which I do now, because with these Qualcomms, I'm under the gun 'cause I don't have enough hours where I can literally finish this load out so I can be on time. I have to watch how I time it.*

"So that's another government force. Within the next four or five years, we're going to be totally communist with regard to trucking. Look at Michigan; they have the right to do a drug test anytime, and the other states will follow, which I don't have a problem with, but you're holding me up, you're wasting my time, and I'm not getting paid for it. When am I going to start getting paid for all my downtime? Apparently they've had a lot of bad accidents up in Michigan, and they're finding truck drivers with beer and liquor in their truck, and they are under the influence of some type of drug; that's what they're saying. Now, I'll say for myself that's one thing I don't do out on the road—I'm not going to go in and buy anything to drink. If I want to drink, I'll go home. You see these guys coming out with several six-packs and sit up there and drink beer all night long and toss the beer cans out the window. And I do have a problem with that—that I do—because you're not showing any consideration for the people out on the road. And it's those bad apples that are making it hard on us. These drivers really don't care, a lot of them don't. But it's only a matter of time before other states adopt drug tests." There are many things to unpack in this response, but most of it centers on her reflection that "within the next four or five years, we're going to be totally communist with regard to trucking." Rather than critique her terminology or political analysis, my goal is to understand what these words mean to this speaker, this trucker, this working-class hero.

Maci feels strangled by a barrage of legislation and policies that she sees as primarily functioning to make her job harder and more dangerous. Hours of Service means she sleeps often at shippers and receivers, which offer no facilities and few protections, and no matter how carefully she manages her schedule, she will break rules and have vast amounts of unpaid work time. And though these regulations place her in positions of increased physical danger, other regulations on transporting weapons prohibit her from protecting herself. Finally, racism out there places a nonwhite body like hers in heightened danger. These are the pressures that Maci describes with the epithet "communism."

A trucker armed with safety vest and attitude.
(Used with permission of the subject.)

From Maci's perspective, a disembodied government puts the good of the many over the safety and income needs of the one: her. Though she is part of the many, and serves us all with her work, she doesn't feel included by government protections but rather feels like a human bulwark positioned to protect and serve other, more culturally valued bodies. This analysis helps explain her "bad apples" theory. There, she's constructing a narrative of why truckers are considered expendable rather than worthy of protection. She's already explained why she rejects a collectivist vision so she can't embrace it here, and instead takes on responsibility, essentially saying, "We are not victims—we did this to ourselves, but we are suffering."

This analysis explains why the beginning of Maci's answer is so sad: what community exists on the road is generated by mutual help, such as going to the aid of fellow truckers whose levers or locking pins are stuck, and providing a second pair of hands so they can slide their tandems, thereby adjusting the weight of the load on the axle to local standards. When truckers like Maci feel isolated by racism and remain ever vigilant about violence and rape, that community disappears. On the minus side, trucking can be lonely and scary. But on the plus side, this isolation is what makes the freedom possible: truckers are unleashed from homeplace, with all its messages about family, stability, monogamy, and heterosexuality. Being over the road results in constant motion and that enables a new way of being—and of being sexual. Gwynneth illustrates the plus side, saying, *"Trucking is my thing. I have a very wandering spirit. I like wandering around and being out in the world. I like driving and kind of being out."* Though Gwynneth probably didn't mean out of the closet but rather out of the house—away from domestic obligation—in motion, her words convey a sexual fluidity as well. Escape from domesticity encourages being out of the closet, which reflexively enables a critique of "houseness"—the unspoken rules that govern what a person can do, whom they can fuck, and how these relate.

Risk and Responsibility

As the twenty-first century unfolds, popular understandings of identity as distinct from sexual practice and of both as chosen and volitional get braided together—and come to seem inevitable and even invisible. "Being" gay, or bi, or trans is enacted by saying that's what you are: by claiming it publicly. However, what is often forgotten is that this vision rests on a sense of personal autonomy that depends on safety: where you are, both geographically and spatially, affects how you imagine both your vulnerability and your identity. Jodie is a Mexican American trucker in her late forties or early fifties. She describes how truck stops shape what she is and does: *"I'll never forget—there was a girl that I was dating, we were in another town. I never brought my girlfriends to my house, and I explained to them why. So she had picked me up at the truck stop in Odessa because I left my truck there, and I was getting out and she came up, and I gave her a kiss and a hug and we were just talking. And this other driver came up, and he was like, 'Cool dykes on trikes,' and we both just looked at him like "Scuse us?' And he's like, 'Do you need a man?' And we're like, 'Oh hell, go away.' That kind of stuff I've seen quite a bit, if I'm dating a woman or whatever.*

"I don't get out of my truck at night, and if I have to, I keep a Taser in my pocket. I try really hard to park up front, and I'll be the first to say I'll buy parking just to be up front, because I don't want to be out in the back—I'm too old now, I don't want to deal with that. I barely talk to anybody. I'm not one to make friends. I just keep to myself and it's easier that way. It's a very lonely life for me right now. It's just me and my dog. That's it. I don't know what I'd do without her; she listens to me cry and bawl and fuss and cuss and everything else. But you know, I shouldn't be like that—it shouldn't be like that for

anybody. But I do it to protect myself because I don't want the bullshit, and it's the only thing I know to do." She has a Taser and loneliness, both of which are required by the geographical, employment-related, and sexual locations in which she finds herself.

Most female truckers (both cis and trans) construct defensive walls that help keep them safe, but they eventually take a psychic toll. Many believe that the risks they experience are not widely understood, since the public thinks advances in feminism and LGBTQ rights mean queer people and women are safe, and even supported. This misperception makes lesbians' and transwomen's support for truckers' campaigns for interstate gun permits and for company policies that allow guns (neither of which is now common) less justifiable. But structural supports that might make women safe don't exist. Rights discourse does not protect them, and collective action is unattainable because they are deliberately geographically and psychically dispersed. Therefore, they are thrown back on individual models because these are the only options offered. When your world does not even try to protect you, you might want a gun.

Not everyone takes this approach, of course. Some truckers say they would never carry a gun and that being alert and acting confident is enough to keep them safe. Others hate the way that trucking's isolated locations and the commercialization of fear push truckers toward conservative political positions. Donovan tells me, *"One night, I was sitting in either Illinois or Indiana, when there was a transwoman shot in the head outside a gas station. Not a gas station I was at, but I sat there and had a thought: I spent my entire life at fucking gas stations. Like, I've gotten into a couple of altercations with truckers, not about that—like I said, I do have the luxury of having some passing privilege—and truckers have come to my aid. But if someone was coming at me for being trans—this isn't an accepting industry."* She laughs sardonically. *"I see it all the time. White male truckers going after immigrants, white male truckers going after people they think might be gay. 'Faggot' gets thrown around a lot, right? One of the things that bothers me a lot in this job is you go to a truck stop, and even the big ones worship the ignorant, white, male, Christian trucker. And by that I mean, if you go into any of those truck stops, you see Rebel flag stickers, Second Amendment–rights stickers, 'Shoot first, ask questions later,' you see shirts making fun of vegetarians and vegans—you get what I'm saying? I'm a liberal, and I do* not *feel welcome in this industry. At all. Like, zero. Even just being a liberal, I just don't feel safe here, add on top of that being trans, add on top of that being gay."* She laughs again. *"That's a big part of why I hate it."* Research on truckers even in this century proceeds as though they are white, Christian men, with Rebecca Upton (whose research focuses on "Christian" companies like Covenant Transport) being most explicit about her subjects' attempts to "reconcile masculinity and religiosity" (105). If scholars fall into these patterns (even while acknowledging that truckers are no longer exclusively male), it's partly because of the messages truck stops themselves convey, as Donovan describes. And these patterns persist because of (even as they create) climates of vulnerability and fear.

Donovan feels threatened because of her gender presentation, though as she says, she passes well enough to avoid automatic suspicion and thus violence. But the climate of fear—which she links to racism, homophobia, resentment about social change, and social status—continually restructures how violence is seen and understood. Violence is usually racialized in U.S. culture, and the culture of transience at truck stops molds what is read as violence, what resistance feels like, and what it means to be safe.

Isabella links a conversation about truck stop safety to race, gender, and guns. When I ask her if she ever feels scared out there, she laughs and elaborates: *"No, I'm too tough. And here's another thing—and I'm probably breaking some rule somewhere—I have a concealed carry permit, and that's something that goes with me. Ever since the motorcycle club, I take my gun with me. There is always a firearm in this vehicle, and this company doesn't care. My last two companies, it was strictly against company policy, but my response was 'I kind of have this policy against being shot.' Now if somebody tries to steal the truck, I'll be like, 'Give me a second to grab my wallet, here's the key, here you go.' There's one truck stop on the 285 north of Atlanta at exit twelve, where locals hang out and play pool. I walked in there on Christmas Eve one day and there were five black guys playing pool. They said, 'Hey, girlie, girlie, girlie,' and I didn't think anything of it. I was just going to eat and then leave, and this guy on a stool leaning against the wall says, 'You know they're talking to you, right?' He's like, 'They're looking for an invitation.' I thought, 'I think I'll get my dinner to go,' and I went right back to my truck."* She doesn't just say she carries a gun, which I heard from many truckers. Isabella also explicitly links this to "probably breaking some rule somewhere" and to her history with a motorcycle club. She wants protection, but also to be seen as an outlaw and a badass. This could be an attempt to impress lesbian me, and it could also be a way of thinking about danger and about how self-protection equals rebellion. In her example story, she's worried about five black guys, locals, whose territory she is passing through. Her transitory state, within a racialized context, is how she constructs the scene: I am alone, you are a group; I am an alien, you are at home. But this scene is only readable that way via the scrim of racial difference, and in our cultural context, the racial meaning is the only real one. Isabella, like the rest of the culture of which she is a part, can't tell this story outside of race but does try to add other layers like mobility. Her story can thus spark another layer of understanding of truck stop violence and of safety.

Those truckers who don't have a hard time usually avoid danger by being very belligerent, thus preempting violence, or by joking their way through it, or both. Ciara says she feels safe at truck stops: *"On the other hand, I know what I can and cannot do at certain truck stops. Sometimes I don't get out of the truck when it's dark out, and that's pretty typical of women, really. If I have a weird vibe, I'll pull out and go to another truck stop. If something should happen, there's usually four or five other drivers that will help me out, usually men. Someone might think, 'Oh, these guys are pigs and they're mean, nasty, and gross.' But that's not really the case; I've met some really great people out here, and I know that if something were to happen, five or six guys would back me up. But I've never really been insecure, especially around men. I grew up with three brothers, I kinda know how they work and I let them know I mean business; if you mess with me, you're going to have a hard time. That's one of the facades you have to put on as a driver. The rest of the time I can be a girl and I'm perfectly fine with it. I met a driver who pushed me around, and I let him have it. I had a mouthful for him. I said, 'If you did that to a man, he'd knock your block off. Why you doing it to me? Cryin' out loud.' A cashier asked, 'Do we need to call the cops?' I said, 'No, you don't need to call the cops, we're done. I said my whole dollar and I'm done.' Other than that I really don't have any trouble."*

Often trucker safety, especially queer trucker safety, is not adequately guaranteed by this type of humorous bravado. Sean told me that, especially after the Pulse nightclub shooting in Orlando during the summer of 2016, he was considering getting a gun. As a gay man who continuously places himself in other people's dangerous spaces, he sought a form of protection that would travel with him.

Often, truckers downplay safety concerns, while acknowledging their validity. Natalia went into trucking to make enough money to support her two kids. She has family members who truck, so she knew how to make the most money, which she mostly did by running into Canada. Truckers need a passport or Transportation Worker Identification Credential, or TWIC card, to cross the border, and you can't get either if you're behind on child support or taxes, or have a felony conviction. This rules out many truckers, so the ones who remain earn a premium. This trucking niche already toes the line between rebellion and domesticity, rule violation and appropriate behavior.

This pattern carries over into truck stops, where, Natalia says, *"I could walk across the parking lot of any truck stop or whatever, and there would probably be ten men following me. They want to know if I'm by myself, if I want to have any dinner, if I want anything. But on the same token, if I got loud enough or said, 'Hey, leave me alone,' there were probably four or three of them standing there to intercede and say, 'You better back the fuck up.' So it kinda went both ways, and I never had any trouble."* She hastens to add that many women do have problems and that her strategy is not foolproof. Indeed, most female truckers I talked to (both cis and trans) had been raped.

Fanny told me about three close calls and added, *"It's only a matter of time. It's just a matter of time."* The first incident occurred in a truck stop at *"like, 10:30 in the morning,"* she says. *"It was a beautiful weekday morning, up in the Red River Valley in Oregon; I was hauling on I-5. And when I pulled into the rest area, there was just my truck and one other truck parked about six or eight trucks over. And when I came out of the restroom, there was an Atlas Van line truck with two males in it parked right next to my driver's door. And they were both standing in front of my truck, outside their truck. All I had was my keys in my hand. As I walked toward them, I realized I am going to have to pass by one of them to get between the trucks. And I didn't want to do that, because once you're between two trucks, you're not visible. So I just kind of stood there, and you know, one of the guys said, 'Hey baby, want to party?' And I just put my hands up, I just put my hands up, like surrender, and I said, 'You know, no, no, I'm not interested, guys.' And I just stood there, and they just stood there. Two seconds later, we heard an air horn. And so all three of us looked over to the one solo truck that was, like, that sixth space over, and it was a driver about my age, and he was not out of his cab, he was half-in, half-out, and he had his tire thumper with him, and his cell phone. And he said, 'Hey guys, that looks like a pretty definitive no to me. Get rolling. Yeah. Get rolling.' So, 'Oh, we were just, you know, messing with her, blah blah blah.' Like, 'Get rolling.' Right. Right. So, because I'm standing there and I'm pondering, what do I do now? If I run forward, I have to run between them, and if I run back to the bathroom, there's no lock. Then, I'm in a secluded place, so I was still kind of pondering what I was going to do to get out of this situation when he intervened. And they got in their truck and they rolled off. And he just looked at me, and he said, 'Are you out here alone?' And I said, 'Yeah, I am.' And he just shook his head. And he said, 'This is not a profession I would ever want my mother, sister, daughter, wife in. Period.' And he said, 'I'd give them ten, fifteen minutes to roll on down the road, and then feel free to take off, but I wouldn't roll for a little bit. I'd let them get a head start.' So I thanked him very much, and he shook his head and got back in his truck, and that was it."* After a subsequent incident, another trucker recommended to Fanny that she always exit her truck on the passenger side. This would encourage anyone observing her to assume that someone else, possibly a possessive husband, is in the truck too. She took this advice and began looking to get out of trucking.

While many of my narrators were planning or hoping to leave the business because the pay was lower than they had hoped and the danger and hours were higher, others found it to be a good fit, between their inner wanderer, their discomfort with being home for sexual or gender reasons, and what they usually call the trucking lifestyle. Vito summarizes these trade-offs when I ask how he sustains a home life while typically running three months at a time: *"Oh, you don't! When you're running solo, it's kind of like a solitary prison, except that you get to get out at the end of the day. There's two things that really deteriorate as a truck driver if you don't maintain it, and that's your physical and mental health. As a gay man driving truck, mental health deteriorates more quickly. Many of these guys will get out and socialize with other drivers, they'll go into Denny's or a drivers' lounge and they'll talk to other drivers, which is something that you need to do out here. It's a need — you need to get out and get with these people. Otherwise, it starts really draining on you, wearing you down. On a personal level, for me, it's really horrible. When I can get a good local job I will definitely do that, because as a social person, it's very hard to have a personal social life. You miss a lot. You miss a whole lot."*

Though stereotypically, truckers are loners who enjoy long stretches of windshield time and don't welcome having to shape their lives around the needs of others, they still need, according to Vito, at least the random social encounters of truck stop life, which are too dangerous for those who are openly gay. Maybe because truck stop culture is so tolerant of male-male sex, it forbids visible gay male identity. These two ways of being in the world become increasingly incompatible as the political and social climate in America changes. As it becomes easier to be gay and out in mainstream American life, we need to remember that this safety does not extend to all people and all places. In fact, as middle-class worlds embrace gay (and trans, though to a lesser extent) lives, there is often backlash in more marginalized, poorer circles. Truckers (and other blue-collar workers) often pay a price for the increased comfort experienced by some queers.

8

ROLLING

DRAGGIN' ASS

Persistence and Endurance Are
Working-Class Values

AFTER THIS MANY CHAPTERS — this many stories — readers may be wondering why truckers persist in such a difficult job. Even more, why trans, queer, and minority truckers stay in these situations where they are so vulnerable, even after traumatic work experiences. The first answer is that they have few other options. Populations like indigenous people, Sikhs, transwomen, and Mexicans are all visible and stigmatized minorities with limited access to higher-status jobs. Kyla Bender-Baird's book-length study, *Transgender Employment Experiences*, speculates that trans people disproportionately occupy low-paying jobs because employers can and do discriminate against them with impunity, and because the fear of that happening shapes workers' choices (41–43). Other visible minorities face similar situations.

The second answer is that working-class culture tends to place a high value on persistence. History has trained poor, minority, and blue-collar groups to "put up with things they don't like" (Hochschild, 80), and they're good at it; persistence in the face of adversity becomes a useful tool, a point of pride, and a source of honor. My mother and grandmother often told me that patience is a great virtue, and when I complained because some circumstance displeased me, they typically responded, "Nobody asked you what you wanted" or "Life isn't fair." Though these comments sound harsh, especially to middle-class ears, they were a crucial part of class training. My family needed me to learn that the world does not care what people like us want or cater to our needs; our best option is to learn that, and learn to live with it.

The trucking lifestyle is hard: accidents, long hours, isolation, rape, low pay, weather. It's hard on the body, the soul, the home life. And it's boring, both during the endless hours of driving during which drivers must somehow stay alert and during the often extensive time they spend waiting. Usually, truckers don't complain about this — they don't want to be seen as victims. They have pride in what they do and want their stories to emphasize their survival rather than their struggle. Most, though not all, of them love the work — the roar of the engine, grabbing gears, unsupervised time, the road. Dwelling on the hard parts, especially to outsiders, would take the sheen off all that. However, the fact that they downplay the hard parts doesn't mean that they accept them or consider them the price of admission. Making a virtue of persistence, and taking pride in your ability to endure hard stuff, is fully compatible with advocating an end to, or diminution of, the hard stuff.

When I ask Sisyphus how she keeps driving in spite of the boredom, she says, *"You just persevere through it."* These are simple words with complex meanings. Sisyphus chose her own alias for this book: she wanted to name the daily experience of pointless suffering and its inevitable, heavy cost. In choosing this alias, she identified this struggle both as something she was doing and identifying with, and as something done to her and resented. Either way, she has no choice but to keep rolling that stone up the hill, to get in her truck each day and face whatever challenges await. When truckers get seriously tired and need to keep driving anyway, they call that condition "draggin' ass."

Reba drives endless loops from her terminal in Michigan to the West Coast. She's out for about twelve days, home for two, and then repeats the cycle. She therefore needs to get lots done on her days at home, and they're her only time with family and friends. Still, she reports, *"Almost every third trip I get some major jet lag, so I don't even tell anybody I'm coming home. It's not tired like I want to take a nap, it's a heavy fatigue. So I don't let people know. I can feel it as I'm driving back, switching to Michigan time."* Not only does the time change, but so do the climate (requiring her to take allergy meds) and the altitude, making her ears pop. Endless repetition of this pattern must be draining, but Reba points out that it's a premium job, available only to experienced truckers with safe records. The guaranteed return freight is what makes the job desirable; the company has a reliable contract and can promise Reba that as soon as she gets to California, there will be freight available for her to haul back home. Adapting is hard, but also about the best you can hope for in trucking.

Brookelene rolling through New York State.
(Used with permission of the subject.)

Reba tells me repeatedly that *"this job used to be physically hard, but now it's mentally hard."* An example of a physical component is that California limits all trucks' speed to fifty-five miles per hour everywhere, while car speed limits go as high as seventy. This difference requires constant clutching, resulting in exhaustion or repetitive-motion injuries. Nevada, by contrast, lets trucks run at seventy miles per hour. Running the same speed as the other traffic, she doesn't need to switch lanes constantly, and thus can put on the cruise control and give her clutch leg a break. Examples of mental challenges while driving are dealing with shifting regulations, timing, disrespect, and isolation. Managing all this at once is typically discussed by my narrators only obliquely — or in a positive light. Reba observes: *"I live a privileged life. Some people save their whole lives for a chance to come to Vegas, and I pass through it four times a month, sometimes seven or eight times. And I could stop, but I work too hard for my money to do that."* She emphasizes her access — her options — and then in the same sentence forecloses it. Last winter, her niece asked her to go ice skating and she had to refuse, because a broken wrist could mean her income or even her career. Though she sees herself as having access to everything, her body and her life are not her own, so that access is only theoretical—the ability to sit there and drive, and to continue doing so, is all that matters.

Just Keep Those Wheels Rolling

Persistence offers both practical and psychological rewards. Driving truck gets addictive—it takes you over. Terell notes, *"I've actually gotten to the point where I've driven truck so much I'm not comfortable in a regular car anymore. I don't get as tired driving a truck; I have better sight lines and more visibility. A million miles does it to you."* And Isabella quips, *"It takes a very special different breed of bird to do this."* She adds that she *"runs a lot harder than most drivers—it's all I've ever done—it's all I know."* Though she uses self-deprecating humor to describe and maintain control of her own work circumstances, she has a critical take on other trucking jobs. She started with a megacarrier, where in her best year she made $40,000. From there, she recently moved to a percentage haul job, where she projects she will net more. This process of sticking with it, gaining experience, and then moving up is an example of the work ethic and persistence that she and other truckers idealize. At the same time, she realizes that *"the large trucking company recruiters lie worse than the military recruiters."* She adds, *"They tell you all this bunch of stuff and then when you come to expect it, it's like, 'Oh, no.' They really are not very honest. The other thing that I feel sorry for is the owner-ops; I think we are witnessing a dying breed. The owner-op has stress. He knows what his bottom line is that he needs to make to move that freight from point A to point B, so he goes and he puts his bid in. Well, John Q. Public wants the lowest bid, and Schneider puts a bid in for nine cents a mile; the owner-ops, who built this country on their backs, get underbid. [The shipper] doesn't think that he's going to get a professional, he just wants to move the freight for $1,500 rather than $2,500. We live in a throwaway society now, and what we throw away isn't just stuff—sometimes it's people."* Though Isabella says she *"really has fun"* out there, she knows that's not possible for these drivers.

Persistence is difficult to locate as a value because it's linked to modesty—the ideal is to accomplish your goals effectively without calling attention to yourself. To name or catalog difficulties is called whining, but without some identification of challenges, it's hard to identify a process of powering through them. Dorothy is a trucker with years of experience and ample pride in her skills. She tells me: *"You'll find out I don't pull any bones. By the same token, I don't like the whiners out here. And I will say this, if you're too feminine—and there's nothing wrong with being masculine, feminine, or anything else, any stretch of the imagination; I like to do my fingernails and have my hair done and stuff—but if you can't handle the job, then don't take it. You find the resources or the ways to manage it. [A friend] has just started doing step deck and flatbed, and I'm teaching her how to do the binders and stuff, because when I first started doing flatbed I didn't weigh more than 125 pounds. I couldn't get out there and get that stuff tight till I found a piece of pipe that extended out about five foot, and with that I could get them tighter than anybody; once in a while I had to get somebody to help me undo it. You figure out a way to do it. This is my favorite expression, and I figured this out, I didn't borrow this from anybody else: 'It's not his job, it's not her job, it's my job, and I do it well.' You figure it out. If you can't do it, male or female—there's a lot of males out here that are whiney-ass. I don't like whiners."* When she says "I don't pull any bones," she means that she doesn't underrate herself—she's taking credit where it's due. Her examples are of modifications she worked out on her own so that she could do the job—work-arounds she devised and now makes available to other women—examples of persistence.

Karen notes that *"it does take somebody pretty strong to be out here alone."* And she's not exaggerating: many women I interviewed had been raped. Surviving rape and sexual violence is part of life on the road, and some truckers report that it saturates life off the road as well. Johanna concludes our interview talking about the Chiricahua Navajo reservation where she spent her childhood, and where poverty and sexual abuse are common. She says, *"One in three women are sexually assaulted out there. And a lot of drug abuse. It's not as bad as it used to be, but when you have nothing to look forward to, what do you do? And I've never been that way, like I said, I had a strong mother. Very strong mother. But, my job, I love it, and I'll keep doing it until I can't do it anymore. Until it's physically impossible for me to climb into this truck. There are bad things that happen out here. I was sexually assaulted out here. It happens, and you can let it kill you and destroy you, or you can dust it off and go on and be stronger for it. [Some women] say, 'I'm too scared to get out of my truck, I won't go into the truck stop.' Those are victims in the making, and it makes me sad. There are things that happen, you just got to be vigilant. But if you need anything, let me know; I'm going to be out here driving. I wish you luck."* I didn't ask follow-up questions because it was clear that, having told me this, she wanted our conversation to end.

Other women who discussed sexual assault with me said they rarely reported it to their jobs or to the police. Transwomen typically ruled out calling the police to report rape because, as Marilu says, *"They'd as likely rape me again as fill out a report, so why bother?"* They try to keep focused on the work and, as Johanna says, *"dust it off and go on and be stronger for it."*

Thelma and Louise are a couple. Louise is a six-foot-six transwoman nervous about using the bathroom without the normalizing presence of Thelma, a lesbian, who says, *"I was in the closet so long I almost found Narnia."* Thelma reports that living with fear is the most tiring part—she rides along in the truck to have time with her wife and because she loves the life, but she deals with PTSD and anxiety, and the added bathroom stress feels like too much. She adds, *"My wife is a rape survivor, and I'm a rape survivor, and we're both on high alert whenever we stop the truck."* That a moving truck provides the only sense of safety these women get is painfully ironic.

Like me, these people wind up trucking in spite of its danger and boredom because their employment options are limited, but many find that they come to love it. My narrators taught me that turning to trucking when at the end of the road (so to speak) is linked to persistence: salvation through trucking is not easy or pretty, and it takes a tough person to make it work, but these facts somehow add to its appeal, especially for the desperate and culturally marginalized. A trans narrator called Jane tells me, *"My wife and I were looking at financial ruin, basically. It seems to be the story of a lot of people right now. So about six years ago I said, 'We just can't do this anymore.' So I went to school and learned how to drive one of these things, which, I already had experience in the military and with farm equipment, so it was not hard to learn. I've been driving going on six years in December for this company, and almost seven years total. I'm making almost $50,000 a year. The hours are intense. You have to be ready for it, and you have to be able to work ten, twelve, fourteen hours a day and be ready for that. And I typically run out of hours in a given week. It does boil down to the person. And you have to enjoy what you're doing. I drive flatbed, so I'm in and out of the truck lots, I'm throwing chains, binders, straps, whatever the load takes. Like I was saying, I'm the exception, not the rule. Weather does not bother me unless it's a tornado, which I was just in last May. I was actually in a tornado in Newcastle, Oklahoma. I hid behind the driver's seat and said, 'Oh Lord, please protect me' over and over again. I was being ornery."* This final comment—the very word "ornery"—names persistence: getting through a challenge just by persevering.

Her persistence comes from desperation as much as desire, and she makes that much money by being away from home for four weeks, followed by three or four days at home, and then out again. When I ask if being gone that much is hard, Jane replies, *"It's harder on the wife than it is me. I went through the military for eight and a half years, and being independent, it's no big deal to me. There are times I just want to get home—we all have it. There's days I wake up and I go, 'I really don't feel like driving today.' I'll lay in bed, looking up, going, 'I know I have to roll—I don't want to, but I have to.' There are days like that, where I have to force myself out of bed and behind the wheel. But then there are days where it's like, 'I can do sixteen hours today. Come on, let's go.' I feel so good that day—sixteen hours—I'm looking at my clock, and it's going ten hours, ten and a half, I could easy go another six hours. And it's like I have to shut down, and it's like, 'Really? I have to shut down? Darn, I want to keep going.'"* The pure joy of driving truck and the competence of feeling like you could just drive on and on coexist for Jane with having to power through the hard days.

Butch Styles, Butch Jobs

When I spoke with Echo, she had returned to trucking because the other work available to her was so emotionally exhausting that mere physical persistence felt like a relief. She says, *"I needed a break from construction and the trades, because it is overwhelming being the only woman—and I'm sure you felt it, too, being the only woman always. I don't know how long you had your hair short, but I just started mine out again after twenty-plus years; I had the shaved-head aboriginal person. Working side by side, all sorts of men—you know, I'd get 2 percent that are maybe okay with me, and the rest don't know what to do with me and then act out accordingly or [are] abusive. I prefer being ignored than being rushed with aggression. It weathers on me quite a bit. At times, one of my best friends—also my ex-partner; we were together eight years? We're still obviously friends, but she would note how I used to come home and feel battered. I'd act out at home, battered-wise, you know, throw a hammer across the yard because I'm so frustrated as I'm trying to do little projects. And where's that coming from? Every day I go in it's like a big, uphill, crazy, soul-destroying battle. And just try and keep strong when I'm in it."* She's made a very gendered statement here, which she feels comfortable making because of experiences she shares with me. We're both short-haired butch women with experience working in male-dominated trades. (I was a car mechanic for many years, which narrators often ask me about, once they conclude from my affect and knowledge that I'm not "just a writer.") Echo draws on that shared history to make her experience legible.

Thus, for Echo and others, it's not only that trucking has its pleasures, but that features of the work make it worth the hard parts, and they reward perseverance. Another butch lesbian, Casey, took time off when her partner

My narrators often challenge the
link between trucking and masculinity.
(Used with permission of the subject.)

needed emergency surgery, and the company tried to dismiss her, saying
that she had abandoned her truck. She kept pushing, and finally they let her
return. *"But it took me a bit to get to that point,"* she says. *"I'd like to say that
when a lot of suckers would give up, I don't give up. I want what I want, so I'll
keep fighting, saying what I got to say, and sometimes I threaten to go to some
government agency. Most of the time it works for you. They might not like you,
but you're fighting, so they'll take you back. Anyway, each to their own."* She
liked her job well enough to fight for it, and she calls attention not just to her
persistence on the job, but also the persistence she had to exert to keep it.

This theme of endurance and persistence in working-class life comes up
often in scholarship, and Augie Fleras and Shane Dixon explore its relation
to gendered reality well. They study four reality TV shows that glamorize
working-class jobs and read them as attempts to anchor blue-collar life in
hypermasculine presentation as it becomes detached from any class-based
meaning. "The workers in these shows are expected to partake in painful
and injurious activities and endure in order to do their job" (587). The heroes
of the shows they study variously redeem working-class jobs and roles by

attaching a more effective masculinity to them. This hypergendered enact-
ment feeds into an erasure of what actual working-class experience looks
like now (service work, precarity, etc.). Risk and endurance are thus recoded
as individual and heroic, masculinized ways of seeming virile at work, replacing any actual control or independence.

This analysis helps explain Casey's work history, though her lesbianism
and butch gender expression add another layer. She started with a megacarrier, she says, *"and then I quit for a short period of time. I thought, 'Are you
sure want to do this?' 'Cause I thought it was really isolating, you know? You
have lots and lots of people around you, but they're nobody, there's nothing
personal. And when you start out in this industry they work you to death, and
you either stay or you leave. And I think that was where I was at that point. Is
this the way I want to go? And I decided that if the opportunity presented itself,
I told myself that I would go ahead and go back into it."* A buddy of hers proposed a team-driving plan, so she told her boss she had an opportunity to
return to trucking. *"And he said, 'You're thinking about doing it?' And I said,
'Well, the thought had crossed my mind,' and he goes, 'I always felt that you
really — you always loved where you were.' And I said, 'Yes, but what a life —
you really don't have one.' And he said, 'I know you miss it.'"* Certainly, her
boss seemed more enthusiastic about trucking than she did, but she returned and loved it.

Ultimately, trucking disabled Casey and she had to quit, but she tells me,
*"I'd go back in a heartbeat [because], out on the road, that was my happiest
time."* While Fleras and Dixon are insightful about how class gets gendered,
to make sense of Casey's narrative, we need to add analysis of how sexuality
gets classed. Elizabeth Lapovsky Kennedy and Madeline E. Davis's *Boots of
Leather, Slippers of Gold* pioneered this research in 1993 with a detailed oral
history of lesbian bar life in Buffalo. They conclude, among other things,
that "butch effectiveness was based on concretely usurping male preroga-
tives in order to assert woman's sexual autonomy and to defend a space in
which women could love women" (383). Casey's boss probably reads her into
a discourse of masculinity because of how sexuality and class intersect in
her body and life history. His willingness to insert Casey in that space ex-
ceeds her own: she attributes to him the observation that she had loved
trucking and wanted to return to it, while her own feelings are more mixed.
Working-class culture needs that space of endurance and sacrifice occupied
by someone who harvests virility and meaning from its very perpetuation.
With white straight men less willing to be that symbol, butch lesbians, indigenous people, and other marginalized bodies get pressed into service.

Having been historically ostracized, the possibility of bearing their culture's meaning is often irresistible, offering indigenous butch lesbians a certain magic. Even if it harms the body, enduring it is then worth something.

And harm to the body seems like a given, though truckers typically don't attribute their health or life trauma to trucking-related causes. Woman narrators had survived cancer (caused by diesel exhaust, etc.), or rape, or both. If I seemed surprised or shocked by this information, they reassured me that it was over, that they were fine. Christina had cancer, and when I express concern, she replies, *"No, no, no. I'm a survivor. Two and a half years. I was out for six months with Triptomal — I took it like a breeze. I won't fool you any; for the first month I sat around and boohooed, thinking I was going to die, so I sat there in my La-Z-Boy watching TV, and then a month went by and I said, 'Well, I guess I ain't dead.' I have a sister who uses my house as a storage shed, and since I'm not there, I don't mind. But then I started looking around and I thought, 'Oh my god, I can't even find any of my stuff without having to boot her stuff out,' so I started organizing. I didn't get as much done as I probably should have, but hey, I had that cancer and chemo, so I did get a whole lot more out than what it was. So it is what it is."* Sisyphus, after our interview, had a mounting list of health problems, including the detachment and explosion of a breast implant and a subsequent infection. I told her I thought the continuous bouncing in the truck had probably contributed to the implant's failure, but she disagreed. Maybe her need to keep driving made it impossible for her to acknowledge that her job was causing her body material harm, or maybe she had some other explanation. Either way, once her infection was under control, she went back to work.

As Kris Paap argues in her book about white men with jobs in construction, workers get job security only by demonstrating their willingness to take risks. This both links them to masculinity and fuels competition between workers, thus minimizing possible collective action. Further, "demonstrating one's value mean[s] that an individual worker sacrifices physical safety in an attempt to seek economic security within organizational structures that do not provide it" (8). The tendency to personalize blame and struggle is tied to ideas like the American dream and the Protestant work ethic, and intensified by neoliberalism, but it's a particularly gendered, classed process in the case of these truckers. When truckers keep their wheels rolling regardless of weather, illness, exhaustion, or harassment, they acquire a timeless masculine nobility.

Adele tells me, *"I was born with arthritis. I was even born with cataracts. I had that surgery done, but till I was twenty-seven, I was borderline blind —*

that's really scary. I was borderline. I had severe night blindness. But I learned to compensate. I learned tricks with myself like—as you saw, I still have my tricks. You know, I try not to squint because I get this nice little lovely dent in my forehead, but you know, just, like, being a woman with all my medical issues, I've learned to compensate." She does not let a scary list of physical problems deter her, or let the struggle show, and there's lots of pride in that for Adele and for others like her.

Daryl has made as much as $60,000 a year. *"But I run,"* he says. *"You have to run, you have to be rolling, to take the loads—you have to be willing to commit. But if you'll put the time and the effort into managing your fuel costs, doing everything you need to do to make sure your truck's operational like it needs to be, this truck becomes your life."* He talks about scheduling problems and lists his divorce as being possibly trucking related, but he adds, *"Once this job is in your blood, it's in your blood."* Using this recurring phrase and calling trucking a lifestyle are rhetorical strategies truckers use to understand their difficult circumstances, their lack of options, and the dearth of collective, structural responses available to them. They personalize the situation and get control of it by embracing stubborn pride and perseverance as virtues, which fits well with their class identification.

When they do express anger and resentment, it's at the government for overregulating and at corporations for profit hogging. Maci says the rules in place to protect truckers are usually disregarded: *"These people are supposed to know this; there's supposed to be a law but they still get around it. We're not supposed to do some of the things that we're doing, but nobody fights it. We got brokers out here—we got way too many brokers compared to years ago, they're undercutting each other. You know, corporate America has really put a burden on us. We don't need more trucks out here, we got more trucks then we ever have, and they're always claiming we need more trucks. No, we don't. That's the problem now—American people don't have jobs, and they are coming out here in the trucking industry, so it's choked everybody, especially the owner-operators. Paradoxically, in the past eight years it's killed us financially—that goes for male, for female, the transgenders, the gays, that goes for everybody that own truck now. In all reality, if I could walk away from this, I would walk away. I came into this because this is what I wanted to do. I like doing this, but if you ever go into the truck stop and talk to these people, they've been out anywhere between a month and three or four years, and the majority of them, if they still had their jobs, they would not be out here. And the government has kinda put this in place; they're trying to regulate what we're making, so corporate America can make more."* She sounds paranoid but she's accurate.

Research documents this race to the bottom in freight rates, and truckers and all other workers in the twenty-first century find the risk and responsibility of their jobs placed squarely on their shoulders (Smith, 302).

Regulations, Again

Labor deregulation, market competition, drastic reduction in staffing for governmental departments like road inspection, and the emphasis on personal responsibility all conspire to leave increasing numbers of safety precautions and their consequences in the hands of the workers—in this case, the truckers. Owner-operators can refuse loads they consider unsafe, thus choosing to make nothing and facing possible retaliation in the form of reduced available freight going forward—or they can choose to accept risky runs and drive for less and less profit. As long as this is framed as a choice, trucking is seen as a job offering independence and control. Maci and most of my narrators see through that language and know they're being screwed. However, lacking any meaningful response, they take pride in enduring these circumstances, while at the same time seeking ways to name, and change, this rigged system.

A network of regulations restricts truckers' lives, but they find a paradoxical pleasure in managing to make the job work anyway. They resent the challenge, yet thrive on it. Eliza laughs when I ask if trucking offers a sense of adventure. She says, *"Every day is an adventure 'cause, you know, you work on the road, there could be accidents, there could be road construction, there could be backups with traffic. Of course, I try to plan my trip where I'm not going through big cities during rush hour if I don't have to, but yeah, every day is an adventure out here, I never know where I'm going to end my day; it could be in the middle of Iowa or it could be downtown Atlanta—who knows? And I also—I try to make it an adventure instead of work, because if you just look at it as work, it seems to be pretty boring, driving city to city, making your runs."* She's letting me know that my question is naïve and filling me in on the real circumstances of her life.

Fanny is more enthusiastic, and less sarcastic. She says, *"I just fell in love with the road."* Then she adds, *"I love being alone, and so I thrive. I mean, it didn't bother me at all to go three, four, five, six weeks without meeting anybody that I knew. I've always loved meeting new people. I don't like the routine of an office, you know, the same people, the same faces, the same routine every single day. I did get off the road once, for about a year when my mom had colon cancer and had surgery. They lived in Fresno, California, so I found a law office job in*

Fresno, and I did it for a year. My mom got better and I thought, 'Well, maybe I'll stay off the road.' And then I went to the doctor and starting crying one day, and she said, 'Either you go back on the road or I'll put you on Prozac.' My life had gotten so small in Fresno that my car wouldn't even hold charge driving just from the house to the office to the gym, you know what I mean? And my friends didn't really understand that. They were like, 'Well, when you're out on the road, you live in such a small space.' And I said, 'But my world is huge out there. My space may be small but my world is enormous.'" Fanny left trucking only when she was almost raped for the third time. She realized that if she kept driving, rape was inevitable, so she got a maritime credential and briefly worked for a tug company that serviced the Shell Oil project on Alaska's North Slope before disability forced her to retire.

In a lifetime of masculine jobs, Fanny says, she learned that *"what goes hand in hand is the more fun you have, the more risk you need to take."* But the risk she means isn't the danger of the job as much as the near certainty of rape. She was given an unusually awful maritime assignment on a fishing boat bound for the Gulf of Alaska, and when she started the job she asked the cook she was relieving about this kind of risk, *"'cause she's a woman about my age and about my size,"* she says. *"And I asked her, 'Have any trouble with the guys?' She's like, 'You know, I'm a single woman in my fifties. I have to make a living. You just shut up and put up with it.'"* Fanny left, if only because her carpal tunnel syndrome required her to, but women survive this and more with little recourse, and little support.

Of course, persistence has not only class implications but racial ones as well. Determining what counts as endurable, or as endurance, and understanding and navigating these borders are practices that are embedded within communities and therefore often have a racial valence. Gwynneth was harassed mercilessly by her trainers, and when a female trucking advocate urged her to prosecute, she says, *"I just told her that, as a black woman, you're kind of accustomed to being harassed. You're just used to it."* She adds, *"I don't know about other women, I can't speak for them, I just know about the black women — we're just accustomed to it, we know how to handle it, you know what I'm saying? I'm not saying that you don't mind, or even that you brush it off, just that we're not likely to file sexual harassment unless, of course, it gets violent or threatening or something."* By her account, learning how to handle unwelcome advances is part of her skill set as a black woman, and she doesn't need the authorities to intervene. The person who urged her to respond was mixed Mexican and indigenous, so also a person of color. Yet Gwynneth may suspect that she just doesn't get it: that if Gwynneth told the authorities that she, a black woman alone in a truck with a white man, merited protection and even retribution, she was likely to get no traction.

Zoe, another black woman, describes the harsh aspects of the job in clear, no-nonsense terms: *"It's a whole different ball game to get in the truck by yourself. Like, my first trip by myself, I went from Georgia to Whitetail Mountain, Pennsylvania. I went to bed and everything was all lovely, I wake up in the morning, there's freaking snow everywhere. I mean, I'd driven my car in snow before, but it's a whole different ball game in the truck. People feel they know so much about trucking, but when you're in the truck driving by yourself, a whole new light comes on, and this ain't what I thought it would be. I don't always get to go home every night, I can't always leave when I want. It's a whole 'nother life out on the highway. They treat us like just a bunch of uneducated hillbillies driving down the highway, but there's people out here now with PhDs, the economy's forcing them into trucking. This is what we do now; life goes on. I'm trying to figure out if this is a man or a woman with nail polish on. It's like everything else in the world — it's changing dramatically. That's how it is, it's sink or swim."* She wants the public to have an accurate image of trucking life — what's possible, and what really happens — and she links trucking's new reality to gender variance ("trying to figure out if this is a man or a woman with nail polish on") and to other shifts in the labor force. Who drives truck and how is changing, but the public perception isn't, and Zoe would like to correct that misunderstanding. She ends up saying, *"If you can find another job that pays decent, jump on it. I don't encourage trucking."* But her focus is, while you're driving, find a way to make the life and the circumstances manageable.

There's a hardheaded realism in people's attitudes about trucking: knowing what the job entails and what it will demand from you is your best armor. You can be realistic about hardships and still not be a whiner or a victim if you describe them dispassionately. Frankie has driven for nineteen years and considers herself one of the pioneer woman drivers. She trains new drivers now, but she remembers her own training. She says, *"When I went through truck-driving school, I met a USA Truck recruiter. I thought he was kind of an arrogant asshole because he stood in front of a class of maybe twenty-six, and he split the class in half and said that only half of us would make it through the year. He wound up saying that only two or three of us would still be doing this after five years, and we'd be in it for life. Now that I've been out here doing it for nineteen years, I totally get what he meant, because either you're cut out for it or you're not. If you make it four, five years, you won't get out of it. You*

Joni, at a customer, waiting for the bill of lading.
(Used with permission of the subject.)

have diesel in your blood. You're one that likes to drive and travel and doesn't have business at home."

For Frankie, truckers who stay in the industry do so because of a natural affinity combined with a lack of home cares. Others stay because they simply don't see a better option. Rhian, who says she has considered suicide often and recently, can't imagine making more money anywhere else, but makes so little trucking that she is very depressed. She made $38,000 last year, which isn't enough to save anything for her transition; surgery begins to seem like a distant dream. She says, *"This year's been kinda tough, and some of the girls tell me, 'It's because you're transitioning, and they don't want to give you good loads.' And I'm like, well, I would like to not think that way, because I've been with this company for eight years now, and there's only one driver with this company that's been there longer than I have. And I really haven't trashed a lot of things, messed a lot of things up; my driving record is spotless, you know."* She considers the suggestion by other transwomen that her freight assignments, and therefore her income, might be low because of antitrans discrimination. But then she notes that all drivers with her company are struggling, and her plan is to work hard and choose loads carefully. She identifies more with truckers and their working conditions than with trans people and their critiques and, after giving her company the benefit of the doubt, just perseveres. Circumstances force her to stay in trucking, but succeeding at it against the odds conveys pride I can hear in her voice.

Strategies for how to persevere include an affective numbing, like that ushered in by witnessing road fatalities. This makes sense, since it's a coping mechanism for a related job stressor. Jodie has worked so hard for so long, driving truck both over the road and in the oil fields, that somewhere along the way, she says she *"learned how to build a wall and not let things get to me."* Men made more than she did for the same work. She adds, *"I was raped at one point, I was almost raped another time; thankfully there was someone else there that stopped it. I was harassed the whole time, mentally, physically; I've gone through it. But it was worth it, because I was able to take care of my kids, and I never looked back."* When I ask if her company did anything to protect her, she scoffs. *"Oh no, oh no. They didn't even know,"* she says. *"Honestly. Because I knew how my boss was. I wore wifebeater shirts; I would wear that in the summertime, and of course I would wear my blue jeans, and I was a lot smaller than I am now, a lot younger than I am now. And he told me several times, 'You're dressed too provocative to be in the oil field.' And I told him, 'It's hot, I'm trying to stay cool, you know? I'm not trying to be sexy out here, I could give a shit about that.' I had my hair up in a cap, ponytail, and it's not like I was wearing makeup or anything like that. My truck didn't have air conditioning. It's 112 degrees outside. So I'm not worried about what I look like, I'm worried about staying cooled off. So anyway, I knew what would happen if I told, or if I even tried to press charges: I'd be blackballed. That kind of place out there, it's a good ol' boy mentality—you just don't, you don't talk about stuff like that. You just don't do it."*

After another rape attempt, this time interrupted by another driver, Jodie was asked by the owner of the company if she planned to press charges. She says, *"I told him, 'If I press charges, what's going to happen?' And he said, 'Honestly?' And I said, 'Yup.' And he said, 'Nobody will hire you.' And I said, 'I know that.' So, you know, I didn't press charges. I've always had guys making passes at me, telling me stuff, you know, 'Come on, baby, let's go here, let's go there.' I'll never forget—one day I was in the office with the owner of the trucking company I worked for, my supervisor, another supervisor, and the shop supervisor, and they were all in there giving me shit about how fat I had gotten and how old I was and blah blah blah. I turned around and looked at all of them and said,*

'I may be fat and old, but it's funny—within the last week, every one of y'all tried to fuck me.' So that shut them up. But that's the kind of mentality I have now. I don't take crap from anybody, and if they want to start talking crap to me, I'll come back at them in a heartbeat. Don't worry about it, but it's because of who I've become."

One reason Jodie decided to leave the oil field and go back over the road was to avoid that level of harassment. The anonymity and transience of long-distance trucking at least help with that. But with the current structure of the trucking industry, this means being out months at a time in order to make decent money. She recently had a frightening experience and would like to quit. She begins to tell me stories of the adventure and excitement—to relive the high points—and she concludes: *"Hopefully my driving days will be finally over. But I don't regret it at all, because I have seen and done more than most people have ever thought of, and I've had the time of my life out here."*

The value truckers like Jodie place on perseverance—the pride she takes from telling me a story like this one—is at least partly a response to stigma. Truckers feel "looked down upon." They mention this often, in these exact words. There's a sense that some abstract, disembodied other does not value who they are or what they do, and they're not wrong. But this invisibility and this prejudice harms the perpetrators more than it harms truckers. The truck drivers' response is simply to hop in the truck and roll off, which gives their life meaning.

Adele reflects, *"There's a lot of hate and everyone wants status quo, but they're really . . . they want change, but they don't. Once you start taking the steps and to take action to go towards making that change, then they are like, 'Whoa, whoa, let's slow this train down a little bit. Do we really want to do this?' Somebody asked me how I would handle making a delivery in Indiana and being turned away because, you know, I have the pride flag on my truck? Guess what? You don't get hamburgers tonight. I'll find somebody else that wants it."* Adele's rebellious claim that she will refuse to deliver her load if her lesbian identification is unwelcome demonstrates how persistence is linked to gender and sexuality. Whether she would actually refuse to deliver 80,000 pounds of meat and "find somebody else that wants it" is irrelevant. What matters is that she tells herself a story that makes her job *and* her sexuality possible. No woman can do this job—no person can do this job—without a large measure of patience, will, and ability to withstand harassment.

In twenty-first-century American work cultures—especially, but not exclusively, blue-collar work cultures—queer people, women, and racial and religious minorities all must fight to hold their own. Most of my narrators establish these skills long before seeking employment; they develop thick skins and bad attitudes before leaving grade school. Donovan stayed trucking for so long because she says she didn't expect to be *"coddled."* When she came out, her family disowned her, and she says she *"found [her] own way."* Then, when things got tough in trucking, she had no safety net but knew she had what it took to endure abuse.

To some extent, all truckers share this toughness, but my narrators report added layers of stigma, to which they respond with strength and pride. Ulrike got stranded in a snowstorm in Wyoming, trapped in her truck for days. She melted snow for water and had a store of canned goods in her cab that she says would have lasted long enough. *"But a local must have seen me, and they came to my truck with sandwiches on a horse,"* she says. *"When they knocked on my door, I was more scared than relieved, not knowing how they'd react when they saw I was a black woman. They did a double take, that's for sure! But then they laughed, and they rode out with food a few more times before I could get the truck clear to move on."* Neither the storm nor the fear of a white man on a horse slowed her down. Both her persistence and her obstacles, and those in so many other stories I heard, are as much about gender and race as they are about class.

9

STOPPING

WHAT'S YOUR TWENTY?

Locating the Queer Trucker's Body

CASEY HAD TO LEAVE TRUCKING because the constant vibrations destroyed her back, but, she adds, clutching didn't help. She says, *"My left knee—boy, it gets real sore some days, you know. It's the position of the shifter, and bending at your wrist and your fingers, that repetitive kind of crap, you know? Sometimes I wonder about other people who drove the model truck I was in. They say they come out okay, but how okay are they? How much do they feel? Sort of like a ballplayer that has concussions and broken bones and torn this and that, you know? I'm forty-five and I could barely get out of bed. So I think certain professions are just awful for our body."* Casey endured all these health problems before ultimately leaving, without taking any measures to address them. Part of trucker culture is to ignore the needs of your body. My narrators know that they eat poorly, sleep fitfully, don't exercise enough, and generally use their bodies hard.

Zoe says it's obvious that trucking is unhealthy. She says, *"I mean, you sit down all day, and you're clenched up and stressed out, and you got to eat like you're an escaped convict because you got to hurry up and be somewhere else . . . so heartburn and all that shit. You get to think in your head that you're invincible, and whatever is wrong you can fix it. That's why you got your drivers having diabetic comas and driving off into the woods and all that crazy shit."* When I ask if some of what she describes as willfulness is inability to keep medical appointments, Zoe says truckers try to avoid asking their companies to schedule around medical needs, because, she says, *"if you have too many doctor appointments, they're going to start working you off their truck anyway, because they don't want the liability."* To protect their jobs, then, truckers avoid seeking medical attention until they're desperate; my narrators take pride in enduring hardship, working through pain and exhaustion, and pushing themselves to the limits of endurance.

Because my narrators are gay, trans, and/or black, they simultaneously participate in a culture that forces the body and its needs into visibility. Here I need to separate the roles linked to sex and gender from those that are related to ethnicity and race. Coming out is often an experience of listening to your body, bringing what it says to the attention of a wider public, and insisting on its value. In contrast, racial identity isn't generally personally discovered or articulated, but it *is* usually visible, and it's part of how the world experiences you. Finally, all the women I interviewed, whether cis or trans, talked about how being in a female body in trucker space forced them to be constantly alert; it made their bodies inescapable.

Each of my narrators manages this contradiction differently. As truckers, they ignore their bodies, often to the point of illness or disability and even beyond. I wanted to sympathize with Christina about her cancer, but she had no time for that, and she shut me down instantly. At the same time, their bodies are a central canvas on which they project transness, queerness, Cree nationality, etc. They need this bodily truth seen and acknowledged, even when making it visible threatens their income and even their lives. This chapter describes how it feels to live these very physical contradictions.

Before they became truckers, my narrators' experiences as some form of outcast trained them to adapt to challenges and built up their resistance to hardship. Many—most—also juggle illness and disability. Even though truckers (especially gay, trans, and black ones) have attitudes that enable them to thrive under the increasing compression of regulations, often their bodies can't take it. No matter how badass you are, trucking has physical effects on your health. Spinal compression is one example; Reba tells me that *"truckers lose an average of one inch of height per ten years of driving,"* with widespread effects (see research by Jensen et al.). And the exhaustion and stress caused by Hours Of Service micromanagement, combined with the mounting parking shortages and decreasing pay, is linked to conditions like chronic obstructive pulmonary disease, hypertension, diabetes, and PTSD.

Trucking itself thus causes illnesses that, if untreated or inadequately addressed, can become disabilities. The Americans with Disabilities Act, passed in 1990, defines a disabled person as someone with "a physical or mental impairment that substantially limits one or more major life activities, a person who has a history or record of such an impairment, or a person who is perceived by others as having such an impairment" (U.S. Department of Justice). The physical labor of truck driving often qualifies workers to fit into this group; however, they don't see themselves this way. Truckers tend to resist labels and avoid medical intervention. Even when they would consider treatment for particular conditions, their constant mobility makes medical intervention next to impossible. Most truckers can't control their schedule enough to keep medical appointments even if they could afford to make them. Several narrators were forced to leave trucking at various points because their illnesses became too severe to continue driving. Others worry about this possibility constantly. Though disability may very well shape their lives, they rarely think of themselves as disabled and believe that the label would limit their ability to work, succeed, and feel pride.

The FMCSA maintains a list of "potentially disqualifying impairments" that justify pulling a trucker's medical card, thereby cutting off the trucker's income. The fear of this happening is as motivating as actual instances where it has happened, since epilepsy, seizures, and psychosis need to be demonstrated to justify termination. But that's on paper. In practice, truckers are routinely fired when they get sick. Maci tells me, *"I did lose my job at the mom-and-pop company when I got sick."* She thought she had cancer, but it turned out to be a treatable condition involving cysts. After surgery, however, she says, *"I couldn't walk, so basically I got fired. I didn't have anything to back my story up except all the doctor's excuses."* Maci doesn't claim that her condition was caused by trucking (though truckers do have inflated rates of cancer and related conditions), but she does claim that the company wouldn't honor its obligation to let her return to work once she recovered. She had to start again with a different company, losing income. Though trucking does directly disable truckers' bodies, it also works to hinder preventative or early medical care through practices like this. And the web of regulations that shapes trucking and more casual, covert practices like starving out truckers suspected of being medically risky, means that truckers need to ignore their health needs if they hope to keep trucking, and therefore earning.

One narrator, Patrick, had to leave trucking because he got hurt at work. He says, *"I was injured on the job. Disabled to a certain degree, I have 15 percent use of my right hand. My right hand was crushed; that was, like, the sign for me to let trucking go."* Patrick is retraining because of this, hoping to get into the web design field. Though an injury forced Patrick to leave, many truckers experience invisible but very challenging mental and physical health problems. Many experience PTSD, depression, or anxiety. Hypertension and carpal tunnel syndrome are common. Bladder problems and diabetes plague many women to the point that some, like Sisyphus, wear diapers while driving. Obesity and related joint problems are ubiquitous. Any of these conditions merit further study; we should understand how each one shapes truckers' lives and work, but I'll use obstructive sleep apnea as my example.

Machines on the Highway

A gay trucker who had worked many years as a maître d', teaching the staff of an elite club about etiquette so that their patrons get the dining experience they desire, was laid off and wound up trucking as a last resort. Hernando wound up liking trucking, though he finds the dirt (personal and environmental) hard to take. Certainly, the regulations drive him crazy. He says, *"The Hours of Service, taking the thirty-minute break, blah blah blah. I think Washington insiders are influenced by the lawyers and attorneys that sue insurance companies. If there's a truck accident, or there's a death, they are pressured to change the rules, and they don't have a clue what it's like. If they rode with you, for a week, driving in Chicago with a big truck? That would change everything. They increase regulations for more break time, required thirty-minute break, blah blah blah, but they haven't added any more parking, so go to a rest area in the middle of the night — and there's thirty truck spots, but there's ninety trucks there, parked all over the freeway, on the off-ramp and the on-ramp — and tell me how safe that is? I can see with CPAP [continuous positive airway pressure], with a sleep apnea type thing, if someone has problems, and they were tired and falling asleep behind the wheel, that would be a problem — but truckers have been driving with sleep apnea for many years and not had any problems."* He tries to identify a valid regulatory structure and briefly concludes that sleep apnea rules are there to protect truckers, but then acknowledges that it's just another bureaucratic smoke screen.

Obstructive sleep apnea (OSA) is a condition in which breathing stops during sleep. It's a serious impairment, and treatment helps many people immeasurably. People with OSA are often fatigued, since their sleep is interrupted frequently. If a test discovers OSA, the most common treatment is a CPAP machine, which is an electric device that continuously keeps the airway open, and thus the patient breathing. It's usually some form of mask, connected to a device that provides air pressure, and many people report that this treatment makes them more alert. However, the truckers I spoke to told me that practically every trucker tested got the diagnosis, and that these odds indicate that the routine testing for OSA required of truckers can be attributed to company profits rather than to trucker health. People who have never experienced sleep difficulties get diagnosed routinely and report that treatments interfere with their sleep as often as they help. I believe that most truckers diagnosed with OSA are fine; rather than benefiting from treatment, they are forced to comply with its coercive regime to keep their jobs.

Truckers are regulated by the U.S. Department of Transportation, which is a branch of the federal government. They do not benefit from protections other workers receive from the federal Department of Labor (the eight-hour work day, just for example). The DOT, in the name of highway safety, imposes a network of laws and rules on anyone who has a license to operate a vehicle over a certain weight. Most of the agency's attention was once focused on setting and adjusting freight rates, but now it leaves that to the market and focuses on micromanaging the daily life of truck drivers. For example, to qualify for a CDL you need to pass a medical exam. There are facilities near megacarriers and trucking terminals, and newly hired truckers get funneled to whichever office their company has an arrangement with. A nurse or certified nursing aide performs a battery of tests: blood sugar, blood pressure, vision, weight, neck circumference. Each new hire must also pass a physical test — lifting a certain weight at arm's length, crawling under a low table, climbing onto a platform, etc. When I did this, if a patient's neck circumference exceeded a set standard, the person was automatically referred for a sleep study. Since then, new guidelines stipulate that if your body mass index qualifies you as obese, you also must undergo a sleep study. Almost everyone who goes in for the sleep study gets the OSA diagnosis.

My narrators tell me that truckers get diagnosed with OSA so often because the people who run the sleep studies are the ones who sell CPAP paraphernalia, and they make a huge profit from truckers. The mask, air hoses, pressure machine, cleaning supplies, and other accessories must be purchased by the trucker and add up to a considerable expense. Other narrators say the best thing to do is research doctors in advance and be sure to find a facility that doesn't have a sleep clinic affiliated with it. If you find your own doctor, you don't need to use the one provided by your company. At least some doctors are not in line for CPAP kickbacks, according to the word on the highway. You then have to pay for the physical yourself, but that is cheaper than seeing the doctor your company pays for, getting the diagnosis, and then paying for the machine and keeping it supplied for the months and years to come. Once they buy the equipment, truckers need to clean it during their very brief breaks, in truck stop bathrooms. Unsanitary equipment is

I took this photo in 2016 at a truck stop in Iowa.
Most truck stops have similar displays.
(Photo by the author.)

commonplace. It causes sometimes serious health problems, ranging from sore and infected throats to pneumonia (Su et al.).

Sisyphus tells me: *"I'm under this CPAP rule, too, that they're really pushing down on all of us. So I have CPAP gear. It was bad enough I originally had to do a sleep study. Not because of any evidence I was having trouble sleeping or anything, but because of neck size. Then I had to buy a CPAP unit, and now they got me. Now I'm going to have to go in for another study because I need a new CPAP unit. So it's a moneymaker for them. And never with any evidence that driver exhaustion has anything to do with the sleep apnea. They still need to prove it. But they would rather set up these rules than deal with the issues that are causing driver exhaustion, like how they do the scheduling so one day you're driving at 7:00 a.m. and then the next day you don't drive till 5:00 p.m. and then you gotta bounce back to 7:00 a.m. They don't want to deal with that issue, which incidentally would cut into their profits, but they say they're serious about driver exhaustion, so they want everybody to get a CPAP machine."*

Truckers diagnosed with sleep apnea are required to be in compliance with a CPAP regimen. Their machines are wired into their home terminals, which send reports to the driver managers revealing how long the CPAP runs each night. People have told me there are ways to make the machine run without hooking it up to your face, but this takes ingenuity, and if you're caught, future trucking work is unlikely. Truckers need to power these machines somehow, and if there is no separate power source in their cabs, that's a problem. In many states, it's illegal to idle your engine, so you run the risk of depleting the truck's battery to run your CPAP. If you don't run it, you will get fired; if you do run the engine, you may get a very expensive ticket, for which you are personally responsible.

Dorothy, a trucker from Arkansas who drives high-value loads, is always armed, and has been trucking for more than forty years. She explains the OSA policy like this: *"You got your health issues, the BMI, the sleep apnea, but those people who are putting this forward, they're investors in these groups, just like [in] these onboard recorders. They're not interested in your safety, they want to make money. At my company we haul [loads worth] between $800,000 and $8 million, and you would think they'd be all over that stuff, but they're not. It is the companies covering their asses. They made [a friend] go for a sleep apnea test, and the sleep apnea was real borderline, but they made her do it. Well, now she's got to have that to get her DOT physical; she's got to turn her stuff in and be on that thing four hours a night. Does she really need it? She just did a study — no, she does not. But now she's got to buy the CPAP herself, she's got to pay them so much to read the stuff every week, and now they've got the fine system — if you don't do this, this, and this, then you've got to pay this amount every week. It's not about her getting rest, it's all about money."*

OSA is just one example of how trucking causes disability. In fact, like many blue-collar workers, truckers often become disabled by their jobs, though they don't typically see themselves as disabled or impaired because they need to keep working, in jobs that blame and target rather than support them. Rather, they become part of a structure in which they take responsibility for learning and following a regime of self-care and compliance. They see themselves as the only part of the structure that is going to flex, and they need the work, so they do what is necessary. The industry, the government, car drivers, doctors, receivers, etc. seem to be the problem, and truckers see themselves as the only solution, and they exercise the only freedom available to them by stepping up, by personalizing that role. Elise, a relentlessly cheerful lesbian, says that she's glad she went into trucking because she had lived her whole life without knowing she had sleep apnea but discovered it because of the required tests. Though she found the apparatus difficult to adjust to, and her partner calls her Snuffleupagus, she believes that it helps her. Since she would need to use it anyway, her cooperativeness is (among other things) a practical response to circumstances.

OSA and other trucking-related ailments are sometimes preexisting conditions that truckers then manage on the road. But they are sometimes caused by the regulatory shit storm of trucking, and these two causes are often hard to pick apart. Are the truckers' medical exams designed to identify or to cause OSA? And once truckers have OSA, pneumonia, or asthma, some seek treatment, but others conceal symptoms in order to keep working. This practice can cause increased health problems that can, in turn, be blamed on the structure of trucking culture.

When I was driving, I met a woman who did not become a narrator here but remained a friend. She started training and then driving at the same time I did, but she was teaming with her husband, and in many ways she had a more traditional trucker experience. She's a grandma, and she hoped the income from trucking would help the family get out of debt (credit card debt is a huge working-class stressor). She says that she got an OSA diagnosis during her training, and in order to keep her job she has to demonstrate compliance with CPAP. She tells me, "I was forced to take an apnea test. They claimed I had hypoxia, shallow breathing. I was forced to wear this god-awful contraption, which I cannot sleep with it on. I do my four hours a day with the machine to keep my DOT reports happy, but I'm not sleeping! Tossing and turning—then I sleep like a baby with it off!" This story and those from my narrators demonstrate that truckers understand what regulations like the sleep apnea bill (Public Law 113–45, which became effective in 2014) do and why: their bodies and lives are being managed for profit.

Illness, Insurance, and Home (Time)

What *is* known is that being queer, or trans, or black increases your chances of having a disability and of getting PTSD, hypertension, or any other illness. Trauma, stigma, discrimination, poverty, and their effects contribute to disproportional morbidity and mortality, which is discussed by public health scholars and sociologists. A good summary of this research, emphasizing both genetic and cultural effects and suggesting strategies to attain health equity, was published in 2014 by Karen Fredrickson-Goldsen et al. Being trans while trucking can further endanger health. One transwoman narrator kept in close touch with me when her second breast implant became dislodged and she bled several quarts into the footwell of the truck. She repeatedly called her dispatcher, who said she had to deliver the load before seeking medical attention. A serious infection had set in before she got medical help. She had to pay for the truck cleanup herself.

Being nomadic exacerbates physical disability, as does being queer, trans, black, and/or indigenous. Because you are in constant motion, you are seen as a threat—someone to be managed because you can't be controlled. Therefore, it's also true that being nomadic places the body in conditions of risk that can lead to disabling illness. Such nomadism is so engrained in the trucking lifestyle that it finds its way into the lingo. For example, when truckers ask "What's your twenty?" they mean "Where are you located?" But the irony is that as soon as they answer, their response is outdated, since they're constantly on the move. How does this chronic movement (geographical, personal, sexual) shape how truckers see and understand home? What sense of groundedness can they draw on? Many truckers are homeless before they start trucking, and when they drive, they have no home outside of their trucks. Some continue to have no residence other than their truck, and others are in it so much that it essentially becomes their home. There's a bed in the cab, food prep happens there, and truckers spend almost every minute of every day there. They get out to fuel, sometimes to pee, and every three or so days to take a shower. Occasionally, they spend a "reset" at a truck stop, at which point they might spend more time out of their truck, but even then, the truck is where most of their hours elapse.

Truckers typically do not have health insurance. The Affordable Care Act is no help to them, because they make too much money for subsidies (most truckers take home between $30,000 and $40,000 per year) but can't afford premiums. Jodie buys her own insurance, and its cost explains why her choice is rare. She says she pays *"$307 a week for family insurance, and that's for me and my children. Because none of my kids' jobs right now are offering them insurance, and to make sure they don't get messed with on their taxes, I put them on my insurance because I'm able to. I can keep 'em on till they're, like, twenty-five, twenty-six, so I'm lucky I'm able to put them in my insurance. I pay up the wazoo, but it helps them in the long run."*

Gloria Anzaldúa is a feminist philosopher who explores the borderlands between Mexico and the United States as they are experienced physically, mentally, sexually, and spiritually. To do this, Anzaldúa has developed a concept she calls "mestiza consciousness" to describe how being Indian in Mexican culture, Mexican in Anglo culture, and lesbian in both involves juggling and "a tolerance for ambiguity" (79). This concept helps me understand how culture positions truckers between public health regulations and difficult-to-access medical remedies, and how queer truckers manage this perilous positioning. Truckers' lives and jobs and Anzaldúa's mestizas are both defined by constant motion. This keeps truckers (especially, but not exclusively, the Mexican, indigenous, and immigrant ones) poised on a seesaw—never settled, never home. In addition to having geographic mobility, truckers dissolve borders between the public and private—their lives are unremitting challenges to that distinction. House equals job, bed equals vehicle. They can't retreat to a private sphere; being working class means their private world (to the extent that it exists) is much more permeable to government surveillance, and their bodies are much more likely to be colonized by the government's regulatory structures. These external border crossings also have internal, mental manifestations. As Anzaldúa describes it, being poised on this thin edge of barbed wire is a perilous type of identity, but one which makes a different way of being visible and possible; "though it is a source of intense pain, its energy comes from continued creative motion" (80). For truckers, isolation from and within culture is both dangerous *and* chosen, embraced, welcome. Nomadism becomes a type of home.

Truckers' Weight

The biggest predictors of obesity are poverty and food insecurity (Townsend et al.). People who study public health understand that these social determinants are predictors for morbidity and mortality on the population level. That is, when people don't know what or whether they can eat in the near future, their relationship to food is troubled. In our culture, we persist in seeing weight and food choice as personal, individual issues, and in tying them to moral virtue. Since ethnography relies on individual stories, it can reinforce that habit. Many of my narrators struggle with their weight and blame themselves for this—and I want to give their voices and interpretations space—but at the same time I also want to understand the causes and consequences of weight structurally.

There's a group on social media called "Meals for 18-wheels" that delivers holiday meals to truckers wherever they are and notifies the community when a trucker is stranded somewhere without food or the money to acquire it. Someone nearby, then, (hopefully) brings them a meal. This group's existence is all readers need to know about truckers and food insecurity.

The link between trucking and obesity is vexing, and truckers are often too willing to take responsibility for their weight rather than blame their schedules, food options, or stress. Jodie says, *"I'm borderline diabetic, my knees are shot, and that's from the oil fields, and climbing up and down on these trucks doesn't help. And my legs, they hurt constantly because of my knees. I've had one operation. I need to have another one, but I can't afford it. I cannot take time off work, I can't afford the copay just to go in the hospital and have the surgery done. I am a bigger woman, and from driving and everything, I've gotten even bigger. I try to get out in the evening, and I walk my dog, but there's times my legs hurt so much, I'm like, 'OK, go pee somewhere, I can't do anymore today.' And that's frustrating. I do cook in my truck a lot; I have a refrigerator that my family gave me for Christmas — it's one of those dorm refrigerators — and then I've got my microwave and stuff, so I mean I've got a lot better setup than a lot of people do, and I know that. I'm able to save money by cooking for myself, and plus I get so sick of this food out here. But still, I'm having a lot of hard times with my health right now, and it's scary for me. My mother died at forty-eight; I'm forty-five. And it was from health reasons, so now I'm getting older, so I'm starting to get scared. I can't afford really to go to the doctor's, because it's so expensive."* I'm appalled to hear this, given what she pays per week for insurance, but she points out that she has a $6,000 a year deductible before the insurance kicks in, so every visit costs several hundred dollars before insurance helps at all — and it's money that she doesn't have.

Research published in 2014 on obesity among truckers concludes that "69 percent of LHTD [long-haul truck drivers] were obese compared to 31 percent in the U.S. adult working population" (Sieber et al., 620). These researchers go on to note that "even with a preponderance of health risk factors, fully 83 percent of LHTD perceived their health to be excellent, very good, or good" (623). There is hand-wringing about this, since the authors observe that, statistically, people who think they're healthy don't get medical care. I agree that truckers don't get enough medical care, and many have health problems, but I resent the way this research personalizes that and links it to poor education rather than scheduling or financial problems. With precious little research about truckers and trucking, obesity is what gets attention. This pattern reinforces, rather than analyzes, emphasis on body size as a personal effect rather than a structural consequence.

Truckers' lives are, as readers now know well, thoroughly regulated and restricted, and they respond with all the grace and attitude imaginable. Some do manage to exercise, and some stay within normal weight. But most don't. Ulrike says, *"[I] was up in Carlisle, Pennsylvania, and I was trying to walk because I'd gained so much weight. And as I was walking, I come across the street from the truck stop, and there's a police officer sitting in the car so I said hello, and I forced him to say hello to me. And by the time I got back to the street, there was three white guys in a car and they're yelling, 'Hey, nigger, what are you doing on our street?' They tried to run me over. They tried to run. Me. Over. With a car. I was running in the street to get back to my truck, and the cop was sitting right there and he never moved, he just sat there and watched. So. I have had people let their dog loose on me. You can't be black and walking where you want in this country. You just can't."* None of the African American truckers I met felt safe exercising in the locations where they wound up; they typically minimized time outside their trucks in order to avoid incidents like this, which are not rare.

Alix ties weight to driving and to other anxieties. He says he's always struggled with obesity. *"But trucking does not help with my weight at all,"* he says. *"In fact, since I started driving, I have actually put on, like, forty pounds or so. And of course, being so overweight, it was starting to affect other things—skin issues, thyroid issues—so that certainly didn't help it, and I'm kind of paranoid that I'll have a heart attack or something and not come home to my kids because I'm so overweight. My biggest fear, though, is postmortem consumption by canine, because I have a dog that rides with me, and I'm terrified that I'm going to die in the truck, and my dog is going to eat me before they find me. My friends always tease me about this, but I don't want to be eaten by my dog before they find me if I die. I just don't."* He laughs. *"But I'm worried about heart issues, and things that my weight doesn't help, and so I'm actively working to lose that."* Stress is also probably a factor: Alix maintains two separately gendered lives, since his kids and other family members don't know he's trans.

Truckers hear the messages of mainstream culture and the media that insist weight is a matter of personal control and a moral issue. Yolanda speculates: *"I would say exercise is the main enemy of trucker health. A lot of obesity and high blood pressures and cholesterol and those kind of things—so yeah, I think you're more at risk of being out of shape and not eating healthy, being in*

Alta's pride, strength, and experience radiate.
(Used with permission of the subject.)

a truck. There's a lot of boredom so there's a lot of snacking, and that's no good. So it does take some discipline, trying to eat some good things, and stopping."

However, truckers also critique the system that profits by regulating them. Isabella says, *"Now at the DOT physical, they measure your neck, and I said, 'Well, what's that for?' And they said anyone whose neck measures over such and such circumference is being recommended for a sleep apnea test. I'm like, well, shouldn't they be asking something else: Do you snore? Do you have problems during the day? If you have a thick neck, why don't they recommend you for twenty minutes' exercise a day? What about these people who are morbidly obese—are you recommending any diet and exercise thing?"* "Why?" indeed. By placing blame, they can sell products.

The disability theorist Alison Kafer observes that in some utopian fantasy fiction, disability gets eliminated: medical and genetic technologies presumably engineer away people with disabilities. Kafer points out how much would be lost in a world that exorcizes the creativity and beauty of disability. She suggests that we should understand disability instead "as a set of practices and associations that can be critiqued, contested, and transformed" (9). This process lets us ask how some bodies and styles come to seem natural, how this process gets manifested as a relation of power, and what seems or feels possible in response. By this reasoning, maybe disability isn't only an alternative to bureaucratic entrapment, not just a strategy for imagining other more cooperative ways to be human, but also a *result* of it—something it produces. As such, it will never be eliminated.

There is a relationship between bodies and bureaucracies. The morbidity and mortality of working-class and poor people from cancer and other major illnesses is disproportional in the population (Dizikes). Additionally, as Virginia Eubanks demonstrates, "The most sweeping digital surveillance technologies are designed and tested in what could be called 'low rights environments'—poor communities, repressive social programs, dictatorial regimes, and military and intelligence operations." I'm arguing here that these trends are related; that surveillance and illness are interconnected. Whenever Reba passes a car or drives in a way that might irritate someone, she worries that they might pick up their phone, call the number printed on her truck, and complain. She and all truckers live with the stress of being subject to constant job evaluation by largely uninformed reviewers. How many workers perform their job duties in public space, with the contact information of their supervisor visible, and the general public encouraged to call and complain? Being watched, measured, and managed, being constantly observed and judged, and being kept in motion while being criticized for transience all foster a lingering dis-ease, and contribute to disability.

My narrators respond to this barrage of stress and surveillance, and the illness it causes, strategically and effectively, but there's still a cost. They could contribute to, and benefit from, disability culture and activism. But there's a problem of communication. Disability culture doesn't reach poor people or truckers any more than queer studies or feminist theory do. Truckers are trying to control their circumstances and live their lives. We need to find a way to hear what they can give us and then work together as a group. They resist seeing themselves as members of groups such as people with disabilities or queers—we need to listen to their reasons and understand how they do see and imagine their contributions and potentials. When I point out to Gabrielle and Xena that many of the trucking problems they describe would be solved by widespread unionization, they agree. But Gabrielle responds, *"I'm wondering if you are ever going to get through to truckers, 'cause if you have to stereotype truckers, they tend to be lone rangers, and the idea of having to join a group or pull together or—"* Xena cuts in with *"Never—it would not work,"* and Gabrielle finishes by noting, *"You know, they are always looking out for themselves. I got my own back, nobody's got my back, I got my own back. I think that would be a way to generalize truckers: very difficult to get them to join a group."*

Xena is correct that one reason truckers don't organize to try to improve their health and working conditions is that they are temperamentally disinclined to group identification, and their companies feed the racism that undergirds that. Yet queer, trans, and black truckers wouldn't identify themselves in these terms if they didn't see themselves as part of a group, and specifically a group linked to embodied experience. Big-rig culture as a whole erases the body because, though the work causes disability, it sheds workers before their oppression (bodily and otherwise) can bring them together. Gina points out that the truck as a structure, specifically the seat and pedal design, is not built for her *"short legs and fat ass,"* so some bodies are eliminated by default. But simultaneously, my narrators can't forget their bodies—the culture constantly sees and won't let them forget their gender, race, fragility. Alix, a transman, experiences this enforced bodily awareness, saying, *"Work is incredibly stressful, especially with the recent uproar over the transgender restroom issue that people are blowing up. While there are a lot of LGBT members out here driving a truck, even more are the old-school, red-necky, antigay types, and God forbid—pardon my French—God forbid there be a faggot in the restroom with them. It's those kind of attitudes that make me concerned for personal safety. I mean, really, I have to watch myself; I'm always looking over my shoulder because of the attitudes and politics, especially in this last year. I do worry about safety because there's always going to be those crazies. I feel like there's more of a target on my back."* This awareness of personal safety contrasts with Alix's normal willingness to sacrifice his body to the truck. He tells me a story of having a kidney stone, calling dispatch, and agreeing to pass the load off to another driver before going straight to the emergency room.

Donovan needs hormone treatments for trans reasons, and when her company doesn't get her home for those appointments, she suffers emotionally, and the resulting anxiety has led to road accidents. She also describes less dramatic issues: *"From not being able to pee, I now have bladder issues, and I had to go to the ER a number of months ago because I was peeing blood. And I was expected,"* she laughs bitterly, *"to deliver the load before I could go to the ER. They don't care about your health in this industry. I don't know if this is the same for, like, all cis women, but for me, our terminals, they have free showers there, but they don't have a mirror and a sink in there. You have to go do your makeup and get ready in front of everyone else. I don't want to do that."* She slides from the brutal story of delaying emergency medical attention to her unwillingness to perform personal grooming in shared space. By putting these two stories in parallel, she demonstrates that her body's demands matter only when gender and sexuality render them dangerous. These two examples feel so different to nontruckers, but for Donovan, they are part of the same conversation: her body is invisible even in acute medical crisis, and the only thing that makes it visible is gender transgression.

Lori is a transwoman who says her experience on the truck and at truck stops is no different from any other woman's. She tries not to signal that she is alone in the truck, and *"that's pretty much what I go through, and it's just all about safety to be honest,"* she says. *"There's a lot of prostitution at the truck stops, and I always try to wear my company ID and a safety vest so that people who see me don't think that I'm a prostitute. Even with the police at the truck stop, I try to always make sure they know I'm a driver and not a hooker."* On the one hand, this is a straightforward story about survival strategies. On the other hand, it radically shifts what is being protected, and from whom. Truckers have safety vests (typically yellow with reflective strips) so that they can be seen in truck stops and customer spaces. Imagine a person surrounded by enormous machines being reversed by people with minimal visibility, who are often exhausted at the end of very long workdays and always work under time pressure. Truckers are run over and killed in these spaces routinely. But what reminds Lori to wear her safety vest isn't the vulnerability of her body to this deadly force; it's how being female makes her visible on a different register if she doesn't. Lori has been incarcerated and done sex work as a dominatrix, so she is familiar with managing her body in threatening circumstances. Though truckers who are sexual or racial minorities must ignore the demands of their bodies in order to keep their jobs, and added layers of stigma add to their exploitation, being visibly outside trucker culture via their bodies shifts what their bodies mean, and how they understand them. Lori wears her safety vest not to make her visible to reversing truckers, but to make her invisible to police searching for sex workers. Trucking doesn't allow Lori to forget that her body communicates, and so she needs to maintain some control over what it says.

Many of the claims and descriptions in this chapter, and this book, are true of all truckers. The messages that truckers get from regulations, their companies, and our culture encourage them to neglect their bodies and wear themselves out until they become disabled or die. However, my narrators are also subject to an additional set of messages about their bodies: that they're dangerous, disgusting, desirable. My job here is not to explain or understand these contradictory messages (which they do far better than I could) but rather to broadcast them: to honor the messy experience of someone like Lori, Marilu, or Donovan.

CONCLUSION

Hammer Down

BOTH AN ADVERB AND AN IMPERATIVE, "hammer down" means to go fast. A truck can be moving "hammer down," and one trucker can instruct another to "hammer down." Speed is thus the job's requirement, but also one of its chief joys. For marginalized truckers, acceleration is an empowering response to mistreatment in other work and social settings, but it also becomes its own trap, since constant rushing becomes the job's imperative. In my conclusion, I use this slang to invoke the countless truckers currently driving "hammer down." For them, it doesn't end. I use the term also, ironically, to signal the coming demise of trucking as we know it, transformed already by the changes I've described and facing the inevitable introduction of autonomous cabs. And it's not just a job that will collapse, because trucking is a way of being in the world and one of the few remaining meaningful employment options for the people who turn to it.

Any job shapes the life, identity, and sexual styles of its workers in one way or another, but since trucking offers essentially no downtime and minimal existence outside of the job, this effect is magnified for truckers. Trucking consumes your life, which isn't necessarily a bad thing. Echo describes how trucking over the road is a form of employment that facilitates personal exploration: *"I do a lot of research about aboriginals. I meet other tribes when I'm out here, and if I can, I take a secondary highway and travel through a reserve, or a colony. I find that different places and areas of the country have different ways of calling where they live. I got a surprise that the Shoshone in western Nevada call themselves colonies — I thought, 'Whoa! Not too far from the tree on that one.' I can focus on my own interests. The best way to meet other tribes is to go to their casinos, so I go there, and there's huge parking lots that are made just for the trucks, and truckers get discounts. I'm not actually a gambler, thank goodness, but some offer twenty or forty dollars free play for a CDL license, so I'll do that, and I'll wander around. I found a plaque in one that says 'General Custer came through here on the way to meet hostile Indians,' so I took a picture of that, and I enjoy little snippets of American history, seen through the lens of, obviously, the settlers. But I'm getting a little groove now when I go to a new tribal center. I just walk in and say, 'I'm a trucker, Cree Nation,' and I just wander around and try to meet other people, learn what they're up to. Most people are pretty interested in talking to me. But I didn't know that some of these tribes even existed. We just know what we see on TV, like, everyone's a Cherokee it seems. So for now, while I'm learning, I actually have my own theater kind of character, trickster, who demonstrates what it means to be aboriginal today and what it might mean for the future."*

Doing this driving and exploring while gay, trans, or a racial minority has two simultaneous yet contradictory effects: my narrators feel alienated from and critical of the people and places within which they circulate, *and* they fit in well because their distance isn't visible the way it is in more urban and middle-class spaces. Both experiences are real, and the friction between them is what sparks — and sometimes explodes — into moments of cultural awareness. This transformative potential of queer trucking is a lot like air brakes. The brake system on cars is hydraulic; lubricant is housed in a master cylinder under the hood, from which it runs in lines to slave cylinders in the wheels, which (when the brake pedal starts a chain reaction) expand to compress pads or shoes onto rotors or drums. It's a precise, closed system. Big rigs use an air-brake system instead. Air is built up and stored, under pressure, and when you mash the brake petal, it gets forced through lines into a similar system of cylinders, pads, and rotors. The air hoses can easily be moved from one trailer to another, using a set of couplings called gladhands. This system is easier and cheaper than a hydraulic system because you can't just detach part of a hydraulic system — it must remain sealed so air doesn't get into the lines and brake fluid doesn't get out. With air, that's not a problem. Air can escape the lines whenever — it's just air. New air is then compressed when the lines are reattached, and the system is ready. However, air brakes easily burst into flames. If a trucker applies the brakes going downhill, the pads and/or shoes can get hot and soft, decreasing brake power. If they get too hot and there are any sparks in their vicinity, they can ignite. This is not a rare event, and it serves as a powerful metaphor for the transformative power of truckers, forced into difficult circumstances and ready to explode.

One form this explosion can take is by igniting questions that unsettle. What does it mean to have your body, sexuality, job, and time regulated by corporations and the government that nurtures them? How does that feel? Why are some forms of regulation visible and some not? The truckers' stories raise questions about what it means to be human. Truckers need to be regulated more than many other laborers because of what they do, but we should start by regulating the corporations and the industry, not by regulating the driver. Further, we should realize that the structure of trucking means the regulations of the work penetrate truckers' whole lives in ways that feel intrusive. When that is added to the micromanagement and surveillance directed at gay, trans, and black bodies in the twenty-first century, you have an intolerable situation. Up until now, truckers have used their skills of adaptation, absorption, and perseverance to prevent the brake fire, though at significant personal cost. Is the moment coming where instead, they will fight back; burst into flames; stop driving?

This book tries to understand how trucking feels — how a small cluster of people living at the intersection of multiple regulatory regimes understand their day-to-day experience. How they respond is important because they are people and they matter. Further, they inhabit an extreme, vanguard version of a world we all share. As surveillance technology clamps down on our lives, bodies, and jobs, we will need the strategies that truckers have developed. They have much to teach us about a resistance that is particular, mobile, funny, and effective. Their stories are their escape, and their freedom.

Are gay people — gay Americans like Walt Whitman or Christina — positioned by some magical congruence of sex acts and cultural outsiderness to see and understand the embodied nature of experience? Are trans people like Kate Bornstein or Felicity primed to resist regulatory systems by virtue of having unregulatable bodies? Are immigrants and queer border dwellers like Gloria Anzaldúa or Echo kept in a state of perpetual unbelonging that challenges our very understanding of home and of place? There isn't one special magic formula. I know that. But there are predispositions. As we all move through this century of increasing precarity and vulnerability, constant motion might be our best option.

Casey, forced to retire by trucking-related disability, uses narrative to construct geographical, national, embodied meaning. She says, *"I grew up a farm kid, so I love the crops, the seasons. I would talk to my dad from the road, asking things like, 'I'm down in Florida, and I saw this plant that looks like corn but it's got this cone-looking thing at the top that's where the tassel's supposed to go, it's not very high up,' and he goes, 'That's sorghum.' I say, 'You serious?' and then I remember hearing the words 'sorghum honey' somewhere, and now I know what it is: it's a type of corn, just a little different than the corn we have up here. I was always looking on the road, my eyes dancing around, always looking at the craziest things. I remember being in Oklahoma or Texas, on the east side, driving down a state route, and seeing this property that was kind of like that miniseries called* Dallas, *with this big beautiful home and a big field. And out at the front, maybe fifty feet from the property line, was a beat-up-looking trailer, older than hills, and these little kids, in just diapers playing in their front yard of dirt—and I mean dirt, they were dirty little kids. You know, somewhere, that man or woman in there works for that property owner. And this is where they live, and this just . . . and the difference. It just was offensive to me. I felt really bad.*

"*So, some of what we see is the worst of society, in that sense, when you're going down these roads. I think where I started really seeing it were these towns of poverty. I would drive by these towns, and storefronts were closed, and you were going through nothing, a few buildings, and what looked like a gas station, and then there was nobody there. I mean, there were houses, but nobody, nothing there, nothing left. I live in South Carolina, but I never knew that there were towns that were exclusively black, next door to towns that were exclusively white, and when you look at that disparity, you're like, 'Oh my god, how do people live like that?' I had grown up up north, so I didn't see that kind of thing.*

"*I got an education while I was out on the road; a different education about what life was about, how things were for people. What poverty felt like. What an education, for me—there was so much good about it. And yes, I hated dispatchers, you know, and shippers and receivers have had a whole damn yard empty and won't let you park there so you can get your sleep. At Ford Motor Company in Atlanta, I make a delivery at this huge property in downtown Atlanta. I came in there and told them, 'Please unload me quickly so I can go get a place before my hours run out,' and of course I sat there for four hours. So then I said, 'There's plenty of places out here, can you just let me pull up? I don't wanna go out illegal, I may get a ticket, have an accident or something, I may lose my job out of this deal.' He says, 'You cannot park here. We don't care. It's not our problem.' That's what they say, and Congress can fix that, to make us safe, mandating if you have a property with room for a driver to sleep, give up that area and let them park. If you think they're lying to you, ask for their logbook. It isn't too hard to figure out they had been driving for eleven hours—you can see that clearly on their mark, that they're not supposed to be driving anymore. Let them sleep. But they won't do that, of course. They're just going to keep restricting us and not solve the problem. You know, you gotta go to the people that will fix this. They don't wanna mess with the shippers or receivers 'cause then they'll have another reason to charge us this much money for products, you know, so yep, that's the way it is.*"

I've quoted Casey at length because the flow of her narrative from adventure and education to regulations and hostile shippers and receivers that constrain her life is significant. Trucking gets restricted because of what Casey's education involved: truckers learn how this country works. They understand our culture's covert narrative: where stuff comes from and what struggles and inequalities undergird that. Culture seeks to silence and curtail anyone with that knowledge, and motion is the only effective resistance.

For Casey, as for Echo, going places—moving across and through the country—makes a kind of belonging possible. It allows truckers to understand, rather than simply inhabit, the country. Often, nonurban, noncoastal America feels pushed aside and rendered invisible and irrelevant. For truckers, Americanness coheres as a resistance to metronormativity—a resistance that takes the form of personal mobility and sexual indeterminacy. Xena says that during *"the first few years driving, it's more exciting."* She adds, *"There's still so much going on we'd never seen, we never knew that world existed. You go out, you see the people, you see the lifestyle, you see how they do, you live in a truck. The first night we went out and we picked up pharmaceuticals in New Jersey. . . . I'm thinking of the first time that you sleep on the side of the road—it's just weird feeling that 'Oh no, we can't sleep here.' . . . Those kind of thing, you have to live it to really know it."*

The connection between motion and excitement, motion and change, motion and brakes/breaks, motion and sex unfolds in the experiences of these sixty-six queer, trans, and minority truckers. In part of a new anthology about the rural queer experience, Ryan Powell analyzes two hardcore porn films about a trucker named Hank, observing that their "portrayal of underground networks of male-male desire that exist in the unmarked, uncharted, and ambiguous 'here' of spaces that are literally in-between (the road, the desert, the truck-stop) carve out ideological spaces where contradictory modes of gender and sexuality can flourish" (194). Powell seems surprised that these modes intersect in blue-collar, trucker space, leading him to identify as "contradictory" the intersection of gayness and truckers, or "man's men." His surprise lingers even though he understands that metronormative ways of having and doing sexuality make nonurban modes of sexual contact invisible or devalued. Blue-collar queers are easy to not see, and thus easy to be surprised by. When we fail to see nonurban queers because we don't know what to look for, or how to understand what we're seeing, or (less generously) because they don't conform to our idea of what "good" queers are and do, we reinforce their invisibility. More important, we fail to learn what they know about resistance, persistence, and pleasure.

The people whose stories fill this book are neither rural nor urban, but rather both, constantly, endlessly circulating. This mobility carries over into how they do sex, gender, race, embodiment. And it is not new. Truck stops, interstates, and casinos have long been locations of sex and risk that don't conform to binary distinctions between straight and gay, man and woman, native and colonizer. John Howard studies the history of roadside parks as they emerged in the 1930s, claiming that men found sex there because "the road for queer Mississippians was less an escape to the seclusion of nature, than a material ingress to a busy network of men and would-be women, homosexuals and trans-sexuals, persons of varied identities and sexualities" (113). You can't leave your house and come back a month later and expect it to be the same. And when you're out there, this motion, this constant change, is anonymizing and therefore freeing. These structural attributes of trucking work challenge binaries, and truckers are not allowed to forget this. Their bodies record it, and they live in it every day.

I began this book by asking whether recent changes in the trucking workforce and the concurrent increase of regulations on truckers and trucking were related, and how. The constant queer circulation enacted by trucking resists (if only accidentally) the increasing surveillance culture. That this surveillance is universal but more fiercely enforced as one's access to power and options diminishes, helps explain the concurrence of these two shifts. Effective resistance to state power (and to corporate and social power sometimes disguised as governmental authority) engenders systematic state countermeasures, ranging from heel dragging to legislative micromanagement. The cowboy renegade trucker had escaped this state backlash for eons by keeping moving and thus being a) less threatening as a result of being decoupled to geography and the iconography of home and b) more difficult to locate and control. As these roles are increasingly occupied by bodies identified as outside the norm (by culture, if not by themselves), the state compulsion to regulate goes into panic mode and doubles down.

This approach can backfire. Doubling down and escaping are maneuvers that truckers are familiar with — that they even invented. Further, many aspects of trucking have persisted while the world evolves around them. Just for example, truckers are paid on a piecework model. Truckers are paid by the mile, not the hour, in a country where that pay structure was deemed exploitative and legislated away almost a century ago. The trucking industry lobbied so that it could keep this unfair system in place, but why did the lobby's vision prevail? When salaries or hourly pay became the national standard, why didn't this extend to truckers, who work countless unpaid hours at shippers and receivers, and whose income is shaped by weather, traffic, vehicle maintenance, road accidents, and other vicissitudes of fortune?

Often, they keep rolling through dangers because they must to survive. Even though this is obviously an exploitative and dangerous policy, the country holds onto it because it doesn't know, and because this keeps the price of everything lower. Truckers themselves embrace it because it gives them some measure of autonomy.

This stasis persists in a culture and a time where change is ubiquitous. As Jack Halberstam summarizes, "Change has occurred on account of the boom/bust economy; advances in computer technology; new medical research; increased mobility; new forms of social contact and social networking; new modes of media including Twitter feeds; new levels of media surveillance and intrusions and new forms of social control; etc." (xx). Halberstam adds that, given this sweeping change, how we understand genders, norms, and intimacies is up for grabs as well. For truckers, sex has in some ways remained consistent. Like piecework pay, truck stop sex is ongoing. How it is seen and understood both by the general public and by the truckers who engage in it has shifted considerably.

As the cultural definitions of what counts as gay, what counts as sex, and how to do gender have shifted, trucking culture hasn't. Truckers don't understand getting a "lube job" at a rest stop, from a person of any gender, as having sex—it's mechanical, not intimate or erotic; its slang name is not an accident. There is a long history of both escape and pleasure linked to the road, and much of that pleasure involves same-sex encounters and gender variance. I had to work hard to build trust with my first intersex narrator, so that I could include her story. But as my research progressed, about 10 percent of my narrators identified as intersex. Perhaps intersex people responded early and disproportionately to my outreach efforts. But I came to believe that there's something in the circulation of trucking—the way that it reconfigures belonging as a process rather than a place—that draws intersex people in and sustains and nurtures them. Similar fits may occur for indigenous people, trans folks, mestizos, immigrants—people whose bodies straddle borders and who don't follow rules well.

Outsiders have always dominated trucking. What's different now is not so much how they see themselves as how they are understood; that is, they now look like a threat because they are no longer invisible (read: white, male, straight) and so they must be contained. Mainstream culture now has a vocabulary with which to name and harass trans people, and that makes it harder (and often less honorable) for them to remain invisible. The web of laws and regulations attempting to regulate truckers clamps down harder and harder until some leave and others find a way to sidestep . . . dance . . .

The author with Idella Hansen. (Photo by Avi Balay-Wilson,
used with permission of the subject.)

keep their trucks, and their culture, moving. One unfortunate effect is the
habit of truckers to blame other truckers (principally Muslims and Mexicans,
sometimes women, people of color, and queers) for calling this regulatory
shit storm down on all of them. One fortunate effect is how many truckers
craft a way out: they've been keeping their wheels rolling for decades under
ever-increasing stress, and they have moves, sexual styles, perseverance, and
humor that we all can copy and learn from.

Dolly Parton, in an interview with Barbara Walters in 1977, explains why
she doesn't mind the travel required by her work: "You need it, it's a way
to survive, just like truck drivers, the motion under your feet or the wheels
rollin'; I like it." She segues to a conversation about her breasts and her extreme styles. Parton emphasizes her inner realness and how she uses humor
to engage the public and make fun of herself. She emphasizes sexual and
stylistic freedom and links it to ambition. Trucking is an obvious metaphor
for her to use to describe this complex web of classed embodiment.

Marilu tells me, *"Years ago, I was on hormones, but not as good looking as I
am now. I was on final probation again because I had failed a DOT inspection.*

I got ticketed because I had gone a little over in my logbook. But my company didn't want to fire me, so they put me on second probation again, said, 'Now you've really, really got to watch yourself.' So I was driving up in Wisconsin, and this cop pulled me over. I was bobtailing, and my tractor was governed at sixty-five, so I couldn't have been going that fast, but the speed limit was under sixty-five, so. But when the cop came up to me, I just started bawling. I couldn't help it. He said, 'What's up with you?' all shocked. I said, 'I can't get another ticket. I just can't. They'll fire me, and then I'll starve.' He looked in at me and said, 'OK, well, what's with the clothes?' I was still crying, and I said, 'I'm fucking transgender.' He said, 'Oh my God, we just had a training on that. Transgender sensitivity training. You're my first.' He seemed just so excited to meet someone to practice on. He didn't write me a ticket or nothing. He didn't hug me when he was leaving or nothing, but I had this feeling that he wanted to. And that's the only time I used crying to get out of a ticket." Marilu brags about her sexual exploits on the road, and about her freedom to do all this while aggressively, visibly trans. But this story has a different valence; someone was happy to see her out there on the road because he wanted to demonstrate tolerance — to be modern. Like every other incident, she weaves this into a narrative of the gendered subversion of norms, and of personal victory.

Marilu's story illustrates how both gender and sexual norms and the trucking industry are changing as the twenty-first century unfolds. Trucking is now called "logistics." Its new identity is intrinsically linked to surveillance technologies, global positioning systems and their satellites, and online personnel management regimes like E-Verify. These all seem like new technologies, but they in turn are about to be eclipsed by autonomous trucks. Soon, most highway trucking will be done by computer, and if humans are present, they will be low-wage, unskilled workers. The few remaining truckers will move freight between large yards on the fringes of cities and its destinations within cities. Short hops only. Available jobs in the trucking industry will be in technology: manufacturing computers, programming and updating them, troubleshooting, and managing logistics. Computers require personnel-heavy maintenance, but these jobs aren't available to the kind of people who drive trucks. A diesel engine and the mechanical systems that support it are comprehensible to most truckers, at least on some level. Computerized trucking builds in many more failure points, inaccessible to even wily drivers. Tech jobs consist of second-order tasks instead of immediate ones, and the working class gets lost in this transition. What was a last-choice job for queer, trans, and minority workers will soon evaporate, leaving millions of people with no means of support.

Looking back at these stories, and at the experience of collecting them and weaving them into the narrative stream of this book, I'm struck by their sadness and by how that's counteracted on the personal level with joy, movement, community, power, and love. No matter what, the truckers have fun. But the frustration that I and my narrators have with the trucking industry, and the deep and systemic institutions that grind people's lives into dust, is not counteracted. As long as Citizens United (a ruling from 2010 that equates corporations with people, thus unleashing their lobbying power) continues to magnify the voices of corporations in legislation and policy, and as long as truckers are a stigmatized segment of the workforce, the megacarriers will get their way, and individual truckers will suffer. As technological change sweeps us all along, it will usher in increased surveillance technologies, which disproportionately affect low-status citizens like truckers. None of this is encouraging. At the same time, I remember the words of Dorothy when discussing taking on a new challenge: *"I'd have jumped right in the middle of that because I've got a lot of common sense; I wouldn't have hesitated a minute. But like I've said time and time again, big equipment, outdoor moving equipment, forklifts—if it's got a key I can run it. Might take me a while, but I can run it."*

That last sentence is where hope sparks, and where a brake fire might erupt. The truckers I know are currently pressing hard to get the government to change course on whether they can be paid for nondriving worked hours. Without going into detail (since the terms and issues will certainly have changed by the time you're reading this), truckers are fighting for the right to collect pay for their meal, break, and waiting time. They want an hourly pay system to be triggered when they are on breaks or waiting to get loaded or unloaded, but the American Trucking Association is resisting by pushing through infrastructure amendments to outlaw any pay structures other than piecework for truckers anywhere in the United States. Ever. Truckers are training each other on social media platforms and hiring graphic artists to create flowcharts that explain the American Trucking Association's plan as it will affect trucking pay and work flow. They are working together to defeat this measure with a new level of unity. What draws me to ethnography is the beauty and poetic range of each particular, grainy story. But what keeps me committed is the process whereby individual stories generate collective action—and political change. It's not a fast process, but it is a powerful one. As Dorothy says, *"Might take me a while, but I can run it."*

ACKNOWLEDGMENTS

SIXTY-SIX PEOPLE contributed their time, their lives, and their whole selves to this book. Just because I asked. My sincere thanks go to them, and I want them all to know that they taught me volumes about courage, humor, and survival. Many have become my friends, and all are my heroes.

I wrote the book in conversation with the people in it, and with a circle of friends and colleagues. I have known Jane Kauer since I was sixteen, and her presence in Philadelphia is one of its chief pleasures. She read every word at least three times and talked me through difficult patches in the revision process. I owe so much of the final version to her. Jesse Shipley single-handedly brought me to Philadelphia and has fostered my career and believed in my work steadfastly. He helped me think through several early ideas, even some unrelated to Bourdieu's baseball article. John D'Emilio has supported my work since before I became an oral historian and gave me the initial confidence to make the switch. He read a late draft carefully and critically, inspiring changes and improving the final version immensely. Linda Gerstein has become my closest friend at Haverford. She read the book and gave important feedback, feeds me often, and connects me to people and ideas that keep me believing in what I do. Finally, Mark Simpson-Vos took on not only this project but also me with patience and enthusiasm. When I began work on the book I didn't have a job or a coherent scholarly community, so an editor who believed in my work and would help me figure out how to make it a reality was a remarkable gift. No author could ask for more helpful mentoring, or more generous friendship.

My children repeatedly drove me to inconvenient locations so I could get in trucks with strangers and ride off into the sunset. They have paid early and continuously for my unconventional career choices, but rather than complaining, they respect me and my work. Emma and Avi are responsible for who I am, how I fight, and what I love. My father died while I was finishing revisions on this book. He demonstrated how to be an ethical worker and never stopped worrying about how I would support myself. My sister, Jean, has talked to me continuously about being a woman in a man's job and being a Balay in a hostile world. These people are my home.

Librarians and the scholars they have connected me to have made writing this book a collective, generative process. Since I still lack a permanent job, my dispersed support network has been invaluable. Gwynneth Cowley and Tim Young at Yale suggested I contact Mona Shattell, who became a collaborator and good friend. Karen Nakamura, Terry Snyder, E. Patrick Johnson, Virginia Costello, Riva Lehrer, Chris

Roebuck, Shana Goldin-Perschbacher, Margaret Schaus, Harrison Apple, Karey Bacon, and Kathleen McGee have all engaged me in conversations about trucking endlessly, and got me to books, people, and places that would help me with thinking and writing about them. Patty Wright designed the graphics with patience and skill. Cate Hodorowicz at UNC Press gave the manuscript a careful revision that not only located problems but also explained how to fix them.

Miriam Frank and Desma Holcomb became my friends after my last book. They help me think about organized labor, and they connect me to a community of LGBT workers that fuels all my writing. Jimbo Lane inspired my first book, and when I didn't get tenure he fought for me fiercely, paying a high price for his advocacy and earning my undying love. The Prindle Institute provided weeks of writing time and vital early feedback. The friends I made there are inarticulate cucumbers. Kaziah White did some transcribing for me and became my first real connection to Haverford College. Kaziah took my class in 2016, wound up being my first senior thesis advisee, and showed me the human side of the place I had landed.

Jane Averill was a lefty, a mom, and a friend. Jan Gentry was a steelworker, a lesbian, and a powerhouse. May their memory be a blessing.

APPENDIX 1

―――――――

THE NARRATORS

THE SIXTY-SIX NAMES listed here are the truckers who agreed to be interviewed for this book. Six are people I interviewed while I was training and then trucking myself. Since we stayed friends, I could go back and re-interview them (with consent) once I decided to write about trucking, rather than continue driving. These initial six also include three of the eight "T-girls" whom I interviewed informally for my article "Sex and Surveillance on the Highway," published in *Trans Studies Quarterly* in spring of 2017. The other five of that group chose not to be included in this research, or I had lost touch with them and could not ask. Of the sixty-six, two (Sandy Long and Desiree Wood) are truckers to whom I reached out for interviews because they are advocates and pioneers in the industry. Their stories are included in the book, but I use their real names because they are not narrators in the technical sense. What I mean by that is that the "narrators" are people who approached me when I asked for input and stories from gay, trans, and black truckers or others who felt like outsiders in the industry. Narrators self-identified, and I agreed to keep them anonymous, so I give only minimal details here, and they are identified by pseudonyms. When race, gender, sexual orientation, or ethnicity are specified in my descriptions, it is because the narrators identified themselves to me in the language I use here. I have alphabetized the aliases so readers can refer to them easily.

ADELE and I had breakfast at a cafe in Gary, Indiana, near a truck stop she frequents. Afterward, I went to hang out at her truck and meet her cats. She's white and about my age (early fifties), with long blonde hair, a ready smile, and a generous heart. There's nobody she wouldn't help, and people who find abandoned cats in truck stops frequently pass them on to her because she trains them to become trucking cats and adopts them out.

ALIX is the first transman I interviewed, near St. Louis. Though Alix isn't on hormones yet, he is heavy enough that people don't question his gender. He has facial piercings and a southern accent.

ALYS is a white, transgender female and a thirty-eight-year veteran truck driver who transitioned in 2003. She pulls long double trailers all over the East Coast and is married with young kids. We spoke in central New York State.

BETTE was a trip. She is a thin, hard-bitten, white transwoman, who looked like she walked right out of a Dorothy Allison book. She is in her fifties. As we talked over several months, she explained that she was born intersex. She also tried to convince me to shoot porn with her, insisting that the pay was good for a trannie-dyke couple and that we could get rich and stop working. After speaking by phone, we met in Southington, Connecticut.

BILLY is a bisexual, disabled trucker whom I interviewed in Indianapolis. He lives with his transgender girlfriend (also a trucker) and a collection of gay male room-mates in what looks like a pretty swinging scene. Billy gave me dittoed copies of newspaper articles about his childhood surgeries and his subsequent trucking success. He had quit driving temporarily but was restless and looking for a way back in. He was generous, and gentle, and very fierce.

BRAD called me from the road and related stories of excitement and hardship. He'd just been through a breakup that he blamed on trucking, and he was thinking about becoming a trainer to beat some of the loneliness.

BRAIDEN was crying when I first called to interview her, since she was in the middle of a scary situation. She explained it when I called back later but was still too trau-matized to talk about much else. She's a light-skinned black woman who has driven for several of the megacarriers.

I interviewed BRIDGET by phone, and we tried to schedule a ride-along, but she left trucking before we could work it out. She's a white lesbian about my age, who had been an art teacher in Arizona public schools but left because of the politics. Truck-ing was worse, though, and she was actively hoping to leave when we talked. She has since returned to teaching, where she says having her own shower and toilet is something she appreciates every day.

CAROLYN identifies as both intersex and trans. We spoke near her home in Walker-ton, Indiana, where her grandniece calls her "transma." She supports her extended family with all the humor and charm that name implies. She was reluctant to be interviewed because she didn't want her body sensationalized or sold out, and it's my sincere hope that I didn't do that.

CASEY is an older Mexican and indigenous lesbian whom I met through a narrator in my previous book. She has retired now, and we spoke in central Indiana. She is a classic, old-school butch, who can tell stories for hours. She remembers everything and longs to be active again.

CHRISTINA is an older white lesbian: heavy, funny, and chillingly honest. She is virulently anti-Trump and generally progressive. She's worked for a series of mega-carriers, and I interviewed her in Oklahoma. She swears a blue streak.

CIARA is a beautiful blonde woman who has a tongue stud and drives tanker. This means she goes to some of the most isolated spots on earth, from which she often sends me photos. She enjoys subverting norms of all kinds. We Skyped.

CURTIS has driven truck as a gay man for many years. We talked in Chicago, where he explained that he isn't transitioning so much as he's exploring his feminine side. So far, this hasn't caused problems at his job. He's married to *"the sweetest man ever,"* and they love sailing and drinking martinis.

DARYL is a white transman who started transitioning in March of 2005 and has always passed well. He has a neat, tailored look and a small goatee. When we talked, near Flagstaff, Arizona, he had his teenage stepson with him.

DESIREE WOOD runs a group called REAL Women in Trucking, set up in response to the limitations of the group Women in Trucking. By "REAL," she doesn't mean "real" women, but rather "real" truckers. She welcomes and adores transwomen both in and out of the group. She was a plaintiff in the training harassment suit, and has gone on to advocate for sane, feminist treatment of woman truckers and has leveraged her social media presence to increase this. I sought her out for information, and she has become a fast friend and ally. She's Mexican.

DONOVAN is a transgender trucker from Portland, Oregon, whom I interviewed by phone. She reminded me of my daughter, and I couldn't get her story out of my head. She has brightly colored hair and big, bold glasses, hipster fashion choices (though she'll probably say I got that wrong), and the saddest story ever. Important queer activists agreed to advocate for her, but apparently nothing about her situation was illegal — it was just really, really bad. She has since left trucking, and is doing better.

DOROTHY is a legend. She drives with a male partner whom she chooses not to marry. She has driven forever, gotten numerous awards, and been featured in the media. She quilts while waiting for pickups and drop-offs, and also always carries a loaded side arm because she runs high-value loads. That contrast is so her: showstopping beauty and the dirtiest mouth I ever heard. We spoke initially by phone and then met in Bensalem, Pennsylvania (among other places).

ECHO is a butch/stud from the Cree Nation, who trucks and lives in Canada. We talked by Skype as she did a reset in Beach, North Dakota. She's a bit younger and sassier than me, with that classic Canadian accent.

I met ELISE in Granite City, Illinois, at Denny's, of course. She is a round-faced, white lesbian with a big dimple and dark, feathered hair. She took me out to see her truck after breakfast, showing me the stuffed animals lining her dashboard that her grandbabies give her to keep her safe on the road.

ELIZA looked like a typical lesbian when we met in Beloit, Wisconsin. She wore cargo shorts and a ball cap, and she looked really tough. But that soon faded as she started telling me stories and the nerves wore off. She's white, in her early forties.

ENID is an immigrant from Jamaica who went into trucking because she couldn't find any other work that paid well enough to support her three kids. She retains a marked accent, and has a stern face that breaks into a warm smile.

FANNY saw a Yahoo News pop-up about my research and called me from Michigan. She had always been drawn to masculine-identified jobs and loved trucking for years, before health and sexual harassment drove her away.

FELICITY is a transwoman whom I spoke with by phone as she drove through central Texas at night. She pulled her air horn for me to prove that she was in a truck at the time. She spoke to me for hours, rarely requiring encouragement, but always keeping me laughing and in shock. She sent me many photos, often of her sitting in the truck in a black miniskirt and skimpy top, with red lipstick and a sultry expression. She's probably in her mid- to late thirties and white.

FRANKIE is a character. She identifies as Indian and is a trainer who prefers to train men because woman truckers get on her nerves. Often, she deliberately tried to get a rise out of me—I'm guessing that conflict is something she enjoys. She is an older, dark-skinned woman with dramatic white hair. There's something refreshing about her enthusiasm and willingness to engage: I liked her instantly.

I interviewed GABRIELLE and XENA together, at their house in North Fort Meyers, Florida. They've been a couple forever, and often finished each other's sentences, which irritated them as much as it charmed me. Gabrielle is very slim, white, and incredibly quiet. Xena is Filipino and much freer with her movements and her laughter. They both loosened up as they told stories about their many years of trucking together as a team. They are in their fifties.

I interviewed GEORGE and GRACIE together in a hotel in New Brunswick, New Jersey, where they were giving themselves a break from the truck for a night. Gracie is intersex, coming to see themselves as a transman, with a small body and delicate face, but knowing how to fight. George tells me he is *an inadvertent gay man, trying to come to terms with all of this.* He is learning about transition, going to meetings, being supportive, reconsidering his own identity. Both are white, very proud of their truck, which they gave me a tour of, and very unsure of anything else.

GINA called me, principally to tell me a shaggy-dog-type story about one particular load that went wrong, when she wound up transporting Budweiser that someone else was meant to drive so she became known as "that beer thief." She says most trucks are not made for someone built like her, *with short legs and a fat ass.*

GLORIA is Mexican and Aztec. She started trucking when her kids left home and loves the independence. The pay is lower than she thought it would be, but more than she says Mexicans can make in any other job, so she's happy with it. Though born in the United States, she has a strong accent, and often slides into Spanish as we talk, just outside Chicago. She dresses high femme with big hair and glittery nails.

GRACIE (see George and Gracie).

GWYNNETH is a force of nature. Her hair changes too much for this white person to be able to describe, but it's always very bold. We spoke in Gary, Indiana, and her enthusiasm—and drive to explain her life in her own terms—really carried the conversation forward.

HANNA is a transwoman and a (white) immigrant from Ireland. She's in her late twenties or early thirties and likes wild hair and snappy fashions. She and I share fan culture interests (Star Wars, Marvel, etc.), and she has a background in CGI, which she still pursues as a hobby. We spoke in Angola, Indiana.

HERNANDO identified himself as a fifty-year-old gay Caucasian, new to the trucking industry, driving for eighteen months. We spoke by phone.

INGRID is a black transwoman who drives for a megacarrier. Though we met in Kansas City, Ingrid is very shy, so much of our communication was done via text over the next few days.

ISABELLA and I spoke in Dodge City, Kansas, which she was passing through with her tanker. She is a straight white woman whose husband also trucks. She often wears a bandanna and looks like a biker.

JANE is a transwoman whom Desiree sent my way. She is white, in her early forties, and easily passes for female, which is not common among my narrators.

JODIE posts trucking-related YouTube videos, and I saw one that tackled an issue I was trying to understand, so I reached out to her. She turned out to be the coolest, toughest, most vibrant lesbian ever. She's Mexican, has trucked forever in a variety of locations, and kept me listening to her stories way past the time I was supposed to meet my kids for dinner.

JOHANNA is Native American: half Choctaw, half Cherokee, raised on the reservation. Her dad drove nitro in the Colorado mines, and she'd go with him and loved it, so she began trucking herself as soon as she could. She has driven ever since, except when she broke her back and had to take time off. She has great comic timing, usually at her own expense. We spoke at the Iowa 80 truck stop.

JOSEPHINE is a Hispanic lesbian with a heart-stopping smile and liquid eyes, whom I spoke to near Rolla, Missouri. She doesn't look old enough to have children, yet her adult son trucked with her when she first started.

While in Iowa, I also met KAREN, who is an older white woman with hair like my mother's. She mainly regaled me with horror stories about training, focusing on things that were hard to learn because she started at a fairly advanced age. She hadn't managed to keep her job, but longed to get back out there.

KATE called me from Oregon and told me long stories about how difficult it was to stay employed through transition. She's a white transwoman in her midfifties, looking for a job that understands those challenges.

LATOYA is a short, black butch from the South. She's very young (maybe twenty-four?), has a warm, flirtatious smile, and loves to talk. I met her during my training, when we both struggled to pass the test.

LIAM is a transman whom I spoke to by phone. He transitioned long ago, and it only ever came up once in the trucking world: when he went for his initial physical checkup, he joked with the doctor that a work-related accident had removed something. He knows his invisibility gives him a safety that is unavailable to many.

LORI was referred to me by Sarah. She is a white transwoman who went into trucking after being incarcerated (not an uncommon pattern), but after she had transitioned. She doesn't mind people knowing her past, yet her stories remain pretty superficial, avoiding controversy and focusing instead on daily struggles. She always has a perfect manicure. She often drives between Detroit and Toledo, which is where we spoke.

LOUISE (see Thelma and Louise).

MACI owns her own truck, which is leased out with a megacarrier. She called me from the road.

MARILU is the most beautiful, hottest trannie around. She has been trucking all her life and transitioned while in the business. She is big and bold and fun as hell. She displays lots of cleavage, drinks double Stoli on the rocks with a Coors Light chaser, and loves to sing karaoke, which she does in her deep voice. Nothing is sexier. We met initially in Gary, Indiana. She's white.

NATALIA is a white woman who told me she had been "free and easy" out on the road, but then had kids, and then got into a relationship with a man. She was taking time off when we met, to focus on her kids, who had gotten out of hand when she was gone so much. We spoke in north Texas.

NATE is a middle-aged white guy who would talk your ear off, which he did to me by phone.

ODETTE is a six-foot-tall, white, pencil-thin, redheaded transwoman from Alabama, who also identifies as intersex. She has a wife and child at home, and leaving them is the hardest part of trucking for her. She always wears a skirt and full makeup, and loves bragging about her thrift-store bargains. We spoke outside Cleveland.

A former student told me that her friend **PATRICK** was a trucker and got us talking in Gary, Indiana. He is a stunning, thirtysomething gay black man who left trucking due to an on-the-job injury. Though he hadn't come out at work, his vocal style makes it obvious, so he was happy to leave a job so rife with harassment.

QUENTINA wants to remain completely anonymous.

REBA is small, wiry, and tough as nails. She smokes, drinks Mountain Dew, and does every damn thing well without taking anything too seriously. She drove me all over the country and was an education in and of herself. She's white, my age, lesbian, and perfect to share an eight-foot-by-eight-foot space with for a few weeks.

RHIAN lives out West, but we spoke in Missouri. Her sense of style and presence are unparalleled. She is a transwoman who has trucked for many years, finally carrying a license with the correct name and gender. Her stories were more poignant than funny — I worry about her.

SANDY LONG called me when I reached out to the group Women in Trucking. This group is despised by many of my narrators because its organizer, Ellen Voie, is not a trucker and makes a high salary off the backs of truckers, but especially because she sided with megacarriers in the harassment suit about training. That aside, Sandy has trucked for years and shared stories and contacts with me.

SARAH is a reclusive transwoman. She shared only one incident with me, via email, but wanted it to be included. She's maybe fortysomething, and white.

SEAN is a gay trucker whom I tracked down on Facebook and then spoke to in Breezewood, Pennsylvania. He's young, white, and baby faced, with a soft voice and intense family ties.

SISYPHUS chose her own alias. She's a transwoman from Wisconsin who does a regular dedicated route through the upper Midwest. She's white, just past middle age, and painfully lonely. Her job gets her home most nights and weekends, but she is often too tired to do much, her health is deteriorating, and she has a hard time finding romance. She's very politically left, articulate, and funny as hell in a biting way.

TAMMY is a transwoman who is itching to leave trucking so that she can fully transition (she still trucks as a man). She is committed to coming out and anxious about how to make that possible. She is white, slim, blonde, and immaculately put together. We met at Denny's in Lake Station, Indiana.

TERELL is an advocate for trucker health, especially mental health. He particularly decries the stigma around mental health care among truckers and seeks to change that. He's a middle-aged white man with a beer belly and mustache, whom I spoke to in King of Prussia, Pennsylvania.

THELMA and LOUISE passed the phone back and forth as they drove through upstate New York. Thelma is a lesbian who rides with her trans wife, Louise, and sometimes with her daughter. Louise had a deep voice and killer deadpan humor. Thelma did most of the talking, often insisting that both she and Louise were loners who required endless quiet hours, which they could only find shut in that small space together. Both are white and in their midforties. Thelma has enormous eyes, and is incredibly striking, while Louise has her lower lip pierced and is the butchest transwoman I've seen out there. As a couple, they sure draw eyes!

With almost 3 million safe miles for a megacarrier, ULRIKE is often used in recruitment materials by her employer. She is a dignified black woman with dreadlocks and a killer smile. She has seen it all and enjoyed telling me stories, but is looking forward to slowing down and retiring, since she's now past sixty. Her company has relocated her to Joliet, Illinois, where we spoke.

VITO is a white gay man I interviewed in Louisville. Like many narrators, he's a diehard Packers fan, with a big, sturdy frame. Nothing seems to piss him off; he has a peaceful voice and vibe. He told me many stories about the lesbian who used to team drive with him.

WENDY is a black trucker from Georgia, whom I spoke with by phone. She speaks often of her grandkids and loves to ask provocative questions, turning the tables on the interviewer. She sent me photos of herself in her truck, sporting facial piercings, long braids, and a big smile.

XENA (see Gabrielle).

YOLANDA is a transwoman from Reno, who was in the final months before sexual reassignment surgery when we talked by phone. She has blonde, feathered hair, and loves to dress up and pose for the camera. She drives a regular run as part of a team, so is home with her wife most weekends.

ZOE was in Winona, Minnesota, when we spoke, just passing through. She's an older black trucker, with a clipped, salt-and-pepper afro. She has a wicked sense of humor and a sly smile.

APPENDIX 2

NOTES ON METHOD

THIS BOOK DESCRIBES the process of navigating trucking's paradoxes by telling the stories of the people who do it. I worked as a trucker, performed formal oral history interviews with sixty-six truckers, and had casual online and in-person encounters with countless others. Unless a narrator explicitly requested that I use their real name, I used pseudonyms, and quotes from their narratives appear in italics. Brief descriptions of each narrator are included in appendix 1, and anonymous transcriptions of the interviews are housed in the Human Sexuality Collection at Cornell University. I met my first narrators when I drove over the road. They referred me to others, as did friends and strangers. It seems like everyone knows a trucker. I also spent time at truck stops, rest areas, diners, bars, and casinos and talked to people there. This is the method anthropologists call "deep hanging out" (Geertz).

I told everyone who would listen that I wanted to write about how trucking was changing, and about who was doing it now, especially queers, trans people, racial minorities, and other outsiders. I recruited the people who became my narrators through a two-step process. I began by engaging someone in conversation, either in person or online. I described the book I was writing and asked if they would be willing to be interviewed for it. Often, I told them that I had started out driving truck myself and found it sufficiently different from what I had imagined that I decided to write about it rather than do it. I added that I had already written about gay, lesbian, and transgender steelworkers, and that I now wanted to share truckers' lives and stories with a wide audience. If they agreed, I set up a meeting, either by phone or in person. At that meeting, we had a conversation that I recorded and later transcribed. Facebook stalking became my ethnographic method of choice, and I recruited many narrators that way. The conversations were unstructured and typically began with me reminding them of my experiences and my goals, and asking them to describe their life on the road. I asked follow-up questions when that seemed relevant, and sometimes pushed for more details, while at other times allowing their hesitance to deter me. Mostly, I just treated them like the friends they soon became.

Truckers' stories and lives have a particularity that grants them urgency and drama. I sometimes reacted to their accounts emotionally, but I tried not to argue with their interpretation of events, since they are best qualified to name their experiences. My openness let them respond to and correct me when they thought I was getting something wrong. My task—the central ethical obligation of ethnographic data collection—was then to move between the acute particularity of each individual story and general claims about my data.

The feminist oral historian Daphne Patai summarizes the practice of ethical oral history. She notes that we elicit intimate, private-sphere information from our narrators, "yet we invite these revelations to be made in the context of the public sphere" (142), symbolized by our tape recorders and notebooks. This is both a methodological asymmetry and a political possibility; by challenging, even violating, the border between public and private spheres, oral history unleashes activism. Ethnography then becomes a powerful motivator of social change.

Trucking is a particularly good fit for this methodology because truckers are often garrulous and fun, but also because their lives and their place in our culture destabilize the line between public and private. As their stories unfold, the conclusions I propose circle around this public-private distinction.

Activism and oral history are mutually constitutive. Once my research was underway, I wanted the things I was learning to receive public attention. I began collaborating with a public health researcher, and we published an op-ed about trucking regulation in *The New York Times* (Balay and Shattell, "Long Haul"). That I had taken a stand (in such in iconic public forum) on an issue that they felt strongly about made it much easier for me to recruit narrators. They knew, from that point on, that I was on their side. Mona Shattell and I also published an examination of PTSD in truckers in *The Atlantic*, which generated even more support. Finally, there was a rally in St. Paul, Minnesota, during which a truck was vandalized and its driver badly frightened. The driver posted a YouTube video describing her experience, and I reached out to her for more details. Subsequently, Mona Shattell and I published an op-ed about the vulnerability of truckers to street protests and riots, and even more truckers were interested in talking to me. None of these publications was calculated to generate interviews, but rather to change hearts and minds. My training is in English literature, and so I find people's stories compelling and important in and of themselves. I write in a journalistic, ethnographic style because my goal is to understand other people's understanding of things and communicate that to a general audience. I try to remain aware that when I do that, I shape big-rig culture as well as describe it.

I also turned to local media outlets to recruit narrators. Jerry Davich is a popular feature writer in northwest Indiana, whom I had gotten to know when writing and promoting my first book. When I described this new work to him, he agreed to meet me and one of my local narrators for lunch, and he based a column on our conversation. The column was picked up by Yahoo News and briefly seen by large numbers of people, many of whom contacted me and some became narrators. Print media, social media, and in-person interactions each contributed to broadening my narrator pool. When I stopped doing interviews, there were still many interested truckers, but I felt I had enough stories to draw conclusions.

The demographic data on my sixty-six interviews is complicated. I did not ask narrators to identify their race, sexual orientation, or gender. When they did, I kept track, and out of the sixty-four total narrators who self-identified, twenty-two identify as transgender, six as intersex, fifteen as lesbians, five as gay men, two as bisexual, ten as black, five as Mexican, four as indigenous, and one as mixed Mexican and indigenous (with some narrators fitting into more than one of these categories). In addition, though they didn't say so, I think it helps to know that thirteen presented as male and forty-nine presented as female. Their ages range from twenty-two to about sixty-five, with the plurality falling between thirty-five and fifty.

I could not have done these interviews if I had not been a trucker, and before that a car mechanic, and if I did not present as blue-collar. I have a job in academia now, but my parents were raised working class, and that culture was transmitted to me even as they tried to leave it behind. I look, walk, and most important, react like a working-class butch. These truckers made sense to me, and I loved talking to them. I believe they were willing to talk to me because I know, both from my mother's endless stories and through my own experience doing dirty, disrespected work, that blue-collar workers are not vulnerable, passive, or victims. The T-girls, crips, women, African Americans, queers, and immigrants I met have taken control of their lives and are proud, talkative, and funny. They often gave me career advice, they completely understood how my work history was shaped by being visibly gay, and they got that I was kind of proud of having paid that price.

As humans, we tend to ignore what's happening to people around us, especially if they are experiencing trauma, and even more so if that trauma is sustained in service of our needs. If we didn't do this, we'd be paralyzed. What I aim to do here is recalibrate my readers' filters—to encourage my readers, if only for the length of this book, to hear the stories of truckers, and get lost in the particulars of their lives. Truckers are proud and standoffish, often conservative, and not always well educated. Many are also part of various other collectives: queers, trans folks, immigrants, veterans, native people, women, Muslims, people with disabilities. Taken as a group, we are a hot mess. Our pleasures and goals are varied, and not always logical. Equal rights are not among them, because equal to whom? What we share is a desire to drive, and to be left alone. Instead, we're subject to a vast network of governmental, corporate, and social management strategies, which can best be resisted via mobile tactics of shifting alliances. Tactics embedded in the actual lives of particular, embodied people. Oral history is an ideal methodology to describe and stimulate such resistance; instead of offering a leader or a hero, it encourages us to become conscious of the structures that repress us, and encourages us to engage directly with those structures. It enables truckers to "find . . . solidarity with other struggles articulated by the forgotten, the inconceivable, the spectacularized, and the unimaginable" (Spade, *Normal Life*, 33). Like the Incredible Hulk, truckers' strength is in a transformation that catches by surprise—that can't be contained. That's its promise as much as its problem.

Too much analysis of contemporary culture treats class and labor issues separately from sexuality and gender issues. New York University professor and writer Lisa Duggan articulated this problem as early as 2004, and scholars are now beginning to address it. By collecting and examining truckers' stories, I hope to add to this emerging body of work, asking how regimes like gender and sexuality are experienced by my narrators as they think about and do their lives, jobs, and bodies. Duggan argues that "a politics that cannot grasp the constraints, coercions, pressures, and deprivations imposed through class hierarchies and economic exploitation, or that fails to imagine the realities of rural, agricultural, and other nonmetropolitan lives" is incomplete (43). The interviews and other data I've collected are my attempt to "grasp" and "imagine" the lived, embodied experiences of these people who are in the thick of it.

Each trucker's story is compelling and important. They want and deserve to be heard — for everyone to know their stories. Though these are the stories of only sixty-six individuals, they provide insight into the structure and shape of big-rig culture. I look for corroboration in my narrators' accounts, scanning for instances in which several narrators share a similar story or pattern. I also turn to the historical archive for confirmation of their stories. For example, Yale's special collections, where I spent a month doing research, contained sources about truckers and sources about gay folks, but few sources about gay truckers. The only documents that concerned this overlap were a dime-store porn novel called *Truckin' Naked*, which purports to be a real-life account of the active sex life of one shy, gay trucker, and the famous "Stud File," a wooden drawer of index cards on which Samuel Steward kept careful track of his sexual encounters over the course of his busy life. His conquests included several truckers. Reading these documents in Yale's glorious and self-important research space reminded me of the invisibility of blue-collar queers to academic space, even as it confirmed what I was hearing from my sources. Juggling this data, keeping the individual stories contextualized, and resisting discourses of blame and rights by staying mobile and local, my work emphasizes the exclusion of truckers from exalted research spaces, and imagines how to change it.

There is a power in trucking; it has its own language and style. Any researcher could describe trucker culture and deliver it to readers with commentary. Many have, and I refer to their work where I find it useful. But truckers also resent having outsiders use their experiences for scholarly ends, and collecting interviews avoids some of that by letting people shape their own tales. Often, truckers feel (and have) a lack of public voice. No one asks their opinion or believes their analysis would be credible if they found a means to present it. This is a class problem; many blue-collar, working-class, disenfranchised people feel it acutely. In fact, it's one of the traits I would list as constitutive of working-class culture. As Karen Olson and Linda Shopes observe in their reflection on doing oral histories of working-class folks, many narrators hope oral history "will provide the means for injecting their own worldview into the elusive arena of public knowledge" (198). At a time in United States culture where most people feel invisible and neglected, they add that working-class narrators seek "to change public consciousness in ways that will make the experiences and agency of working-class women and men more visible and important to society at large" (198).

Telling the stories of sixty-six gay, trans, black, Mexican, and female truckers enables me to describe their too-often overlooked lives as they are being lived. This book serves as a snapshot of what's happening now, and asks what that tells us about surveillance, sexuality, and trucking.

WORKS CITED

Agar, Michael H. *Independents Declared: The Dilemmas of Independent Trucking.* Washington, D.C.: Smithsonian Institution Press, 1986.

Anderson, Carol. *White Rage: The Unspoken Truth of Our Racial Divide.* New York: Bloomsbury, 2016.

Anzaldúa, Gloria. *Borderlands/La Frontera: The New Mestiza.* San Francisco: Aunt Lute Books, 1987.

Apostolopoulous, Yorghos, Sevil Sönmez, Jennie Kronenfeld, Donna Jo Smith. "Sexual Networks of Truckers, Truckchasers, and Disease Risks." In *21st Century Sexualities: Contemporary Issues in Health, Education, and Rights*, edited by Gilbert Herdt and Cymene Howe, 112–14. London: Routledge, 2007.

Apostolopoulous, Yorghos, Sevil Sönmez, Michael Kenneth Lemke, Richard B. Rothenberg. "Mapping U.S. Long-Haul Truck Drivers' Multiplex Networks and Risk Topography in Inner-City Neighborhoods." *Healthplace* 34 (July 2015): 9–18.

Asgarian, Roxanna. "Rigged System: Women Truck Drivers Are Paving Their Own Way Through an Often Hostile Industry." *Utne* (Fall 2015): 43–45.

Badgett, M. V. Lee. *Money, Myths, and Change: The Economic Lives of Lesbians and Gay Men.* Chicago: University of Chicago Press, 2001.

Balay, Anne. "Sex and Surveillance on the Highway." *Trans Studies Quarterly* 4, no. 1 (February 1, 2017): 96–111.

———. *Steel Closets: Voices of Gay, Lesbian, and Transgender Steelworkers.* Chapel Hill: University of North Carolina Press, 2014.

Balay, Anne, and Mona Shattell. "Long Haul Sweatshops." *New York Times*, March 9, 2016.

———. "PTSD in the Driver's Seat." *Atlantic*, March 22, 2016.

Beck, Ulrich. *Risk Society: Towards a New Modernity.* Translated by Mark Ritter. London: Sage, 1992.

Belzer, Michael H. *Sweatshops on Wheels: Winners and Losers in Trucking Deregulation.* Oxford: Oxford University Press, 2000.

Bender-Baird, Kyla. *Transgender Employment Experiences: Gendered Perceptions and the Law.* New York: SUNY Press, 2011.

Bérubé, Allan. *My Desire for History: Essays in Gay, Community, and Labor History.* Chapel Hill: University of North Carolina Press, 2011.

Caldwell, Clay. *Truckin' Naked.* San Diego: Surrey House, 1972.

Califia, Pat. *Public Sex: The Culture of Radical Sex.* Pittsburgh, Pa.: Cleis, 1994.

Canady, Margot. *The Straight State: Sexuality and Citizenship in Twentieth-Century America*. Princeton, N.J.: Princeton University Press, 2009.

Chauncey, George. *Gay New York: Gender, Urban Culture, and the Making of the Gay Male World*. New York: Basic Books, 1994.

Cole, Alyson M. *The Cult of True Victimhood: From the War on Welfare to the War on Terror*. Stanford, Calif.: Stanford University Press, 2007.

Crenshaw, Kimberle. "Demarginalizing the Intersection of Race and Sex: A Black Feminist Critique of Antidiscrimination Doctrine, Feminist Theory and Anti-racist Politics." *University of Chicago Legal Forum* 1989, no. 1, art. 8. http://chicagounbound.uchicago.edu/uclf/vol1989/iss1/8.

DeGenaro, William, ed. *Who Says? Working-Class Rhetoric, Class Consciousness, and Community*. Pittsburgh, Pa.: University of Pittsburgh Press, 2007.

DePillis, Lydia. "Trucking Used to Be a Ticket to the Middle Class. Now It's Just Another Low-Wage Job." *Washington Post*, April 28, 2014. https://www.washingtonpost.com/news/wonk/wp/2014/04/28/trucking-used-to-be-a-ticket-to-themiddle-class-now-its-just-another-low-wage-job/.

Dizikes, Peter. "New Study Shows Rich, Poor Have Huge Mortality Gap in U.S." *MIT News*, April 11, 2016.

Duggan, Lisa. "Crossing the Line: The Brandon Teena Case and the Social Psychology of Working-Class Resentment." *New Labor Forum* 13, no. 3 (Fall 2004): 37–44.

Dunn, Jill. "In-Cab Filming of Drivers for Disciplinary Reasons OK'd by Calif. Attorney General." *Overdrive*, February 21, 2014. https://www.overdriveonline.com/in-cab-filming-of-drivers-for-disciplinary-reasons-okd-by-calif-attorney-general/.

Eubanks, Virginia. "Want to Predict the Future of Surveillance? Ask Poor Communities." *American Prospect*, January 15, 2014. http://prospect.org/article/want-predict-future-surveillance-ask-poor-communities.

Federal Motor Carrier Safety Administration. "Large Truck Crash Causation Study." Updated April 17, 2014. https://www.fmcsa.dot.gov/research-and-analysis/research/large-truck-crash-causation-study.

———. "Tips For Driving Safely Around Large Trucks Or Busses." Updated 7/19/2017. https://www.fmcsa.dot.gov/ourroads/tips-driving-safely-around-large-trucks-or-buses

Fleras, Augie, and Shane Dixon. "Cutting, Driving, Digging, and Harvesting: Re-masculinizing the Working-Class Heroic." *Canadian Journal of Communication* 36, no. 4 (2011): 579–97.

Frank, Miriam. *Out in the Union: A Labor History of Queer America*. Philadelphia: Temple University Press, 2014.

Fredrickson-Goldsen, Karen L., J. M. Simoni, H. J. Kim, K. Lehavot, K. L. Walters, J. Yang, C. P. Hoy-Ellis, A. Muraco. "The Health Equity Promotion Model: Reconceptualization of Lesbian, Gay, Bisexual, and Transgender (LGBT) Health Disparities." *American Journal of Orthopsychiatry* 84, no. 6 (November 2014): 653–63.

Fringe62. "CB Radio—Trucker Slang Definitions." *Rubies in My Mirror* (blog), June 22,

2012. https://rubiesinmymirror.wordpress.com/2012/06/22/cb-radio-trucker-slang -definitions.

Geertz, Clifford. *Available Light: Anthropological Reflections on Philosophical Topics.* Princeton, N.J.: Princeton University Press, 2000.

Grant, Jaime M., Lisa A. Mottet, Justin Tanis, Jack Harrison, Jody L. Herman, and Mara Keisling. *Injustice at Every Turn: A Report of the National Transgender. Discrimination Survey.* Washington, D.C.: National Center for Transgender Equality and National Gay and Lesbian Task Force, 2011. http://www.thetaskforce.org /static_html/downloads/reports/reports/ntds_full.pdf

Halberstam, J. Jack. *Gaga Feminism: Sex, Gender, and the End of Normal.* Boston: Beacon Press, 2012.

Hamilton, Shane. *Trucking Country: The Road to America's Wal-Mart Economy.* Princeton, N.J.: Princeton University Press, 2008.

Herring, Scott. *Another Country: Queer Anti-urbanism.* New York: New York University Press, 2010.

Hochschild, Arlie Russell. *Strangers in Their Own Land: Anger and Mourning on the American Right.* New York: New Press, 2016.

Hollibaugh, Amber, and Margot Weiss. "Queer Precarity and the Myth of Gay Affluence." *New Labor Forum* 24, no. 3 (2015): 18–27.

Howard, John. *Men Like That: A Southern Queer History.* Chicago: University of Chicago Press, 1999.

Hsu, Stephanie. "Number of Female Truckers Slides as Women Face Industry Hurdles." *Trucks,* September 28, 2016. https://www.trucks.com/2016/09/28/female -truckers-face-industry-hurdles/.

Hubbs, Nadine. *Rednecks, Queers, and Country Music.* Berkeley: University of California Press, 2014.

Humphreys, Laud. "Tearoom Trade: Impersonal Sex in Public Places." In *Public Sex / Gay Space,* edited by William L. Leap, 29–54. New York: Columbia University Press, 1999.

Isenberg, Nancy. *White Trash: The 400-Year Untold History of Class in America.* New York: Penguin, 2016.

Jensen, Anker, L. Kaerlev, F. Tüchsen, H. Hannerz, S. Dahl, P. S. Nielsen, J. Olsen. "Locomotor Diseases among Male Long-Haul Truck Drivers and Other Professional Drivers." *International Archives of Occupational and Environmental Health* 81, no. 7 (July 2008): 821–27.

Johnson, Colin R. *Just Queer Folks: Gender and Sexuality in Rural America.* Philadelphia: Temple University Press, 2013.

Kafer, Alison. *Feminist, Queer, Crip.* Bloomington: Indiana University Press, 2013.

Kennedy, Elizabeth Lapovsky, and Madeline E. Davis. *Boots of Leather, Slippers of Gold: The History of a Lesbian Community.* New York: Penguin, 1993.

LeMasters, E. E. *Blue-Collar Aristocrats: Life-Styles at a Working-Class Tavern.* Madison: University of Wisconsin Press, 1975.

Mason, Carol. *Oklahomo: Lessons in Unqueering America.* New York: SUNY Press, 2015.

McLean, Amie. "'Four Guys and a Hole in the Floor': Racial Politics of Mobility and Excretion among BC-Based Long Haul Truckers." *Transfers* 6, no. 1 (Spring 2016): 45–61.

Michaelson, Edward D. "Sleep Apnea and Trucking: Where Are We Now?" *Sleep Review*, October 28, 2014. http://www.sleepreviewmag.com/2014/10/sleep-apnea -trucking-now/.

Olson, Karen, and Linda Shopes. "Crossing Boundaries, Building Bridges: Doing Oral History among Working-Class Women and Men." In *Women's Words: The Feminist Practice of Oral History*, edited by Sherna Berger Gluck and Daphne Patai, 189–204. New York: Routledge, 1991.

Paap, Kris. *Working Construction: Why White Working-Class Men Put Themselves— and the Labor Movement—in Harm's Way*. Ithaca, N.Y.: ILR Press, 2006.

Parton, Dolly. Interview by Barbara Walters. *Barbara Walters Special*, 1977. https:// youtu.be/3Vj3Bb9aCvA?t=3m16shttps://youtu.be/3Vj3Bb9aCvA?t=3m16s.

Patai, Daphne. "U.S. Academics and Third World Women: Is Ethical Research Possible?" In *Women's Words: The Feminist Practice of Oral History*, edited by Sherna Berger Gluck and Daphne Patai, 137–54. New York: Routledge, 1991.

Perkins, J. Blake. *Hillbilly Hellraisers: Federal Power and Populist Defiance in the Ozarks*. Champaign: University of Illinois Press, 2017.

Powell, Ryan. "Queer Interstates: Cultural Geography and the Social Contract in Kansas City Trucking Company and El Paso Wrecking Corp." In *Queering the Countryside: New Frontiers in Rural Queer Studies*, edited by Mary L. Gray, Colin R. Johnson, and Brian J. Gilley, 181–202. New York: New York University Press, 2016.

Rojas, Rick. "The Uphill Battle for Minorities in Trucking." *Pacific Standard*, February 4, 2016. https://psmag.com/the-uphill-battle-for-minorities-in-trucking -d708339665fe#.ttdnnrlo1.

Rubin, Gayle S. "Thinking Sex: Notes for a Radical Theory of the Politics of Sexuality." In *Deviations: A Gayle Rubin Reader*, 137–81. Durham, N.C.: Duke University Press, 2011.

Schifter, Jacobo. *Latino Truck Driver Trade: Sex and HIV in Central America*. New York: Routledge, 2014.

Schilt, Kristen, and Matthew Wiswall. "Before and After: Gender Transitions, Human Capital, and Workplace Experiences." *B. E. Journal of Economic Analysis and Policy* 8, no. 1 (2008): Article 39. http://www.bepress.com/bejeap/vol8/iss1 /art39.

Schweighofer, Katherine. "Rethinking the Closet: Queer Life in Rural Geographies." In *Queering the Countryside: New Frontiers in Rural Queer Studies*, edited by Mary L. Gray, Colin R. Johnson, and Brian J. Gilley, 223–43. New York: New York University Press, 2016.

Shattell, Mona, Yorghos Apostolopoulos, Sevil Sönmez, and Mary Griffin. "Occupational Stressors and the Mental Health of Truckers." *Issues in Mental Health Nursing* 31, no. 9 (2010): 561–68.

Sieber, W. Karl, C. F. Robinson, J. Birdsey, G. X. Chen, E. M. Hitchcock, J. E. Lincoln, A. Nakata, M. H. Sweeney. "Obesity and Other Risk Factors: The National Survey of U.S. Long-Haul Truck Driver Health and Injury." *American Journal of Industrial Medicine* 57, no. 6 (2014): 615–23.

Smith, Sharon. *Subterranean Fire: A History of Working-Class Radicalism in the United States*. Chicago: Haymarket Books, 2006.

Sönmez, Sevil, Yorghos Apostolopoulos, Amanda E. Tanner, Kelley Massengale, and Margaret Brown. "Ethno-epidemiological Research Challenges: Networks of Long-Haul Truckers in the Inner City." *Ethnography* 17, no. 1 (2016): 111–34.

Spade, Dean. *Normal Life: Administrative Violence, Critical Trans Politics, and the Limits of Law*. Durham, N.C.: Duke University Press, 2015.

———. "What's Wrong with Trans Rights?" In *Transfeminist Perspectives in and beyond Transgender and Gender Studies*, edited by Anne Enke, 184–94. Philadelphia: Temple University Press, 2012.

Standing, Guy. *The Precariat: The New Dangerous Class*. London: Bloomsbury, 2011.

Stevens, Maurice E. "Trauma Is as Trauma Does: The Politics of Affect in Catastrophic Times." In *Critical Trauma Studies: Understanding Violence, Conflict, and Memory in Everyday Life*, edited by Monica J. Casper and Eric Wertheimer, 19–36. New York: New York University Press, 2016.

"Stud File." Samuel Steward Papers. Beinecke Rare Book and Manuscript Library, Yale University.

Su, Vincent Yi-Fong, C. J. Liu, H. K. Wang, L. A. Wu, S. C. Chang, D. W. Perng, W. J. Su, Y. M. Chen, E. Y. Lin, T. J. Chen, K. T. Chou. "Sleep Apnea and Risk of Pneumonia: A Nationwide Population-Based Study." *CMAJ* 186, no. 6 (April 1, 2014): 415–21.

Terkel, Studs. *Working*. New York: MJF Books, 1972.

Townsend, Marilyn S., J. Peerson, B. Love, C. Achterberg, S. P. Murphy. "Food Insecurity Is Positively Related to Overweight in Women." *Journal of Nutrition* 131, no. 6 (June 1, 2001): 1738–45.

U.S. Department of Justice, Civil Rights Division, Disability Rights Section. *A Guide to Disability Rights Laws*. July 2009. https://www.ada.gov/cguide.htm.

Upton, Rebecca N. "What Would Jesus Haul? Home, Work, and the Politics of Masculinity among Christian Long-Haul Truck Drivers." In *Work and Family in the New Economy*, edited by Samantha K. Ammons and Erin L. Kelly, 101–26. Bingley, England: Emerald, 2015.

Valentine, David. *Imagining Transgender: An Ethnography of a Category*. Durham, N.C.: Duke University Press, 2007.

Vance, J. D. *Hillbilly Elegy: A Memoir of a Family and Culture in Crisis*. New York: Harper Collins, 2016.

Viscelli, Steve. *The Big Rig: Trucking and the Decline of the American Dream*. Oakland: University of California Press, 2016.

Warner, Michael. *The Trouble with Normal: Sex, Politics, and the Ethics of Queer Life*. Cambridge, Mass.: Harvard University Press, 1999.

INDEX